THE INSTITUTION OF LITERATURE

THE INSTITUTION OF LITERATURE

Edited by
Jeffrey J. Williams

State University of New York Press

Published by
State University of New York Press, Albany

Printed in the United States of America

For information, address State University of New York Press,
90 State Street, Suite 700, Albany, NY, 12207

Production by Christine L. Hamel
Marketing by Michael Campochiaro

Library of Congress Cataloging-in-Publication Data

The institution of literature / edited by Jeffrey J. Williams.
p. cm. —
Includes bibliographical references and index.
ISBN 0-7914-5209-3 ISBN 0-7914-5210-7 (pbk.: alk. paper)
1. Criticism—United States—History—20th century.
2. Literature, Modern—20th century—History and criticism.
3. English philology—Study and teaching (Higher)—United
States. I. Williams, Jeffrey, 1958.

PN99.U5 I57 2002
801'.95'09730904—dc21

2001020753
CIP

10 9 8 7 6 5 4 3 2 1

Contents

Acknowledgments vii

Introduction: Institutionally Speaking
Jeffrey J. Williams 1

I. The Institution of Theory

Framing Theory: The Disorganization of Historiography
Vincent B. Leitch 19

The Theory Junkyard
James J. Sosnoski 25

Orbiting Planet Foucault
Paul Trembath 43

This Feminism Which Is Not One:
Women, Generations, Institutions
Devoney Looser 61

II. The Question of Cultural Studies

Cultural Studies: Literary Criticism's Alter Ego
Grant Farred 77

Peer Pressure: Literary and Cultural Studies
in the Bear Market
Michael Bérubé 95

The Work of Cultural Studies in the Age of Transnational Production
Crystal Bartolovich 111

III. Professional Channels

Dancing in the Dark: A Manifesto against Professional Organizations
Lennard J. Davis 153

The Star System in Literary Studies
David R. Shumway 173

The Life of the Mind and the Academic Situation
Jeffrey J. Williams 203

IV. The Job of Literature

Time Out of Mind: Graduate Students in the Institution of English
Louise Mowder 229

Getting Hired
Terry Caesar 241

The Educational Politics of Human Resources: Humanities Teachers as Resource Managers
Evan Watkins 265

Contributors 289

Index 291

Acknowledgments

I would first like to thank all the contributors to this volume, not only for their fine essays but for their endurance in awaiting completion of the volume. Special thanks go to Eric Leuschner at the University of Missouri for timely research assistance, and to those who helped with the production of *the minnesota review*, where many of these essays originally appeared, particularly to Jan Forehand. And thanks to James Peltz and the staff at SUNY Press, who showed remarkable patience as well as care with the manuscript. On a more personal note, I'm grateful to my daughter, Virginia Williams, who had to bear with manuscripts strewn on the kitchen table many nights after dinner.

Grateful acknowledgment is due *College Literature* for permission to reprint chapter 10, "The Life of the Mind and the Academic Situation"; and to *PMLA* to reprint chapter 11, "The Star System in Literary Studies," by David Shumway.

Introduction

Institutionally Speaking

Jeffrey J. Williams

I

What is literature? is perhaps the preeminent theoretical question of literary studies. Akin to What is philosophy?, it promises to define our object of study and by extension the grounding rationale for our field. Theorists from Aristotle to de Man and present-day "new formalists" have answered it, usually specifying (and often celebrating) distinctive attributes of a class of linguistic objects. Against this current, *The Institution of Literature* raises a different line of questioning, looking not at the autonomous traits of literary works but at the institutional parameters and places demarcated by the rubric of literature. In a sense, it inverts the question in a pragmatist way: instead of ascertaining the core of a thing called literature from which our activities in literature departments derive, it examines what people in contemporary literature departments do—what are our regularized practices, what are the professional mandates that inflect our practices, and what are the institutional locations that mediate our work. A premise of this volume is that the institution, in its various senses, generates what we call literature, or more modestly, that the question of literature is inseperable from our institutional practices and locations.[1]

Institution is of course a freighted word, frequently carrying unsavory connotations. Swimming in the same school of words as *bureaucracy*, *disciplines*, and *professionalization*, it signifies the structures of regulation and management of contemporary mass society and culture, running in the opposite direction of words like freedom, individuality, or independence. At one extreme, it suggests literal imprisonment—being confined to a mental institution, correctional facility, drug rehab facility, or the like. More generally, it designates seemingly implacable state or civil bureaucracies, like the IRS or schools, which we inhabit and which regulate what we do. This might be called the brick-and-mortar sense of institution, calling up the image of the actual buildings, as well as the regulation of life associated with those buildings, of modern bureaucracies, and it has two permutations: the more pervasive sense of a permanent structure that we inhabit, and the more transitory sense of a structure that we pass through, to be disposed of once we have completed the bureaucratic business there—like the DMV or the payroll office, which one must traverse to get to the heart of the matter, whether driving a car or getting paid. In this latter sense, institutions are momentary thresholds, considered external to if not distractions from the activity at hand, like waiting on line at the DMV.

Professions jockey between both of these senses. On the one hand, a professional institution designates the apparatus through which one has to pass to be accredited, for instance, to practice law or to profess literature, presumably granting a degree of autonomy once one has attained that credential. Such thresholds might include law school, or the bar exam, which enable one to hang out a shingle to practice law, but do not necessarily bear on the everyday practices of lawyers. Still, lawyers are regulated by and inhabit the court system. Or professors must pass through various institutional hurdles—grad school, comprehensive exams, the dissertation—before attaining a Ph.D. and being granted autonomy to practice one's intellectual pursuit. However, professors are embedded within the university and its system of rules and management.

"Institution" also has a looser, less concrete meaning, designating an established practice or tradition. As the Oxford *Dictionary of Modern English Usage* notes, five-o'clock tea in British culture is an institution. Or marriage, cricket, or Eton. On the American scene, we might say that baseball is an institution, or Harvard, which signifies more than the campus in Cambridge, Massachusetts. One might even say that a person is an institution, as Robert Moses was and Al Sharpton is in New York politics, or M. H. Abrams and Edward W. Said have been in the field of literature. While usually less pejorative—we might even venerate such practices, places, or people—this dimension still ties to the harder sense of institution, in that custom and tradition are generally regulated through formal, societal structures (as, say, marriage is mediated through both religious and legal institutions, baseball is regulated through little leagues, schools, and its professional organization and rules, and reputation is tied to institutional position and provenance).

This volume looks at a cross-section of the various senses of the institution of literature. The first half focuses largely on the softer sense of institution as custom, investigating how the critical practices and discourses designated by theory and more recently cultural studies have become established, especially in the American university, these past thirty years. It looks at the organization and circulation of theory in standard devices such as theory anthologies, in the attribution of theory brand names such as "Foucault," and in the tensions over feminism's attaining established status. It also looks at the implications of the putative paradigm shift to cultural studies over the last decade—ties to the establishment of global corporatism, as well as the ways in which it continues the normal literary practice of close reading. The second half of this volume turns more explicitly to the concrete sense of institution, investigating professional organizations like MLA or regulative processes like tenure. It also examines the position of graduate students, the hiring process, and the extraliterary role of English departments in managing personnel in the postindustrial university.

An undercurrent of argument throughout is that we need to look more directly and concertedly at the institutional vectors of literary studies, seeing them not as distractions, momentary, or external, but as constitutive and deeply formative of what we do. Related to this, we need to depolarize the charge against institutions; they are not an evil cage created by a perverse genie, but the modern mode of organization of people. Some of the practices promulgated by our current institution no doubt fulfill the unsavory associations of the word, and many of the chapters here point to its failings, but the point is to reconfigure the institution in better ways. As Bruce Robbins astutely advises, we need "to pronounce the word institutionalization without the usual sinister innuendo, [and to] distinguish particular institutional alternatives from each other rather than condemning (or praising) them all together" (768).

The purview of this volume by no means exhausts the investigation of literary institutions, and one could perform complementary examinations of the nonacademic and popular precincts of literature (for instance, magazines like the *New Yorker* or prizes like the Pulitzer), and the material institutions of publishing, book reviewing, and bookselling.[2] This collection aims to demarcate salient pieces of the academic puzzle—the function of theory, professionalization, the job market—but one could also imagine companion volumes devoted to rhetoric and composition and the apportionment of labor it marks, or to creative writing and its growing place in English departments, or outside of the institutional megalopolis of English, one focused on the fate of foreign languages and their relation to the reign of "globalism." Paper enough and time. I hope that this book, though, suggests directions for this line of questioning, as well as provides an analysis of some of the facts of institutional life c. 2000.

II

The chief problem with talking about institutions is that they are often taken as exogenous and hence ignored—the university roofs over our heads that we rarely give a thought to, or measures like yearly reports that we might grumble about but forget as soon as possible. One can see this especially in the typical definition of our "work." If asked what you do, what do you say? Most likely, you don't talk about the courses you are teaching, except perhaps the graduate seminar dovetailing with your research, but probably not the literature survey, not to mention the composition course. You certainly do not adumbrate the proceedings of the six committees you are on. And you probably do not talk about the cadre of workers with whom you work, whether the Romanticist down the hall or the grad students herded downstairs and staffing a majority of your department's courses, not to mention the physicist or administrator who is part of the same university plant. Rather, "work" typically equates with one's field of research, the scholarly and critical writing that one does, what one's book is on, the topic of one's latest paper. This is not necessarily out of bad faith or delusion—we might be trying to put the best light on what we do, in the midst of quotidian tasks, and do not want to bore our interlocutor. Still, we gravitate toward an abstracted and individualized conception of our work, apart from our workplaces and institutional roles.

In a well-known passage in *The Philosophy of Literary Form*, Kenneth Burke spins out a striking vignette for what we do, one that also tacitly fleshes out an image of the institution:

> Imagine that you enter a parlor. You come late. When you arrive, others have long preceded you, and they are engaged in a heated discussion, a discussion too heated for them to pause and tell you exactly what it is about. In fact, the discussion had already begun long before any of them got there, so that no one present is qualified to retrace for you all the steps that had gone before. You listen for a while, until you decide that you have caught the tenor of the argument; then you put in your oar. Someone answers; you answer him; another comes to your defense; another aligns himself against you, to either the embarrassment or gratification of your opponent, depending on the quality of your ally's assistance. However, the discussion is interminable. The hour grows late, you must depart. And you do depart, with the discussion still vigorously in progress. (110–11)

This vignette holds a certain power and charm. One great virtue is that it characterizes our work—criticism for Burke—as a vibrant, engaging, and attractive activity. On first sight it taps into the somewhat stereotyped scene of the cocktail party; however, it makes what happens there not frivolous but significant and eventful, the object of substantial investment, even heated argument. It dispels the image of tweedy pedants worrying over comma splices, or of refined aesthetes throwing off choice apercus, replacing it with a tableau of people with stake-laden interests and serious concerns. It makes what we do seem less disembodied and obscure, less a dry, formulaic, quasi-scientific academic pursuit, and more lively and challenging.

Another virtue is that this vignette provides a brief but powerful account of the nature of criticism, both over time and at one moment. Countering the sense of criticism as a series of static documents or isolated monuments, it portrays criticism as constitutively dialogic, a dynamic of history, people, and concepts. It places our work in a live historical tradition; its model of tradition is anything but staid and confining, but active and ongoing, forming what Burke calls the "unending conversation." And it gives bodies and voices to positions, fleshing out the commonplace metaphor of the conversation, in characteristic Burkean fashion locating it within a dramatistic scenario. It underscores the theoretical point that criticism is a process rather than end, and operates through a kind of call and response or, as Burke puts it, "answer and rejoinder" (109). This parallels the Bakhtinian point that any utterance is an answer to another utterance, situated within a speaking situation, or, as we might put it now, the critic is always positioned. (One can see an update of this model in Gerald Graff's program for teaching the conflicts, that we introduce students to the rough sport and interchange of the critical conversation, the back and forth.) Overall, Burke's vignette emphasizes that the conversation always occurs in the midst of an intellectual community with a history and represents alliances as well as antagonisms. It thus argues against isolation, attesting that we are always defined in relation to others in the room, past and present.

Another great virtue of this vignette is that it presents an open and democratic model of criticism. It casts entry as easy and egalitarian: one does not need a special pass or permission, but simply has to walk in, listen, and speak up, and others will presumably listen and respond. And it suggests that merit—one's arguments rather than credentials—carries the day. This presents perhaps the best hope of our critical field, that anyone, regardless of where he or she comes from, can first speak in seminar, lecture, or conference, or first publish an article and join the conversation, and one's arguments will be enjoined according to their value. In fact, I often read this passage aloud in the first weeks of a criticism or theory course, to emphasize the vibrancy of what we do, its conviviality, its historical and dialogic nature, and especially its beckoning welcome.

Still, for all its virtues, this sketch leaves a lot of questions unspoken, and more consequentially its representational slide is such that one might forget to ask them. For instance, how do you find out about the parlor? Do you get invited or do you crash the conversation? Are there bouncers? Who does the inviting and why? How do you have the time to hang out there? Where do you pick up the idiom spoken there? What ensures that people listen, or that they don't? Simply what you say? How do you get allied with one group? Who owns the room and pays the insurance and light bill? Who cleans it? What relation does it have to other rooms? The town it is in?

By posing these questions, I do not mean to detract from the usefulness of Burke's model as a heuristic that underscores both the dialogic nature of criticism and the possibilities for entry, but rather to expand it to account for the parlor and the institutional conditions of conversation. In keeping with his persistent focus on rhetoric, Burke foregrounds the drama of critical argument, directed as an answer to "poetic" or static models of criticism. The problem, however, is one of representation; insofar as "the conversation" has become the prevalent figure synecdochically naming what we do, it occludes other dimensions of our tasks as literature professors. These pose a different avenue of answer.

First, the representation of our work. The standard professional self-definition of our work—what goes on in the parlor—is criticism or scholarship. The figure of "the conversation" tacitly conflates our work as scholarly debate, as a self-contained genealogy of discourse, obscuring the very real parameters and effects of the institutions that mediate our work. This figure abstracts our particular and in fact rarefied activities—according to MLA statistics, most faculty publish very little—from the very real tasks that comprise our jobs, like teaching or myriad other academic duties. Although the image of conversation situates criticism socially rather than individually, it still poses a narrow public, of those in the parlor or field, unrelated to a larger public, larger histories, or to its own situation in the university. We thus need to redefine our work, bringing these other dimensions into the terms of the conversation.

Second, the special nature of the conversation. The conversational figure, connoting a scene of everyday language and interchange, glosses over the specialized languages of those in the parlor. At midcentury there might have been literary journalists in the parlor (and the idiom probably was more colloquial), but now the conversation takes place almost exclusively among academic critics and within professional precincts. It assumes specialized idioms in which, accepted topics on which, and normative positions from which one speaks and hears. Even if one grants the centrality of the critical conversation in representing our work, it is not a level field of exchange, but inflected by professional credentials and position, circumscribed by the specific terms of institutional hierarchies. Some people have more of a purchase to speak, with others clustered around listening intently (think, for instance, of how this is coded by the affiliations on MLA badges). We thus need to look at our professional protocols and terms of argument, and their ties to institutional hierarchies.

Third, the door to the room. The colloquializing tendency of "conversation" construes entry as open: one simply speaks up. In Burke's scenario, it seems one freely walks through the door, gleans the general tenor of what is being said, and puts one's oar in the water. But there are obviously professional terms and institutional conditions of entry—graduate school, credentials, and mentors, as well as discourse. The conversation, in this sense, is not purely intellectual but performs a professional function, designating the official language of the parlor as well as the medial terrain through which we adopt professional behavior and are recruited into the social psychology of relations of the academic institution of literature. This dimension of the conversation has become all the more apparent in the present the job market, when there seem to be far more obstacles than invitations to entry; many of us have been turned away at the door, or have to navigate and inhabit a series of outer rooms—basements, the coatroom, and so on—while knocking, like Augie March, sometimes softly and sometimes not so softly at the door of the main parlor. We need to relentlessly examine the conditions of entry, and to work toward opening rather than closing the professional door.

One notable acknowledgment of this dimension of the conversation can be found in John Guillory's well-known essay, "Preprofessionalism: What Graduate Students Want." Guillory focuses on the medial position of graduate students, exacerbated by the current job market; however, by defining their position as "preprofessional," he places them in an anteroom, reinforcing the boundaries of the field. The problem, for Guillory, lies with graduate students and their misrecognition of their position, rather than with those of us who have fully franchised professional positions and might open or close the door to the parlor. One could, after all, see graduate students as professionals, given that they frequently teach 2-2 while doing their course work, especially at state universities. Are they not already professionals? Burke's model, in contrast, provides a salutary image of the permeability of entry; it not only welcomes but confers legitimacy on those who come knocking.

Fourth, jobs and time. The abstracted image of the conversation precludes the issue of jobs and time. It requires substantial leisure or a certain construal of worktime, not available to those of us with part-time or adjunct positions (not to mention working at a coffeehouse while sending out cvs), to visit the conversational parlor. Even for those with full professional positions, there is an internal differentiation of time: those relatively few of us at research universities have time and resources to participate in the critical conversation, whereas those with less research-oriented berths can only squeeze in a few fugitive hours amid teaching and service. As James Sosnoski shows in *Token Professionals and Master Critics*, the imaginary system of professional rewards purports to be egalitarian, based on our equal place at the critical table, but very few of us actually work under the conditions that enable us to participate. That is, most of us are "token professionals," but measure ourselves, debilitatingly, according to "Master Critics" who get to spend most of their time in the parlor or library carrel. To put it another way, the parlor is first and foremost a place of employment, that permits us to join the critical conversation but that also encompasses much other work. It also regulates the work time of students, as Evan Watkins emphasizes in *Work*

Time, whom we in English (given that everyone takes comp) circulate through the university, channeling them into the advanced labor pool. We need to examine the issues of time, of where and how we actually spend our time, and of who gets time.

Fifth, the university. While attuned to the rhetorical dynamic of critics, the image of the conversation is seemingly set, as in a stage play, in an otherworldly space apart from the concrete locales of our work; it is usually conceived as self-contained, with its own history and for its own benefit. But our work occurs within the university, regulated by the disciplinary apportionment of our departments, funding, and administration, and the division of university labor, and governed indirectly by community needs and corporate and state mandates. Criticism, in one sense, functions to legitimate the distinctiveness of our field within the context of the distribution of university resources, as well as in a larger public sphere. We need to turn our attention to the university, which houses our parlors: how it is administered and funded, and how it relates to the so-called real world, not as an ivory tower but in fact as the most prominent public institution post-World War II, arguably one of the last vestiges of the redistributive Great Society.

This volume sheds light on these other dimensions of the parlor, in particular the institutionalized terms of its languages and topics, its professional protocols and regulation, and its actual ground as employment. Dispelling the image of the conversation as a stage set apart, it aims to look at the ways in which our institutional location forms our work, and how we are institutional actors.

III

It is hard to hear the word *institution* without thinking of the writing of Michel Foucault. Yet, though we do not lack for Foucauldian studies of, say, the broad epistemic shift embodied in the modern novel, we have largely foregone the study of the institution of literature that we inhabit. As Lennard Davis points out in this volume, we have often left unexamined our own disciplines and workplaces. There have been some notable exceptions, such as Richard Ohmann's still unsurpassed *English in America*, Gerald Graff's *Professing Literature*, and Evan Watkins's *Work Time*, as well as a series of special issues of *the minnesota review*, from which a number of the following essays are drawn.

Parts I and II, "The Institution of Theory" and "The Question of

Cultural Studies," deal with the ways in which our predominant critical practices operate institutionally. Against the tendency to see theory as a train of concepts and doctrines, akin to what one might find in the history of philosophy, the first section deals with the way theory has become institutionalized as part of the normative practice in literary studies, and in turn how institutional modes and structures govern the practice of theory. In the first chapter, "Framing Theory," Vincent B. Leitch, the leading historian of contemporary criticism, turns a historiographical eye on the way in which theory is organized in textbooks, anthologies, and histories, pointing out different modes of organization—great figures, monumental texts, schools, and so forth. He shows how our understanding of theory is shaped by the institutional molds in which we place it.

Continuing his contrarian and antielitist view of criticism from *Token Professionals, Master Critics*, James J. Sosnoski examines the nonlogical protocols of theory in chapter 2, "The Theory Junkyard." Using the analogy of a market, he argues that theory adopts a commodity form, so that certain schools, approaches, or representative individuals come to represent "signature concepts" or designer labels. Focusing on the institutional cycle of obsolescence in criticism, he also examines the junkheap of the tradition, and how signature concepts become last year's news or forgotten terms might be revivified. In chapter 3, Paul Trembath analyzes a specific example of how "signature concepts" operate—those gathered under the name of "Foucault." With a bit of wit, Trembath titles the chapter "Orbiting Planet Foucault" to indicate the institutional circulation of Foucault's name in the current critical galaxy, deciphering historicist, pragmatist, ethical, and empirical or deleuzian orbits.

Turning to look at a "school," the fourth chapter, "The Feminism Which Is Not One," examines the current institutional situation of feminist theory. In it, Devoney Looser, coeditor of the pioneering anthology *Generations: Academic Feminists in Dialogue*, foregrounds the issue of institutional generations, in particular the tensions between second-generation feminists, who struggled for an institutional toehold and who seem to resent younger feminists or see them as careerists, and third-generation feminists, who find themselves entering an established but job-deprived field. One line separating the two generations is that of theory, the older generation questioning the professionalization signaled by an absorption in theory, the younger generation claiming theory as the locus of struggle at hand.

Part II examines the seemingly pervasive shift over the past decade "from literature to culture," from defining our object of study as high literary works to the larger realm of cultural practices and from summarizing our practice as literary theory to the broad rubric of cultural studies. Though cultural studies is often cast as more worldly and socially relevant than theory, this section turns a critical eye on some of the complications of cultural studies' establishment. Grant Farred, in chapter 5, "Cultural Studies: Literary Criticism's Alter Ego," unpacks some of its contradictions, exposing how cultural studies often continues the close reading practices of the New Criticism, thus absorbing it into traditional literary studies. As an antidote, Farred argues that cultural studies needs to attend more concertedly to class, which it has largely foregone in its frequent focus on identity politics.

In chapter 6, "Peer Pressure: Literary and Cultural Studies in a Bear Market," Michael Bérubé, one of the most prominent public spokespersons for the humanities in recent years, turns his sights on our public image. In answer to conservative attacks on the imputed relativism of cultural studies, he calls for renewed attention to the issue of value, arguing that our eschewal of considerations of value debilitates our public authority. He also cautions against the misrecognition of our work as cultural studies, remarking in a pithy and memorable line: "The discipline thinks it's going from literature to culture, and the market tells us we're going from literature to technical writing."

A panoramic overview of the state of cultural studies, chapter 7, "The Work of Cultural Studies in the Age of Transnational Production," examines the assimilation of cultural studies both within literary studies and outside the academy by the corporate world. In it, Crystal Bartolovich unearths a range of management texts and advertisements that surprisingly adopt cultural studies for the service of transnational corporations. And, in a close analysis of the recent MLA volume *Redrawing the Boundaries* that claims to represent the state of the art of our various pursuits, she shows how the prevalent academic use of cultural studies largely retains traditional disciplinary boundaries and a nationalistic rhetoric. Arguing that these two strands neutralize the progressive impulse of cultural studies, she, like Farred, calls for a renewed left cultural studies that critiques the material inequalities of capitalism.

Part III, "Professional Channels," shifts from an analysis of our critical practices to one of the professional institutions that directly regulate what we do. In chapter 8, "Dancing in the Dark: A Manifesto against Professional Organizations," Lennard Davis takes to task the entrenched form of our professional organizations, like MLA, which, he argues, function as bureaucracies to maintain hierarchies of power. Some of the problems he cites include plenary sessions featuring "stars," distinctions between graduate students and senior faculty, and rigid periodization. Taking the example of the newly created Group for Early Modern Cultural Studies, which he helped start, he offers some practical proposals for change, aiming at genuine "thinking through," more professional conviviality, and less reproducing the extant hierarchy.

Chapter 9 focuses specifically on the present-day "Star System in Literary Studies," conducting a groundbreaking examination of its rise and effects as a model of career. In it, David Shumway traces the historical image of authority in literary studies, evolving from turn-of-the-century scholarly figures like George Kittredge to the current celebrity of figures like Jacques Derrida and Stanley Fish. To help explain this phenomenon, he looks to the larger model of celebrity in theater and film, as well as specific institutional factors, such as the rise of conference circuit and the explosion of literary theory from the 1960s on. In his final diagnosis, Shumway sees celebrity as a sign of weakened authority and public legitimation, and calls for more collective approaches to knowledge, not reliant on the authority or aura of an individual star.

In chapter 10, "The Life of the Mind and the Academic Situation," my contribution to the volume, I investigate models of professionalism and the ways in which our institutional conditions circumscribe our work. Discriminating between what I call "insular" and "consultant" versions of professionalism, I focus on how, especially in the humanities, our ideal image of "the life of the mind" and disciplinary devices gathered under the rubric of tenure serve to promote insular intellectual work. In contrast, I propose a model of "secular professionalism," which acknowledges our institutional setting in both its disadvantages and privileges and allows for a more socially engaged criticism.

Continuing the investigation of our professional institutions, Part IV, "The Job of Literature," looks more directly at the material terms of employment—for graduate students, in the job process, and in the reconfiguration of our roles as human resources managers. In chapter 11, "Time Out of Mind: Graduate Students in the Institution of English," Louise Mowder debunks the stereotypical image of the graduate student. Against a widely influential report by William Bowen and Neil Rudenstine offering remedies to lengthening "time to completion," she draws a different and more accurate picture of the present-day grad student from demographic studies—more returning students, more women, more minority students, and so on. Based on the actual situation of grad students as well as on her experience in the Graduate Student Caucus of MLA, she offers several proposals to improve the plight of grad students, starting in one's own department and extending to a larger political level. Her bottom line: always unionize!

Over the past decade, Terry Caesar has persistently shone light on the hidden aspects of professional life, especially for those of us who work at "second-rate" universities. In chapter 12, "Getting Hired," he meditates on the hiring process, delving into the mysteries of interviewing, campus visits, and ensuing departmental politics. He underscores the intangible and irrational nature of the process, beyond pure judgments of merit, comparing it to an amorous relationship whereby one is wooed or rejected. Exposing otherwise invisible factors of our institutional channels, he sounds a note against the elite representation of the profession.

In chapter 13, "The Educational Politics of Human Resources: Humanities Teachers as Resource Managers," Evan Watkins turns the tables on our standard self-definition (as professing literature) to investigate our actual function in contemporary corporate culture. Extending his original study of the role of English in circulating labor in *Work Time*, he shows how our professorial roles are changing to "specialized services" and that we now serve as "resource managers." Like Bartolovich, he surveys a number of management texts and their multicultural rhetoric, but unlike Bartolovich, he argues that we need not blanch at such corporate policies. Rather, we should recognize our positions, which might enable us to intervene more effectively; as he puts it, we need to "understand literary and cultural studies as a profession inserted within the multiple, diverse market field of professional service providers."

The institution of literature has come a long way from Cardinal Newman's humanistic enclave, and these chapters help to redefine some of the ways it has evolved. They argue in tandem for a greater recognition of the institutional dimensions of our work, dimensions that in effect make us. Though many are cautionary, they do not throw up their hands in despair but offer timely advice to redress contemporary politics of the profession and the university. To offer a roughshod paraphrase of Marx, the point is not simply to theorize institutions, but to change them.

Notes

1. As Pierre Bourdieu remarks, "Philosophers like to ask: 'What is thinking?' But they never ask what are the necessary social conditions for that particular way of performing the activity of thinking" (5). And he reasons: "If there is a question that philosophy, itself so questioning, manages to exclude,

this is the question of its own socially necessary conditions. Resembling the artist in this respect, the philosopher sets himself up as an uncreated creator, a creator whom there is no getting around and who owes nothing to the institution. The distance from the institution (and, more precisely, from the socially instituted post) which the institution itself allows him, is one of the reasons why he finds it difficult to think of himself in the framework of an institution" (4). This suggests that the tropism against thinking about institutions might be tied to the general belletristic ethos of letters.

2. For a model of such an investigation of publishing, see Richard Ohmann's still relevant "The Shaping of a Canon." That Ohmann's account, originally published in 1978, remains a rare example of this line of research speaks to the dearth and hence need of such research. It also speaks to the limitations of our training, largely preparing us to decipher the traits of literature rather than the historical institutions of literature. For one update of Ohmann, see Neilson's "Commercial Literary Culture," as well as the special issue of *the minnesota review* in which Neilson's essay appeared, "The Academics of Publishing" (n.s. 48–49 [1997]).

Works Cited

Bourdieu, Pierre. "The Philosophical Institution." Trans. Kathleen McLaughlin. *Philosophy in France Today*. Ed. Alan Montefiore. Cambridge: Cambridge UP, 1983. 1–8.

Burke, Kenneth. *The Philosophy of Literary Form: Studies in Symbolic Action*. 3rd ed. Berkeley: U of California P, 1973.

Graff, Gerald. *Professing Literature: An Institutional History*. Chicago: U of Chicago P, 1987.

Guillory, John. "Preprofessionalism: What Graduate Students Want." *ADE Bulletin* 113 (1996): 4–8.

Fowler, H. W. *A Dictionary of Modern English Usage*. 2nd ed. New York: Oxford UP, 1965.

Neilson, Jim. "Commercial Literary Culture." *the minnesota review* 48–49 (1997): 71–90.

Ohmann, Richard. *English in America: A Radical View of the Profession*. 1976. Hanover: Wesleyan UP, 1996.

———. "The Shaping of a Canon: U.S. Fiction, 1960–1975." *Politics of Letters*. Middletown, CT: Wesleyan UP, 1987. 68–91.

Robbins, Bruce. "The History of Literary Theory: Starting Over." *Poetics Today* 9.4 (1988): 767–82.

Sosnoski, James J. *Token Professionals and Master Critics: A Critique of Orthodoxy in Literary Studies*. Albany: SUNY P, 1994.

Watkins, Evan. *Work Time: English Departments and the Circulation of Cultural Value*. Stanford: Stanford UP, 1989.

Part I

The Institution of Theory

Chapter One

Framing Theory: The Disorganization of Historiography

Vincent B. Leitch

There are many ways to frame theory, as, for example, concocting syllabi, course descriptions, and pedagogical goals; putting together packets, casebooks, and anthologies of readings; constructing maps and models of the field; compiling area bibliographies and reviews of research; writing histories of the discipline; composing glossaries of key words; drawing up reading lists and exams; and producing specialized guides, introductions, and handbooks. Each of these genres of scholarship engages in the work of framing. To be sure, there is always already, in Derridean terms, a play of frames in arbitrary and determinate relations with one another. Invariably, these other frames turn out to involve some linkages with matters economic, social, political, historical. When it comes to frames, there are also questions not simply of inclusion and exclusion, concatenation and configuration, but of privilege and prejudice, memory and amnesia, highlights and blind spots, profit and loss. Because the various academic forms of framing named above have separate histories and require individual consideration, I shall limit this inquiry to one—writing histories of literary and critical theory, particularly of the contemporary period. Given our present moment of restructuring and transformation, I believe in the merits of a disorganized mix-and-match postmodern mode of history writing, but I am getting ahead of myself.

❦ ❦ ❦

To start, let me offer a simple heuristic scheme. There are five ways to construct histories of contemporary theory. One can focus on either leading figures, or key texts, or significant problems, or important schools and movements, or some mixture of the others. I shall comment briefly on each of the four main modes.

History of major figures scrutinizes the careers of a relatively few selected geniuses. Composed of a series of intellectual biographies, this kind of account suggests that cultural history and value are generated by gifted individuals whose special insights deserve care and reverence. It aggrandizes the concept of career and the associated idea of individual growth where the complete works afford evidence of decisive stages of development. Minor work can possess value in this context. Connections between and among luminaries may appear fortuitous or unimportant. In history as pantheon one is encouraged to admire. Not surprisingly, quotidian forms of theorizing don't register, and institutions seem vague backdrops.

One of the most salient features of history of key texts is that it deemphasizes professional biography and preoccupation with complete works and lines of development. Also it opens space for outsiders, as, for instance, Heidegger and Fanon, who work primarily in other domains, but who arguably have made significant contributions to literary and critical theory. History of theory here figures as a string of blockbusters, taking one's breath away. As in a world-class art museum, the masterworks risk decontextualization. To counter this shortcoming, sequences or groupings must be fashioned, possessing at least minimal plot or sense of progressive movement. Chronological order, if nothing else, implies forward motion. Still, monumental works appear to emerge at random. Among the things that disappear in this framework are histories from below made by minor figures and collectivities. A partial solution to this difficulty is to expand the category of key works to include coauthored texts and collections by diverse hands. Sooner or later, however, one has to interrogate the idea itself of great work, just as one has ultimately to put in question the notion of major figure.

History of theory that focuses on significant problems—like the conceptualizations of authorship, of literary language, or of reading—offers the "virtue" of coherence and the pleasure of managed variety. On the question of authorship, for example, one can trace intricate lines of reflections from, say, Wimsatt and Beardsley to Poulet, Gadamer, Hirsch,

Barthes, Foucault, Bloom, and Gilbert and Gubar. But the history of ideas approach—which often has a sequence of highly cohesive unit-ideas at its center—is open to existing critiques of traditional intellectual history. It dwells in the rarefied realm of concepts, separating ideas from complex intertextual networks as well as material contexts; it places too much emphasis on innovation; it privileges philosophically oriented theory, disregarding popular forms, as, in the present case, anonymous and collective modes of authorship typical of TV, cinema, advertising, street ballads, and hypernovels. History of problems is, in addition, frequently committed beforehand to liberal pluralist agendas where the teleology of theory purportedly leads to both improved argumentation and respect for all points of view. The difficulties of position-taking tend to be deferred.

History of schools and movements, a favorite mode among historians of contemporary theory, has much to recommend it. It provides a means of assembling numerous major and minor figures, influential texts, key problems, and institutional issues within coherent spaces—although these diverse materials must be made to exemplify significant features in school portraits. With the postwar enclosure of theory inside the universities and the diminution in the ranks of nonacademic critics and theorists, history of contemporary theory has had to attend, sometimes reluctantly, to such institutional factors as the formations of disciplines and programs, professional organizations, significant conferences, university presses, and journals. Histories of leading figures and major texts programmatically ignore such crucial matters. Given over typically to studying a wide array of groups, history of movements can dispense with teleology. Accordingly, history of theory need exhibit little evidence of any prearranged unity, evolution, cyclicality, devolution, or continuity. An obvious drawback of history of schools is its exclusion of mavericks, independents, and antidisciplinarians. Another limitation is its evident inapplicability to earlier eras, for instance, the Classical and Enlightenment periods. Also the categories "school" and "movement" can become so flexible that strange and strained configurations occur, as when critics like Riffaterre and Culler hold simultaneous memberships in two "schools"—structuralism and reader-response criticism. What happens to a cross-disciplinarian like Spivak? Is she a deconstructor, Marxist, feminist, postcolonial theorist, or advocate of cultural studies? The schools and movements approach also exacerbates the contemporary tendency to valorize theory and metacriticism and to devalue "practical criticism" and scholarship (especially textual editing). Finally, like histories of leading figures, key texts, and significant problems, histories of schools and movements run the risk of deemphasizing relations among theory and economics, politics, and other cultural spheres.

❦ ❦ ❦

With the restructuring now occurring inside and outside literary studies and the university, it is becoming less and less plausible to talk about *literary* criticism and theory. Literature is merging into the categories of discourse and culture. Many departments of literary study are being explicitly transformed, more or less grudgingly, into departments of literary and cultural study. Framing histories of contemporary theory from this vantage requires contractions, expansions, and novel arrangements. A new array of figures, works, problems, movements, and sites comes to the fore—and doubtlessly new modes of history writing will ensue. Polemical histories, especially from members of new social movements, are playing significant roles in this stage of transformation. The emergence of new disciplinary charters and paradigms entails historical revisions, reconstructions, and reframings. History of theory as a mixture of more or less incommensurable microhistories of precursors, texts, issues, schools, and institutions—variously intersecting with relevant social and cultural factors—strikes me as the best alternative for postmodern times. However urgently and problematically, it is a matter of unevenly yet innovatively desacralizing/resacralizing expanding archives of knowledge.

In my view, theory is undergoing less a simple expansion than a transformation. Not surprisingly, the agendas of current histories, textbooks, and other such framings often have more to do with memorialization and replication than charting vital knowledge. Meanwhile, the increasingly common reinscription of theory into new modes of practice signals the dissolution of ("pure") theory. It is in some ways a moment of posttheory. Today theory is to be found scattered through the fields of postcolonial studies, semiotics, women's studies, narratology, ethnic studies, media and cultural studies, pragmatics, queer studies, rhetoric, and indeed, national literary studies. Here literary studies is reconfigured not as a master discipline but as a regional discourse amidst a host of others. And yet this scattering, this dissemination, signifies not theory's demise, but a particular triumph through rhizomatous transformations, graftings, hybridizations. The modern framers of theory have usually found it a semiautonomous interdisciplinary field influenced by a limited range of established disciplines, especially philosophy, anthropology, psychology, and linguistics. Postmodern framers, however, continue discovering unstable and proliferating cross-disciplinary sites where new fields of inquiry as well as older disciplines (being restructured themselves) intersect in ways that render questionable the old terms "literary," "criticism," and "theory." In recent times "literature" has come for many intellectuals to mean not poetry or *belles lettres* but discourse. Similarly, "criticism" exceeds exegesis and approximates cultural critique. "Theory" increasingly designates neither method nor approach but both self-reflexive practice and productive pragmatic tools. Consequently, framing histories of contemporary literary and critical theory is, I believe, best done through disjunctive forms: such history approaches anarchistic romance, decentralized, carnivalesque, heteroglot, pluralized, irreverent, counterhegemonic, contentious.

While "theorists" started encountering more allies in the *fin de siècle*, I do not mean to suggest that we all become theorists by now (though everyone's views have theoretical implications, however inchoate), nor do I wish to declare victory for theory. Although shrinking, the number of holdouts remains large. The point is that theory among literary intellectuals has shifted from something like a relatively enclosed subspecialty to broadly diffused strands found in all specialties and subspecialties. This transformation testifies perhaps less to a happy destiny than to exhausted disciplinary paradigms seeking reinvigoration at numerous points. As a moment of "expansion," the shift in question strikes many commentators as a form of imperialism and others as a stage of Balkanization. It is neither. The incommensurabilities among different theory groups and figures undermine claims of imperialism. And the singular mode of dissemination of contemporary theory has ultimately more to do with the proliferation of new territories than with the struggle over existing ground, which, of course, continues unabated.

In these circumstances, framing theory as a scene of parochial turf battles misconstrues its mode of development. However disruptive they may be, departures are not simply takeovers. It is worth pointing out also that certain theorists regard the "expansion" of theory as a sad spectacle, signifying dilution, vulgarization, loss of rigor. Writing histories of theory that take into account innumerable intricate conflicting perspectives and lines of development profits from both lateral multiplications and intercut frames. The politics of this form seeks to dethrone teleological history in the name of a seriality without guarantees. Such a disorganized historiography does not deny that events are determined—after the fact and subject to dispute.

Chapter Two

The Theory Junkyard

James J. Sosnoski

> junk . . . [colloq] useless stuff, trash, rubbish.
> —*Webster's New World Dictionary*

Junk is a useful commodity. The term usually refers to old paper, metal, or rags but can include most anything we wish to discard. Junk is useful because it is worthless. It is useful to designate something as trash or rubbish. That allows us to replace it. We junk clothes, appliances, newspapers, magazines, and theories to make room for new ones. Throwing away ideas is as useful as throwing away newspapers. Both tend to accumulate rapidly and it is nice to have room for what is current. Critics notice when theories get "too old" and replace them ASAP. But where do old theories go? Surely theory junkyards exist—at least in our imaginations. I imagine our "theoretical archives" as personal junkyards—hard-to-reach basement shelves, boxes in attics, files that our current word processors barely recognize if at all. In my study, for instance, there is a huge closet full of blue, plastic milk cartons from Office Max crammed with folders containing fading photocopies of articles by Northrop Frye, Claude Lévi-Strauss, and other old-fashioned critics. That such places exist raises the question: Do theories become obsolete? Are there "theory junkyards"? The premise that there are such places allows me to raise the question: What is in the theory junkyard that should be reclaimed or recycled?

Many critics, for instance, have junked structuralism and along with it a lot of narratology. Yet, though designated as junk by poststructuralists who distrust them as linear and reductive, some structuralist theories of narrative are still deemed viable by other critics, a circumstance much in evidence in journals such as *Narrative*. Does this mean that the work of Greimas, Genette, or the early Barthes can be recuperated? (Maybe I should take them out of my blue milk cartons.) Or does it mean that one critical school's junk is another's wealth? Still, would either hypothesis account for Jameson's recycling of Greimas, Frye, Propp, and others in the "Magical Narratives" chapter of *The Political Unconscious*—is his use of their terms a reclamation, a recuperation, a rewriting, or a rereading of old and worn-out theory? Are these theories recovered in their former state or are they mended in some way? Are they altered so substantively that they require new authorship or have they merely been reinterpreted? Are they obsolete? Do Propp's terms survive Jameson's use of them? Do Frye's? Do Greimas's? What about Lacan's?

Lacan's terms are frequently used in current discussions. So, Jameson's use of them seems to require no explanation. But Propp's, Frye's, or Greimas's are not. For instance Propp's use of the term "plot" (a specific arrangement of narrative functions) would appear to be a clear instance of an "obsolete" concept long since tossed into the theory junkyard. It seems fair to say that Jameson is not using Propp's term in the way that Propp used it in *The Morphology of the Folktale*. Most critics regard Jameson as a poststructuralist, associating his work with a critique of the formalist assumptions on which Propp's work depends. When Jameson uses the term "plot," his readers are likely to assume he reinterprets it or rewrites it as a poststructuralist term. Or so the argument goes. I take a different view of the matter.

When we discuss a term's relation to other terms, we often locate it in a conceptual network wherein the use of any one term allegedly depends upon the use of all. In a conceptual framework (like deconstruction or New Criticism) the use of any term is said to depend on its link to the terms that form a "discourse" with it. Thus Jameson's use of the term "plot" should be classified differently than Propp's use of it. But is the former's usage grouped with Marxist usages and the latter with Russian formalist usages? Probably not. Yet if terms belong to a school of thought or discourse community and are thereby integrated in a communal "discourse usage," then the Marxist Jameson ought not to be using "plot" in the same sense as the formalist Vladimir Propp. Still, as we all know, it is not a simple exercise in classification to mark such differing uses. For instance, when Jameson uses Lacan's terms, he is often understood to borrow from psychoanalytic usage. This assumes—perhaps too readily—that Lacan's uses of the words in his texts are easily understood to function as a set of terms and that such integrated usage can be defined. It also seems to conflate the contexts in which these terms might be used—Jameson does not employ them to interpret psychoanalytic situations involving patients whereas Lacan, presumably, did.

Accounts of the effects of membership in a discourse community on its members tend to be exaggerated—perhaps because it is difficult to separate our perceptions of shared beliefs from the assumption that they form a community of interests. (This assumption is tantamount to inferring that Chicago Cubs baseball fans are Democrats. Who would accept the inference that because persons share a common interest in the Cubs, they must thereby hold beliefs in common?) Unfortunately, when a common denominator is found, unity seems to appear out of plurality. Though such "denominations" (classifications) can be handy, they are often arbitrary and misleading.

In literary study, the notion that using terms associated with a particular school of thought is an index of a shared practice is quite common. Yet one of the peculiar effects of assuming that persons who use the same "jargon" belong to the same school (also use the same methods of reading) is that such a view ought to mark its proponent as a member of the structuralist school of thought since the underlying conception of terms (that they draw their meaning from their function in a terminological system) is palpably structuralist. It would, therefore, be odd if a poststructuralist thinker held such a view. Contrast this formalist attitude toward terminologies to Derrida's warning that his terms are constantly shifting, even in the same work. (One might wonder, then, why critics schooled in deconstruction would worry about the way nondeconstructionists use Derrida's terms in their comments on his work; or, why they would accept the term *deconstruction* as a description of their reading habits.)

The notion that terms belong to terminological sets is the foundation of the belief that critical schools exist. Here is the logic of it: a critical reading is a description of how a text has been read. Thus a given reading is warranted by a specific conception of how texts can be read. In sum, the concepts which provide a model of texts form a theory from which a method of reading can be derived, since concepts of textual features allow one to describe reading acts, and any description of a text is, in effect, a set of instructions about how to read it. *In principle* theoretical models yield critical methods even though *in practice* they are blurred genres. However tautological the notion is that schooling produces schools, persons are unpredictable. Being schooled in a specific theory usually results in allegiance to its critical practices even when critics so schooled do not exemplify them. Critical allegiance is often a fashionable matter and the signature terms of schools are often invoked in ways that are incompatible with the implied authors they allegedly signify.

The preceding observations suggest the following provocation: the theory junkyard is a symptom of the schools and approaches mind-set according to which the former authorizes the latter. This attitude makes theory more or less equivalent to method. Like other machinations, methods wear down. They get old. As vehicles, they no longer take their owners where they wish to go in the same style at the same rate with the same panache. Or, like clothes, theories get ragged. Before that they go out of fashion and become worthless to the fashion conscious. They have to be junked, or so it would seem.

Let me digress for a moment and offer a hypothesis about the motives for "junking" terms (the materials from which theories and methods are constructed). If, like Wittgenstein, we described literary terms as tools, this would be a useful metaphor, particularly if we consider that tools are invented or altered in response to the changing conditions of the work they do. Electric drills replace hand drills, staple guns replace hammers for certain tasks, but hammers remain in the toolbox (though redesigned). Changes in tools correlate with changes in building materials and technology which, in turn, correlate with changes in cultural expectations. So we might say by analogy that terminology is the toolbox we carry to work and that it carries tools we replace when they no longer suit the materials available to us or no longer measure up to the expectations of our clients. Though I cannot explore this matter in any depth here, it seems germane to note that just as the use of tools is correlative to both the changing conditions of work and of cultural expectations, so also are terms in literary study correlative to changes in institutional commitments and in public expectations.

Perhaps influenced by a long-standing "knowledge for its own sake" educational rationale, we have a tendency to believe that the development of our intellectual frameworks derive from "paradigm shifts" in philosophy, anthropology, psychology, sociology, and linguistics which are independent of employer or client interests. I would suggest, however, that theoretical developments influence our work in large measure only to the extent that they match correlative changes in institutional goals and public pressures. Postcolonial theory (as a response to the public debates about multiculturalism) is an interesting case in this regard. Its advocates have adapted theoretical frameworks already in place to concerns that have more to do with intra- and extramural pressures than "paradigm-shifting" theoretical developments. Similarly the theoretical tools advocates of New Historicism use are already at hand. Indeed, many have wondered what is "new" about New Historicism. In the current climate, any shift in critical interest is likely to be described as "a new approach." Unfortunately we have inherited a publishing market that promotes new, just-out, up-to-date, current, lately issued, novel, original, fresh, and especially cutting-edge concepts to which the four recently published, major glossaries testify.[1] They also testify to the prevalence of schools and their approaches.

The schools and methods ideology that permeates histories of literary criticism (as well as encyclopedias, glossaries, and dictionaries) promotes the notion that theories become obsolete. Thus new theories can take the place of older ones just as newer critical readings replace older ones. Since new readings are often the product of new methodologies, it is useful to regard older methods as obsolete. This is a strategy that benefits a publishing industry tied to an academic market. As a consequence, the schools and methods conception of critical work commodifies terminology. Instead of treating terms as "working terms" appropriate to historically specific conditions of work, it codifies them as the "signature concepts" or "trademarks" of a particular school of thought. (Understanding that readings of literature to an extent have given way to readings of theoretical texts, such commodification of terms is a likely result of the book industries' marketing of *new* readings.)

New methods and new readings are disseminated as new schools or movements. When a critic forms a new method, often by extrapolating from interpretive procedures judged to be effective in neighboring disciplines, he or she can produce novel readings of literary texts. If these readings are imitated widely, he or she becomes, in Paul Bové's phrase, "a sublime master" (265). This pattern is palpable in the strange case of New Historicism. Stephen J. Greenblatt is the master reader of the school having become for many an "exemplary" critic (Vesser 244).

> Following Clifford Geertz [, Victor Turner,] and other cultural anthropologists, the New Historicist critics have evolved a method for describing culture in action. [Taking] Their [cue from Geertz's method of] "thick descriptions" [they] seize upon an event or

> anecdote—colonist John Rolfe's conversation with Pocohontas's father, a note found among Nietzsche's papers to the effect that "I have lost my umbrella"—and reread it in such a way that the analysis of tiny particulars reveals the [behavioral codes, logics, and] motive forces controlling a whole society. (Quoted from the back cover blurb of H. Aram Veeser's *New Historicism*; the brackets indicate what was omitted from Veeser's preface.)

As the cover also points out, "the rise of New Historicism" is "one of the most talked about developments in contemporary criticism." This verdict seems justified. According to a recent MLA survey, 39.7 percent of MLA members now regard New Historicism as an "influential theoretical approach." Until the 1990s, anthologies of literary criticism did not include New Historicism in their texts. Such texts are excellent barometers of institutional influence. This is reflected in recent anthologies. The percentage of New Critics represented in these anthologies has been dropping rapidly even though the school is still regarded by 64 percent of MLA members as influential. We can expect that soon New Critics will disappear as humanists did—Irving Babitt is no longer much included in anthologies and humanism is not even listed as a "theoretical approach" in the MLA survey. As the cover of Veeser's collection indicates, New Historicists are "seeking alternatives to the orthodoxies ranging from New Criticism to contemporary Franco-American literary theory."

Taking the notion that New Historicism is an alternative to New Criticism as my starting point, I wonder what is being thrown into our theoretical junkyard. Assuming that New Criticism is a name for a group of critics who shared common practices and terms, in the next section I first raise a question about the sense in which the careers of critics exemplify schools of thought and then raise a question about the extent to which the terms they use in their work can signify a particular practice. Specifically I ask: Is Cleanth Brooks a New Critic and is "irony" a New Critical term?

II

Cleanth Brooks, the quintessential New Critic, is surely the best instance of a matchup between an American critic and an American school of criticism. It is this pervasive fiction that I wish to address. Though Brooks is regarded in textbooks and histories on literary criticism as *the* New Critic, statistically speaking a larger percentage of his work is devoted to philology and historical study. Of his forty-year career, only eleven of those years saw the publication of close readings. In his later writings Brooks expresses concern that his emphasis on the text has been misread as a disregard for its various historical contexts. In an interview I conducted with him in 1985 not only was he quick to point out that a substantial portion of his scholarly work has been devoted to understanding the social, political, moral, religious, and biographical contexts of Faulkner's, Milton's, and Percy's work, but he insisted that the critics who complained that he disregarded history simply did not read all of his work.

Brooks's first book published in 1935 was on philology—*The Relation of the Alabama-Georgia Dialect to the Provincial Dialects of Great Britain*—as was his final project *The Language of the American South* (1985). In the early fifties, after he wrote the texts with which we associate him (1938–49), Brooks contributed "Part IV," to *Literary Criticism: A Short History* (1957), focusing on Richards, Empson, Eliot, Pound, Ransom, and Winters and the influence of Nietzsche, Freud, and Jung on literary critics. In 1963 Brooks published *William Faulkner: The Yoknapatawpha Country*, the first of three books on Faulkner, which represents a departure from his earlier work. This initial study attempted "to deal with William Faulkner's characteristic world" (vii). In it, Brooks shows how Faulkner developed out of a particular milieu and how this manifested itself in terms of ethical and religious themes in his work. The same year he published *The Hidden God: Studies in Hemingway, Faulkner, Yeats, Eliot, and Warren*, in which he defends modern writers on grounds quite "extrinsic" to the formal properties of the texts he studies, an enterprise that we would not typically associate with New Criticism. The same is true for *A Shaping Joy: Studies in the Writer's Craft*, published in 1971. By then Brooks's work had been the subject of so much commentary that he felt it necessary to remark:

> The pigeonhole assigned to me carries the label "The New Criticism." Now, it is bad enough to live under any label, but one so nearly meaningless as "The New Criticism"—it is certainly not new—has peculiar disadvantages. For most people it vaguely signifies an anti-historical bias and a fixation on "close reading." (xi)

Brooks hoped in *A Shaping Joy* to "mitigate the effects of an overshadowing generalization" (xix). Unless we wish to disregard Brooks's own testimony, it is difficult to consider his practice (in which materials *extrinsic* to texts are crucial) as an instance of New Criticism.

Indeed, Brooks's response to his typification as the quintessential New Critic ought to give us pause. With him we might well ask, Why do we employ these "overshadowing generalizations?" Ultimately to help us organize our work into manageable categories. There are thousands on thousands of critics writing millions of essays and books. We need some way of managing this information glut. Consequently we fall back on our accustomed matrices—the alphabet, chronology, and language. These help considerably. However, it is difficult to sort out the connections among critics and so we have to find other ways of organizing their works. Under the influence of disciplinary thought, we organized our work alpha-numerically according to fields, identifying Arnold, Austen, Barnes, Beddoes, Borrow, Bowles, Braddon, Brontë, and so on as nineteenth-century British writers. As the information glutted, we added additional categories—genre, for instance. To cope with "the theory industry," we borrowed again from our colleagues in the scientific disciplines and added the category, method, or, more humanely, approach. This gave us schools of thought. In his history of criticism, *Republic of Letters*, Grant Webster gives a capsule history of the "schools and methods" mode of organizing rapidly multiplying theoretical works:

> Among the most common sources of critical ideologies in the post-World War II period have been terms and values drawn from the contexts of other disciplines and applied to literature. These sources of literary charters are usually referred to as "approaches" to literature or "perspectives" on it, and the most common approaches were first expressed in John Crowe Ransom's *The New Criticism* (1941), where, despite his title, he classifies Richards as a psychological critic, Eliot as a historical critic, and Winters as a logical critic, and titles his last chapter "Wanted: An Ontological [or New] Critic." This formula was extended in precision and influence by Stanley Edgar Hyman in *The Armed Vision* (1948), in which twelve critics are discussed as representatives of possible approaches to criticism on the thesis that "what modern criticism is could be defined crudely and somewhat inaccurately as *the organized use of non-literary techniques and bodies of knowledge to obtain insights into literature*" (3). Thus Yvor Winters represents evaluative criticism, Constance Rourke folk criticism, Kenneth Burke the criticism of symbolic action, Caudwell marxist criticism, and so on. By centering on a single person and showing how he represents a kind of criticism (the past history and current use of each approach is traced explicitly), Hyman takes into account both the individual accomplishment and its representative

> nature. These various approaches were also considered by Wellek and Warren in *Theory of Literature* under the heading "The Extrinsic Approach," where the relation of literature to biography, psychology, society, ideas, and the other arts is treated fully with the purpose of showing the limitation of these approaches compared with the (to these authors) central study of the work itself (the "intrinsic approach"). In a 1961 essay, Wellek reclassifies the tendencies of modern criticism as Marxist, psychoanalytical, linguistic and stylistic, organismic formalism, mythic, and existentialist, but reaffirms his continuing belief that "formalist, organismic, symbolistic aesthetics . . . has a firmer grasp on the nature of poetry and art [than existential or mythic criticism]." (363–64)

In an effort to make literary criticism a reputable academic discipline, New Critical theorists ushered in an emphasis on method or approach, which indeed was the title of Brooks's most famous work, *An Approach to Literature*.[2] The passage from Grant Webster's *Republic of Letters* reveals some of the schools that have been thrown into the theory junkyard. Organismic Formalism and Folk Criticism sound discarded and Myth Criticism sounds at best antique whereas New Humanism has the ring of the archaic. What may have begun as an attempt to identify various approaches to literature has given way to a reified classificatory system which does, if Brooks's testimony is any evidence, pigeonhole critics into schools of thought. In my view, the usefulness of this system (which ought to be its *descriptive power*) is no longer a sure thing.[3]

Hoping that I have established in your minds a "reasonable doubt" that Cleanth Brooks was really a New Critic, let me point out that it is then even more questionable that a term like *irony* can be considered a "signature term" of a school called New Criticism. We can readily admit that many critics use "signature concepts"—that is, concepts that not only warrant their ad hoc practices but also identify them, however misleadingly, with a school of thought. "Signature terms" evoke in readers implied authors of theoretical consequence who are associated with particular schools of thought. In his *A Glossary of Contemporary Literary Theory*, for example, Jeremy Hawthorn begins the entry on "hegemony" with the remark: "A term used by Marxists to describe the maintenance of power without the use, or direct threat, of physical force; normally by a minority class whose interests are contrary to those over whom power is exercised" (103). As a consequence of such remarks, the term *hegemony* becomes a signature of a Marxist writer. Moreover, when a critic uses this term, its implied author is often taken to be Gramsci unless Laclau and Mouffe are referenced. Given the tendency to link a theorist's use of a term with a particular school of thought, we have to raise not only the question whether Brooks is a New Critic, but also whether the terms that he characteristically uses, such as *irony* and *paradox*, are thereby New Critical terms? Before I undertake to answer this question, however, I want to take up the most obvious objection to my previous observations, namely that while it is surely true that critical schools are invented categories or fictions used to organize our history, they are nonetheless useful fictions.

III

The "schools and approaches" frame we give to the development of literary study suggests that discourse communities dominate our work. As I have suggested, this is a dubious surmise. The histories we have invented for ourselves, organized around shifts from one school of thought to another, disguise highly individualistic critical work in the cloak of interpretive communities. This cloak may be the invisible one *only its wearer sees*. Is Foucault a structuralist? Is Fish deconstructive? Is Mary Louise Pratt a speech act theorist? Is Derrida Derridean if J. Hillis Miller (who has explained deconstruction in the *New York Times Book Review*) also is? To which school of thought does Kenneth Burke belong, choosing from among the several in which he has been included (formalist, psychoanalytic, Neo-Aristotelian, Pragmatist, Marxist, and of course dramatistic)? We are accustomed to labels. It is time to defamiliarize them. Is Lacan Freudian? Is Jane Gallop Lacanian? Wouldn't it be easy to marshal evidence against such claims?

Our recognition of schools is rooted in the recognition of signature terms—*hegemony*, *trope*, *paradox*, *unconscious*, *ideology*. Yet the uses of terms are notoriously disparate. The criticism of criticism is a stockpile of accusations that critics are unfaithful in their espousal of terms. Critics often call attention to the disciplinary force of signature terms: that they warrant critical practices. "Deconstruction" not only tells us which school of thought a critic refers to, but it also names a now legitimate critical practice.

Schools of thought allegedly have "disciplinary force" in the sense that they produce methods of reading. This is characteristic of a discipline. That is the good news, but there is bad news as well: once critics are institutionalized as a school—no matter how vigorously the founders may disown a shared methodology—their practices are converted into methods in the name of pedagogy. This is why textbooks and journals play such crucial roles in maintaining schools. Through selective excerpts, they promulgate an apparently unified methodology. Students are taught to read after a fashion. We do not often speak favorably about "method reading" because the terms collide when juxtaposed. Yet we seem to promulgate "method reading" by the way we have organized our "discipline," that is, by narrating the history of criticism as a succession of schools and approaches. But what about disclaimers from critics who are strongly associated with a school of thought. Cleanth Brooks is not the only critic to have cast some doubt on the relations between schools and their master critics.

Indeed, when we turn to "Towards a Poetics of Culture," an essay by the putative founder of New Historicism, Stephen Greenblatt, we read:

> I feel in a somewhat false position, which is not a particularly promising way to begin, and I might as well explain why. My own work has always been done with a sense of just having to go about and do it, without establishing first exactly what my theoretical position is. A few years ago I was asked by *Genre* to edit a selection of Renaissance essays, and I said OK. I collected a bunch of essays and then, out of a kind of desperation to get the introduction done, I wrote that the essays represented something I called a "new historicism." I've never been very good at making up advertising phrases of this kind; for reasons that I would be quite interested in exploring at some point, the name stuck much more than other names I'd very carefully tried to invent over the years. In fact I have heard—in the last year or so—quite a lot of talk about the "new historicism" (which for some reason in Australia is called Neohistoricism); there are articles about it, attacks on it, references to it in dissertations: the whole thing makes me quite giddy with amazement. In any case, as part of this peculiar phenomenon I have been asked to say something of a theoretical kind about the work I'm doing. So I shall try if not to define the new historicism, at least to situate it as a practice—a practice rather than a doctrine, since as far as I can tell (and I should be the one to know) it's no doctrine at all. (1)

What emerged from Greenblatt's essay was a "poetics" of culture that provided a method, a way of generalizing a practice. The practice shifts attention away from texts as such to their various social contexts. It is a reaction to prior practices. It existed without a name for years in the work of Stephen Orgel, Roy Strong, and D. J. Gordon to mention only the scholars identified by Veeser. If we add the work of Foucault, Jameson, and other prominent poststructuralist thinkers, the list gets longer.

According to Louis Montrose the term seems to have been introduced into Renaissance studies in Michael McCanles's "The Authentic Discourse of the Renaissance," but "gained currency from its use by Stephen Greenblatt in his brief, programmatic introduction to 'The Form of Power and the Power of Forms in the Renaissance,' a special issue of *Genre*" (32). The puzzling aspect of the "conditions" under which New Historicism was invented is the role advertising played—the marketing of a conception. No less an authority on New Historicism than its "alleged" founder considers it one of many "advertising phrases" whose "kind" are names of schools of thought or, to stay with his idioms, "theoretical camps."

I think Greenblatt is right. New Historicism gives a name, a logo, to work that "has always been done with a sense of just having to go about and do it, without establishing first exactly what . . . theoretical position [it] is" (1). Giving a name to work done by several hands comes *post facto*. The conditions under which schools of thought appear to be necessary are historiographical. Historians seem to need ways of linking critics together into critical movements. In the nineties having a history has given way to inventing one. Since stories about the past are stories, then my story becomes possible if it can also be your story. The message is the medium, a "sound bite." The "schools and approaches" is less an ideology than a mythology—a *mythos*, thoughts about thoughts embodied through narrative. What is this myth about?

All the talk about interpretive communities notwithstanding, criticism is still practiced as a highly individualistic enterprise in the academy. The reward system operative in the American university system is designed to breed specialists whose work is conducted in isolation. The governing assumption is that the results of highly specialized work will contribute to the accumulation of knowledge about a given subject if they conform to a disciplinary "paradigm." However, this goal is not a viable one in the study of cultures (of which the study of literature may be said to be a part). Interpretations are not easily reassembled as a body of knowledge about cultures (or about the texts called literature) since interpretations (no less than the texts from which they are derived) are an aspect of the culture under investigation. Nonetheless, histories of criticism are written as if the results of literary criticism were a valid if not enduring body of knowledge. In my view, work in cultural study is ad hoc, historically specific, local, and disposable. From this perspective, histories written about literary criticism are *Kritikromane*, that is, historical fictions bordering on a mythology that maintains belief in the *institution* of criticism.[4] Central to the myth of a *discipline* of literary criticism is the belief that critical work can be coordinated systematically into a body of reliable knowledge. The schools and methods ideology supports this belief because it seems to explain how a coherent body of knowledge about literature could be accumulated. It encourages us to believe that critics, however individualistic their practices, nonetheless form schools of thought which produce readings that can be considered reliable or definitive of a canon comprised of cultural wisdom. This myth is part of an elaborate mythology about universal cultural literacy.

If the schools and approaches ideology encourages individualistic work in literary study, should we not discourage efforts to describe our work in its terms in order to promote a more realistic, collective view of it? I believe that answering our "main question" will shed light on how we might answer this one. So, let me return to it: Which terms should be placed in the theory junkyard?; Which should be kept there?; Which should be recycled?

IV

The promotion of schools and approaches seems to invite us to replace one school of thought with another. This is tantamount to replacing one group of terms with another, for instance, Propp's with Jameson's. To consider what is involved in replacing one use of a term with another, I will construct a scenario in which a new school starts up. Let us stipulate that Peter Brooks's *Reading for the Plot* is the inaugural moment for a group of like-minded critics who find themselves being called Neonarratologists. Let us situate Brooks's practice by situating one of his key terms, *masterplot*.

This tactic forces us to admit that the term "masterplot" is a bit troubling. It is designated by Brooks as a "model for the uses of plot," "a model that would provide a synthetic and comprehensive grasp of the workings of plot" (90). It is not a master-narrative. Neither is the conceptual equivalent of Vladimir Propp's term, nor Lévi-Strauss's, nor Roland Barthes's, nor Tzvetan Todorov's. It seems almost the obverse of Ross Chamber's "story," but it is hardly the concept about which Gerald Prince writes. Despite the title of Brooks's chapter "Freud's Masterplot:

A Model for Narrative," we wouldn't want to say it is a Freudian term. Nor would we wish to suggest it means what archetype means in Jung. However we situate this term, there would be no apparent motive for replacing any of these conceptions of plot or story with Brooks's or vice versa. But, if there is no reason to throw away, say, Ross Chamber's term *story* and replace it with Brooks's *masterplot*, what reason could make us throw away Propp's use of *plot* and replace it with Brooks's *masterplot*? I cannot think of any lexicographic motive. There is no obvious reason for putting Propp's view of plot in the junkyard. In fact Brooks uses Propp's sense of a plot to clarify his model.

What if we argued that Propp's method is outdated and Brooks's is not. Would this count as a reason to throw away Propp's usage and replace it with Brooks's? We might say that Brooks uses Propp's term without employing his method, that he updates Propp's use of the term. If we take this position, however, then we have to admit that Brooks's use of the term is also already dated. All terms are dated. They all have histories. This raises the question, Is the use of a term dependent on its history?

Surely no term being used is an *old* term as long as it is used. Used now, it makes sense now. The use of a term is situational. This use is this use. Or to express this tautological relation in another way, if my use of the term plot corresponds to Propp's conception of repeated narrative functions, this does not make it any less a conception I use. Though I might express indebtedness to Propp, chances are that the way I use the term is not identical to his use, and chances are that his use is inconsistent. If I choose to use a term in a sense approximate to Propp's, the usefulness of that term for my project is not dependent on the original context by which the term was defined. Terms are not defined by proxy. They are reformulated by the inquiry undertaken. The term "plot," for instance, is negotiated by the persons who use it when they are using it. It does not necessarily depend on the earlier discourse for its meaning.

Method reading confuses this issue. The promulgation of methods derived from schools of thought leads easily into the meat grinder style of reading. Any text read is ground up into the theoretical terms applied to it. Methods produce new readings as surely as recipes produce meals. However, that Propp's method of analyzing texts is no longer much in vogue does not make the terms he used useless to us. Old terms do not become useless until they are "archaic," until they have no senses useful to present-day speakers. Schools sometimes have a noxious effect on the free use of terms. We sometimes think critics are misusing terms because they use the same words other critics use in different ways. Schools often seem to claim the right to use terms distinctively. What could count as a privileged use—that someone else used it? In such a contract, authority or authorship becomes ownership.

Recently we have been marketing terms. Critics have learned from businesses that concepts can be sold. Persuading your clients that a product is old is the first step toward persuading them to buy a new one. It is an old marketing technique. Though it seems to promulgate innovation, it actually promotes imitation. To sell a new product, you must first create a market for it, and to market a new product line, you must reproduce the same desire tens of thousands of times. The success of a new term is measured by the number of new readings it generates. It would be fascinating to search the *MLA Bibliography* for titles of articles invoking a signature term in the years immediately after the publication of the theoretical statement in which it was tellingly used. How many "The Implied Reader in . . ." or "The Narratee in . . ." or "A Postcolonial Reading of . . ." essays would we find? And would the disappearance of these terms in subsequent issues signal their demotion to the theory junkyard? Hardly! Fashion is not to be confused with function. Neither is the word "function" in the preceding sentence to be confused with the term *function* as it has been allegedly appropriated by structuralism.

Critical practices tend to be ad hoc and historically specific. Generalizing them into methodologies is a distortion and a fiction even when it is a helpful one. I believe the schools and approaches mode of organizing our work is no longer helpful—it disguises individualism in a cloak of collectivity. It has given us the theory industry and that has produced the buying and selling of signature concepts. We need to rethink our mode of historicizing ourselves. Rather than cloak self-aggrandizement in the fiction of interpretive communities, we need to show how concurrent projects have thrived on critical differences. We need to show that the rewards given by institutions to individual critics depend on collective work. Instead of schools and their master critics, we could think in terms of projects and the problems they address. Instead of thinking that theories end up in junkyards, we could think of theorizing as the persistent recycling of tools for the cultural work confronting us in the discursive forms of sexism, racism, isolationism, and elitism.

Notes

1. *The Johns Hopkins Guide to Literary Theory and Criticism* (1994), *Encyclopedia of Contemporary Literary Theory* (1993), *A Glossary of Contem-*

porary Literary Theory (1992), and the sixth edition of *A Handbook to Literature* (1992). A good example of the many glossaries published in the nineties is *An Encyclopedia of Contemporary Literary Theory*, which the University of Toronto Press published in 1992. The volume is divided into approaches, scholars, and terms that are listed for the readers' convenience. Meticulous in her efforts to be discriminating, Irena Makaryk, the editor, identifies 49 approaches to literature still current in literary studies and 134 scholars who exemplify them. That this is a considerable increase over Vincent Leitch's identification in *American Literary Criticism* of some 13 schools of criticism (though he does identify 157 scholars who exemplify them) is easily explained. The Encyclopedia covers the world of criticism and Leitch only covers America. However, since Leitch admits in his Introduction that he left out many schools, we arrive at the number 46 if we subtract European schools such as Croation Philological Society, Nitra school, and Tartu school from Makaryk's list.

In her Introduction, Makaryk writes that "this volume is intended to suggest the immense scope of current theoretical approaches." She determined her list on the basis of the "most frequently cited" schools in various bibliographic indices, certainly a useful indication of contemporary literary critics' views. Remarking on her list of scholars, Makaryk notes that they were "Not always neatly pigeon-holed into any particular school or approach" (viii). I take it then that sometimes they were considered to be an exemplar of a particular school of thought. And, of course, many of the essays do this. For example, Cleanth Brooks is "described as 'the quintessential New Critic'" (quoting Robert Con Davis; 264). This is a judgment which Leitch shares.

2. I. A. Richards in England and John Crowe Ransom in America were both adamant in their writings about the need to make literary criticism more disciplined. Ransom, in particular, called for a science of criticism.

3. Rather the classificatory category "approach" as it is employed in reference works like the MLA Bibliography and textbooks on critical theory has become meaningless—just as Brooks warned. Recall that Makaryk used as the basis of her identification of approaches the counting of citations. This does not ensure that because a group of critics are lumped together into a category, for instance, the one called the "Yale school," that their critical practices are in fact tantamount to a shared method.

4. I describe this process in detail in Part One of *Token Professionals and Master Critics*.

Works Cited

Bové, Paul. *Intellectuals in Power: A Genealogy of Critical Humanism*. New York: Columbia UP, 1986.

Brooks, Cleanth. *An Approach to Literature*. 3rd ed. New York: Appleton-Century Crofts, 1952.

———. *The Hidden God: Studies in Hemingway, Faulkner, Yeats, Eliot, and Warren*. New Haven: Yale UP, 1963.

———. *The Language of the American South*. Athens: U of Georgia P, 1985.

———. *The Relation of the Alabama-Georgia Dialect to the Provincial Dialects of Great Britain*. Baton Rouge: Louisiana State UP, 1935.

———. *A Shaping Joy: Studies in the Writer's Craft*. New York: Harcourt, 1971.

———. *William Faulkner: The Yoknapatawpha Country*. New Haven: Yale UP, 1963.

Brooks, Peter. *Reading for the Plot: Design and Intention in Narrative*. New York: Random House, 1984.

Greenblatt, Stephen. Introduction. "The Form of Power and the Power of Forms in the Renaissance." *Genre* 15.1–2 (1982): 1–4.

———. "Towards a Poetics of Culture." Veeser, ed. 1–14.

Groden, Michael, and Martin Kreiswirth, eds. *The Johns Hopkins Guide to Literary Theory and Criticism*. Baltimore: Johns Hopkins UP, 1994.

Hawthorn, Jeremy. *A Glossary of Contemporary Literary Theory*. London: Edward Arnold, 1992.

Holman, C. Hugh, ed. *A Handbook to Literature*. 6th ed. New York: Macmillan, 1992.

Jameson, Fredric. *The Political Unconscious: Narrative as a Socially Symbolic Act*. Ithaca: Cornell UP, 1981.

Leitch, Vincent. *American Literary Criticism from the 30s to the 80s*. New York: Columbia UP, 1987.

Makaryk, Irena, ed. *Encyclopedia of Contemporary Literary Theory: Approaches, Scholars, Terms*. Toronto: U of Toronto P, 1993.

McCanles, Michael. "The Authentic Discourse of the Renaissance." *diacritics* 10.1 (1980): 77–87.

Montrose, Louis. "Professing the Renaissance: The Poetics and Politics of Culture." Veeser, ed. 15–36.

Propp, V. *Morphology of the Folktale*. 2nd ed. Trans. Laurence Scott. Ed. Louis A. Wagner. Austin: U of Texas P, 1968.

Sosnoski, James. *Token Professionals and Master Critics: A Critique of Orthodoxy in Literary Studies*. Albany: SUNY P, 1994.

Veeser, H. Aram, ed. *The New Historicism*. New York: Routledge, 1989.

Webster, Grant. *The Republic of Letters: A History of Postwar American Literary Criticism*. Baltimore: Johns Hopkins UP, 1979.

Chapter Three

Orbiting Planet Foucault

Paul Trembath

> As to those for whom to work hard, to begin and begin again, to attempt and be mistaken, to go back and rework everything from top to bottom, and still find reason to hesitate from one step to the next—as to those, in short, for whom to work in the midst of uncertainty and apprehension is tantamount to failure, all I can say is that clearly we are not from the same planet.
>
> —Michel Foucault, *The Use of Pleasure*

As any seventies "theorist" turned millennial "historicist" can probably still recall, Nietzsche was fond of asking the following question: "Have I been understood?" His own implied answer was always something like "Well, of *course* not. Who, after all, has ears nowadays to *hear* me?" We can well imagine Foucault, perhaps Nietzsche's greatest elaborator, asking us the same question: "Have I been understood?" The answer to Foucault's query, given our current cultural-critical rubric, could only be "Well, yes and no." For we academics *do* have ears for Foucault, but they are "certain" ears, ears that can only hear certain things.

This is no doubt due to Foucault's academic reception—a reception by now as "overdetermined," in old-fashioned theoretical terms, as it is diffuse. Despite all our important "materialism," we revisionists of Foucault seem to work less well "in the midst of uncertainty and apprehension" than did Deleuze's "self-appointed archivist" (*Foucault* 1). We of course have our "practical" reasons, but we are starting to hear *in* Foucault the kinds of ideas and justifications that can accommodate the Post-Theoretical easy-listening habits of a growing critical intelligentsia. Such habits would indeed be "tantamount to failure" on Planet Foucault—an earthbound satellite that nearly all contemporary critics "orbit" partially, even as they manifest strong centripetal inclinations to return to the very Humanist Commonsense that Foucault's centrifugal thought forever asks us to question.

Foucault is undeniably a major player in the swerve toward critical "historicism" that captivated academic inquiry in the 1980s and continues to animate criticism up to the present. As Frank Lentricchia explained (or perhaps invented) in the by-now "classic" *After the New Criticism*, the influence of Derrida's "deconstruction of metaphysics" on Yale-influenced literary theory was beginning, toward the end of the 1970s, to appear increasingly "hermetic" after the collapse of Eliot-inspired New Criticism in prestigious 1960s English Departments. What was left? Since nobody felt inclined to return to "aesthetic" approaches to literature that would reconstitute "pre"-poststructuralist emphases on authors and autonomous texts, Foucault seemed a viable way to engage History while maintaining the poststructuralist emphasis on the contextual constitution of categorical authors, texts, readers, critical procedures, and readings themselves. That is, the relevance of poststructuralism could be both reaffirmed and improved by emphasizing a concrete "historicism" (Foucault's) over what was increasingly seen as an idealist "textualism" (de Man's, Hartman's, and Miller's versions of deconstruction). This is of course old news;[1] yet without some account of what motivated the "Foucauldian" sublation of "literary Derrideans" in American universities and journals, the bizarre pertinence of the anti-Hegelian Foucault to our professionalized academic environment since 1980 cannot be sufficiently grasped or even addressed.

Foucault is usually diced, spliced, and doled out by contemporary critics in ways that encourage us to read Foucault (if we continue to at all) as the inventor of a three-part philosophy (Hoy 3). These parts are either gloriously reconcilable or irreconcilable, depending on the attitudinal preference of the "Foucauldian" hermeneut in question. Deleuze recently argued that philosophers (as "friends of wisdom") were friends and creators of concepts, but that philosophers were also each others' antagonists, since concepts cluster around proper names ("Conditions" 471–73). Well, in this register Foucault established three friendships on the planet that bears his name: one with discourses and epistemes (as an archaeologist); one with disciplinary surveillance or power/knowledge (as a genealogist); and one with ethics or the practices of the self (as an "aesthetician of existence"). This tripartite version of Foucault is the one we find in most critical synopses of the philosopher's work as a whole, yet it is the first two "Foucaults" with whom criticism is currently on "friendly terms," since they are both more or less compatible with the present emphasis on cultural politics that is central to contemporary criticism. I see this as a brilliant *extension* of the eighties reaction against the "hermeticism" of literary deconstruction, if it nonetheless puts Foucault to "use" in ways that dull the subtlety of his thinking, while blinding us somewhat to the growing predictability of our own.

So who specifically is orbiting Planet Foucault (besides "all of us"), and how? Perhaps no critic did more to encourage scholars to consider the political consequences of literary scholarship and criticism than the extraordinary Edward Said. It was Said more than Lentricchia who had given Foucault the nod and Yale Derrideans the kick as early as *Beginnings*, and who continued to mount an argument for an engaged literary criticism through his seminal *Orientalism*, *The World, the Text, and the Critic*, and other writings. The important "Post-Colonial Turn" that a lot of contemporary criticism has taken over the past fourteen years owes a great deal to Said's astute directing of Foucault's thought, as well as to the postcolonial work of Homi Bhabha and the more Derridean-Marxist feminism of Gayatri Spivak. What is central to Said's use of Foucault is a tendency to revise what many critics consider to be Foucault's "descriptive quietism" with the engaged pragmatics of Gramsci's postscientistic Marxism—a Marxism that can transform Foucault's emphasis on the "specific intellectual" into Gramsci's communally (but not transcendentally) based "organic intellectual." Additionally, the emphasis on a politically/academically *engaged* Foucault has been productively developed in Paul Bové's ambitious *Intellectuals in Power* (in a way that leans more toward Foucault than Gramsci), as well as in Jonathan Arac's *Critical Genealogies*. All in all, the comparison of Foucault with Gramsci has produced valuable "activist" results (at least in Theory), but in a selective fashion that sometimes suggests, not without a certain legitimacy, that a lot of Foucault is just "transgressive" aesthetic posturing. In an era of daily stock market reports, Gramscian Foucauldians argue compellingly that critics are in no position to endorse cultural theories that, as Marx blistered earlier of Hegel, cannot transcend speculation into practice.

Other no less Foucauldian materialists see things a bit differently. Their categorical interests remain more overtly literary than political, but they would align themselves with the Gramscian activism of Said and Bové, I suspect, if theoretical push came to revolutionary shove. I am referring, of course, to the New Historicism that emerges in the eighties literary scholarship of Greenblatt, Dollimore, Sinfield, and others—a historicism which, at least in the case of the latter two critics, owes as much to Raymond Williams's *Marxism and Literature* as it does to Foucault's *Discipline and Punish*. Foucault's emphasis on the constitutive materiality of cultural representations comes to the foreground in such work, but usually in a way that refurbishes discussions of Renaissance authors while implying that "cultural works" continue to be coextensive with the legitimation or subversion of political regimes in the present. What is loosely called "cultural materialism" has its popular academic origins (at least in the U.S.) in the New Historicism and in journals such as *Representations*, although an emphasis on a textual-based reception historicism emerges concurrently in the work of Romantic scholars such as Marilyn Butler and Jerome McGann. What remains Foucauldian in these various historicisms is the focus on the unconscious coextensivity of cultural representations with the "normative" tendencies of any political or literary-canonical status quo. Many critics discern an attitudinal difference between the likes of Greenblatt and Dollimore. As Philip Rice and Patricia Waugh suggest, Greenblatt is closer to the passive "pessimism" of Foucault whereas Dollimore is closer to the activist "optimism" of Marx (260); that is, the former supposedly sees power as all-appropriating, while the latter does not. Yet we must remember that one moment's discursive version of action is another's passion, and resist universalizing the potential benefits or bankruptcy of Foucault's "political" thought, since new versions of what "activism" entails might well be in the discursive works.

Foucault, of course, was important to other eighties theorists, critics, and philosophers, if only as somebody to one-up, or again as a "proper name" in a constellation of Stars within which philosophers, if clever enough, could situate orbits of their own. I am reminded of a provocative moment in eighties criticism—namely, that of the New Pragmatism. To judge from the examples of Richard Rorty, reader-response critic turned pragmatist Stanley Fish, and Walter Benn Michaels, Foucault at his best had moved us away from Philosophy (often conflated with Pure Theory) toward a "historicism" whose least common denominator became "communal consensus." Where Foucault had productive "consequences," his work could be read as an antifoundationalist dismissal of all "transcendental guidelines" that might claim to distinguish between "right" and "wrong" interpretations of texts or of the "world." Where he had bad ones, Foucault (like deconstructors) took the "textbook problems of philosophy" too seriously (Rorty 104) and refurbished the Kantian metaphysics of "conditions of possibility" all over again. Foucault, in effect, was something like a Bloomian strong poet who had invented a "new description" of the world for our democratic edification, but it was a mistake to confuse this "new description" with an insight into the workings of power or a theory of "history" (as did Foucauldian Marxists). New Pragmatists thus conflated their critique of philosophy as a "mirror of nature" with historical criticism as a "mirror of society," the better to reduce *all* criticism to the well-received and marketable category of creative writing.

I "suggest" (I wouldn't want to "argue" with a New Pragmatist; I could not "win") that this somewhat Bubbathustrian reading of Foucault collapses Dewey and Foucault into something like "Fouey"; it is a reading of Foucault that recycles our passive common sense (either in the name of Rorty's hypersecular Philosophy as Creative Writing, or in the name of a "moral solidarity" that tolerates "private artistry" [193–98]) while neglecting the possibility of a *constructive* pragmatism that might prepare the conditions for an alternative, and perhaps better, common sense (Deleuze and Parnet xii). I think Foucault would have diagnosed our "micro-political" tendency here—our *liberal* desire to be led—in slightly less than a microsecond. Yet it promises to take some brilliant exegetes and "practical" engineers of Foucault years, if not decades.

To be fair, however, to the genuinely political merits of New Pragmatism—at least where it seriously overlaps with Foucault—one must acknowledge the compelling political theories of Laclau and Mouffe, and of the "Neo-Gramscian Pragmatist" Cornel West.[2] Laclau, Mouffe, and West—as well as the feminist socialist Nancy Fraser—owe a great deal to Rorty's revision of Dewey, and to Rorty's convincing view that it is both thoughtless and dangerous to confuse one's individual self-fashioning with an absolutist mandate that encourages political transgression. Whereas Laclau and Mouffe use Rorty's Pragmatism to criticize the transcendental claims of structuralist-inspired marxisms, West revises Marxism as an ethics whose root workability, as in the Foucauldian Said and Bové, must be based on the organic experiences of collective groups. The "Pragmatism" that we're offered here owes as much to Foucault as it does to Rorty, if only because the liberal distinction between "public" and "private" life is not taken at face value, nor as a metaphor that provides any reliable descriptive alternative to Marxist emphases on collective "individuality." Nor am I overemphasizing Pragmatism's important relation to Foucault here; it is significant (not least of all because it suggests the Girardian state of contemporary criticism) that Lentricchia's Foucauldian historicism should have found its way to Pragmatism by way of Kenneth Burke, whereas the New Pragmatism of Walter Benn Michaels turned more and more toward "New Historicism" as cultural materialism became the dominant trend of criticism in the late 1980s and 1990s.[3]

The Pragmatist response to Foucault is additionally central to Foucault's (non)position vis-à-vis the "postmodern debate" of the 1980s—a debate that centered around the thought of Jürgen Habermas and Jean-François Lyotard, as well as around Rorty (more orbits, folks). Nowadays this debate seems pretty dead, but it was crucial in the development of what we now refer to as cultural criticism (at least, once again, in the United States). It was in the exchange between Habermas, Lyotard, and Rorty that the word "postmodernity" came to the fore in political discussions concerning the limits of democratic "consensus" (Habermas insisting we needed communicative foundations for consensus, Lyotard equating all consensus with "terror," and Rorty refounding "democratic" antifoundationalism on *laissez-faire* consensus). This debate fueled an interdisciplinary interest in cultural materialism, and then disappeared. Foucault's emphasis on constitutive representation fared well in this climate, and the techniques of materialist criticism were applied, from 1983 up until the present, to all spheres of "cultural production." Moreover, the New York Art world moved quickly in the mid-1980s from an appreciation of Barthes and Lacan to Foucault, as exemplified by the journal *October*. NYC's increased interest in Foucault, Baudrillard, societal postmodernity, identity politics, and so on is a brilliant, albeit manufactured, part of this postmodern package.[4]

But by far the most important applications of Foucault—Post-Colonialism aside—have occurred in feminism, multiculturalism, ethnic and gender studies, as well as in Birmingham-inspired analyses of popular culture. There can be no question about this. Foucault has provided a materialist arsenal (with its Bakhtinian emphasis on "margins" and "centers") without which the most urgent issues of contemporary criticism would have little or no academically sanctioned voice in our "postdeconstructive" America, despite the earlier articulation of "cultural materiality" in the work of Stuart Hall and Richard Hoggart. As Naomi Schor argues, the first volume of *The History of Sexuality* prepared the ground for Eve Sedgwick's and Judith Butler's important emphasis on the priority of gender-positioning to sexual preference (276–78). Additionally, this insight has been brilliantly developed in Gay and Lesbian Studies in the work of D. A. Miller, Diana Fuss, and others. And the use to which Foucault has been put in current cultural criticism—as the latter collapses the distinction between "high" and "low" culture in order to examine the political effects that cultural works produce on living individuals—is best exemplified in Grossberg's, Nelson's, and Treichler's anthology *Cultural Studies*. This anthology is a cornerstone in the academic production of cultural studies, as the 42 anthologized cultural critics productively address the realities of racism, homophobia, eco-devastation, sexism, and class discrimination that are manifest in our unwitting consumer *and* canonical Euro-American culture. All of these criticisms owe something to the emphasis on constitutive representation that is central to Foucault's work as a whole.[5]

None of this, however, does much with the later "ethical" emphasis in Foucault—the third and thus far neglected "friend" whose only expression finds conflicted voice in the work of Charles Taylor, James Bernauer, Geoffrey Galt Harpham, but above all in the truly exceptional work of John Rajchman. Rajchman is absolutely singular in his dealings with Foucault; it is Rajchman who addresses Foucault's notion of the "difficulty" of "becoming what one is"—an ethical difficulty without transcendental guarantees that requires the "countereffectuation," the Nietzschean affirmation, of one's ungrounded "self" in a way that criticism at present overlooks, and which is also articulated in Deleuze's work on the Stoics in *The Logic of Sense*. In contrast with Rajchman's Foucault, the "ethical" Foucault that James Miller describes in *The Passion of Michel Foucault*, for all its thematic brilliance, is an Existentialist in poststructural togas. And Miller's biography of the Great Philosopher ultimately provides less information about the "practices" of Foucault's "self," for those of us who are interested, than the more "detailed" biography by Didier Eribon.

The proper name of Deleuze keeps cropping up here, largely because it is my growing hunch that Deleuze "heard" Foucault, knew the planet, in a way quite unique in Foucault's reception. Foucault did not hear Deleuze quite as well (how *could* he have through all the accolades?), but he often, perhaps too easily, expressed his allegiance, his shared Nietzschean debt. I think Deleuze can help us move beyond the one-dimensional "materialist" morass within which we are caught—not the "antipsychiatric hedonist" of "total flows" that most 30-something cultural critics dimly recall only to dismiss, but the *unheard* Deleuze who rejects the simple emphasis on either textualism (Derrida) or historicism (Foucault) in favor of a "radical empiricism"—the *affective* Deleuze who sees no *qualitative* difference between "organic" and "cultural" materiality, as do all cultural critics.

What Deleuze might yet bring to Foucault's reception can be found in his books on Foucault, Nietzsche, and Spinoza. The Foucault text argues that Foucault's archival scholarship emphasizes the "statement" over the "proposition" or the "phrase." This means roughly that traditional scholarship either *abstracts* its content from already "molar" categories that it can paraphrase (the proposition), or *sublates* categories it finds "ideological" in dialectical ways (the phrase). The Foucauldian "statement," in contrast, accounts for the invention of the categories it examines while inventing new ones, and is thus protentive and singular in a way that the *reactive* vocabularies of "phrasers" and "proposers" are not. Most critics, in this sense, are proposers and phrasers who either reproduce the authority of inherited categories by iterating them, or who provide them with additional descriptive urgency by sublating them (back to Hegel and early Marx).

The problem here is that proposers and phrasers reembody the very conditions of *signifying* containment they oppose. They lack the affective power to hear in Foucault an unreceived version of aesthetics—one that does not invoke "art" by way of phrases or propositions, and which describes the body as a locus of affective power (a local aesthetics).[6] Difficulties arise, however, given that "cultural" rhetoric—in both its evaluative *and* analytic modes—can only make sense of the word "aesthetics" in relation to categories like "art," "aesthetic intentions," and so on—categories that Baumgartian formalists celebrated, and which Benjamin-inspired critics of "ideology," at least on the dialectical surface, seem to oppose.[7]

Deleuze's *empiricist* Foucault, in contrast, can suggest that formalists and cultural materialists *share* a reactive allegiance to the metonymic association of "art" with "aesthetics"—formalists by way of the proposition (repetition), and materialist critics of ideology by way of the phrase (dialectic). The word "reaction" functions in Deleuze's empiricism in the same way that the word "ideology" functions in cultural historicism, but it resignifies aesthetics (as affective power) without "reproposing" art, and thus diverges from the "reactive" metonymies that embody "cultural" work in general. Indeed, Deleuze's philosophy suggests that everyday life[8] can be understood in terms of affective (creative) power without being "primordial" (i.e., without being "prior" to what historicists would call "the mediations of culture"); that contemporary "historicist" or "cultural critical" vocabularies might themselves be instances of "reactive" affective power; and that everyday life can take on an "aesthetic" (affective) meaning without taking on the reactive identity of "art." Our *active* consideration of this might prepare the conditions for an analysis of how the word "culture," like its predecessor "art," is itself coextensive with postmodern consumer markets: markets that convince us again and again that "creative power" (or its critically acclaimed sublation as ideology) is always elsewhere—that is, with *fame*, whether we find it in "cultural works" or critical articles. And it could position the body (with its power to affect and be affected) as the active/reactive mediator of world events in place of the "simple" exteriority of culture. But in these back-to-Trilling times, Deleuze's dense mixture of Foucault, Nietzsche, and Spinoza does not get much attention, neither do journals seem very interested in publishing research that develops it.

There are reasons for this, and they have to do with the state of critical inquiry as we expect it. Critics are starting to revise Foucault in the mimetic name (did it *have* to happen?) of Necessity—a necessity certainly refined beyond any transcendental notion of "universal" aims or causes, but re-universalized in terms of the reactive, *instrumentally* constrained common sense within which we actively prosper and suffer. Everything in Foucault's thought suggests we might also write to overcome this common sense, and thus many of the concrete social problems with which it coextends. But we, in our competitive academic empathy, are beginning more and more to accommodate the going common sense in the name of "social responsibility" (we do this by "reading" MTV), the better to convince ourselves professionally that the unexplored regions of Foucault are old, while our overdetermined applications of Foucault are new. And we call this "practice."

Maybe for now we're practical, but we will not be for long.[9] More than Marx, Foucault always knew how ineffectual our inherited definitions of practice could be. The facile recognition of what constitutes "practice" is the principal condition for a marketable idealism, and if we do not guard ourselves practically against this danger we will end up pretty much where we left off—paying lip service to institutional "culture," only now within the conceptual matrix of a new critical orthodoxy. I sometimes fear this has already happened, and there is no better indication of this than an academic constellation of star-level "materialists" against whom the raising of such a charge would simply seem unfathomable. What next? Foucault, protentive *and* materialist to the marrow, never said.

I am nonetheless most hopeful about the social and intellectual potential that Foucault's work still provides us and grateful for the important critical work that has already developed, both explicitly and implicitly, out of his thinking. But I have doubts about where this will all lead, culture being what it is. I see brilliant critics using Foucauldian ideas in the name, and in the important concrete service, of social reform. I see absolutely extraordinary "historicist" scholars of canonicity, class structure, the arts, popular culture, gender, ethnicity, and sexual preference absorbing Foucault's thought to bring about, to advocate and struggle for, a more tolerant and responsive collective social reality. I see the old poststructuralist vocabularies revised in ways that encourage sensitivity to *all* diversity, and I see this as an urgent, absolutely requisite task of contemporary criticism, activism, and everyday thinking.

But I also see the containment of all this sneaking in quietly in the form of professional academic careerism, facile "posttheoretical" historicisms, the reputable commodification and marketing of critical "geniuses" in the institutional (and ultimately economic) inertia of avant-garde Modernism. Their dialectical passion for art aside, Adorno and Jameson know what they are talking about—they are talking about themselves, about *us*. We are smart—all of us cutting-edge critics transforming old-fashioned "literary theory" into cultural critical "practice"—but we are stupid, too. It is our fame, our success (or *desire* for it), that makes us stupid, that makes us passive and fetishizable; for our professional self-admiration can encourage us, in our currently "practical" mode, to sometimes think we have exhausted Foucault, when it is more likely *we* who risk becoming exhausted, commodified—returned precisely to the "flattened" postmodern conditions that we sincerely strive to oppose.[10] We risk transforming difference into mere diversity, into fifteen minutes of famous Otherness. And all of this in the service of a categorically "cultural" rhetoric that, let's face it, critics from both the Left and Right welcomed with open arms after the difficulties of Theory. Surely this tells us more than we might want to know.

I can imagine how Foucault would have declared war—unconditional war—on the word "culture" (since it is the *working* concept of culture, after all, that packages marginal and centrist "identities" alike), as readily as he declared war on the word "Man," and no doubt for historicist reasons. And why not? There is nothing in the word *culture* that automatically resists homogenization, any more than there is in the word *Man*. But we do not see it; we are not yet *asked* to. Cultural theorists run as readily to the institutions that refurbish and profit from familiar "cultural" categories (the novel, painting, cinema, poetry, music, scholarship, Theory, etc.) as did old-fashioned "aesthetes." It is their inherited right of contract. And political Foucauldians are becoming famous with a good Kantian conscience—something I do not think Foucault, for all his enormous "difficulties," ever did.

Foucault must remain open: *that is what he is for*. But we risk closing him off in the name (and practice) of immediately workable versions of difference: versions that cannot do much more than multiply familiar categories and identities (such as Art); solicit "genealogies" or "reception histories" of these categories; or address these categories as "ideological products and producers"—the better, of course, to sell them (along with all the "articles" in question) all over again. Despite all our academic smarts (and they are more than considerable), we are presently recuperating the same "cultural" categories that the centrifugal *example* of Planet Foucault so generously suggests we might overcome. Given the luck that "naturally" follows from hard work in our consumer culture—and this culture extends into academia—we are in a legitimate position to remarket both these categories and ourselves, if we are not careful, in a way that we just might come to deserve.

Notes

1. It seems to me that academic criticism has by now overnarrated deconstruction as a "quietistic" form of critical inquiry. Critics would do better to think about what deconstruction might yet contribute to progressive criticism. For example, cultural criticism has tended to downplay the significance of Derrida's critique of the categories within which we think and act (literature, consciousness, the subject, Art, etc.), while doing genealogies or *ideologiekritiks* of specific *works* that are circulated through our sense of these categories. Yet criticism would benefit from a continued "deconstruction" of such categories, provided that our widespread "experience" of such categories is explained in terms of the capital that inscribes their sense in our very bodies—that is, so long as Derrida is aligned with Marx and (someone I take to be the missing link in this equation) Deleuze. Such a criticism could maintain Foucault's insistence on historicism while aligning it with a structural (or relational) element that his "politics of transgression" so sorely lacks. Additionally, it could explain how certain capitalized affects are perpetuated in the otherwise progressive projects of cultural critics—those in particular that derive their "cultural authority" from an engagement with artworlds and their packaged aura of radicalism.

2. In quite productive ways, Laclau, Mouffe, West, and Fraser preserve the antifoundationalism developed in the work of Rorty, Fish, and Benn Michaels, but they do so without falling into the ideological "liberalism"—with its facile

and uncritical distinction between the public and private—that is so all-pervasive in Rorty's pragmatism. See Fraser's *Unruly Practices* (93–110), West's *The American Evasion of Philosophy* (208–10), and in general Laclau and Mouffe's *Hegemony and Socialist Strategy*.

3. A version of mimetic desire revised through Marx and Deleuze might account for the competitive state of academic criticism. In a more or less reactive state of professional competition ("I want it because you want it"), academic bodies compete for the attention bestowed on academic "stars" by bodies such as their own. The body whose critical capacity receives the most "attention" is the one simultaneously invested with the most cultural capital, and this produces our collective experience of that body's greater *value* (with its coextensive powers of thinking and doing). The ability to use critical language in ways that acquire capitalized attention is *the* affective power of the academic body, and order-words such as "art," "ideology," "aesthetics," and so on signal the shared affective range of the competing bodies in question. What is at stake—at least for academic/cultural capital itself—is the degree of capitalized critical attention that bodies can virtually *become*.

4. If it seemed for a brief alterian moment that theory might challenge the concept of Art itself, NYC gave us MLA deconstructions, genealogies, and sublations of "modernist aesthetics" instead, and we ended up with categorical Art all over again (only now as "cultural work" with both "materialist" and "antifoundationalist" seals of approval). To witness how "theoretical" criticism can challenge Modernist versions of aesthetics while *revitalizing* the corporate hegemony of the New York Artworld, see the art criticism of Hal Foster, Rosalind Krauss, Michael Newman, and contemporary anthologies such as Kirk Vaarnedoe's and Adam Gopnick's *High and Low*. Perhaps "aesthetics" *wasn't* the definitive—or even pivotal—perpetrator of "cultural hegemony" that we took it to be. Perhaps the business of Art is far more "plastic" (if less "organic") than any Modernist could have theorized in His wildest imperial dreams.

5. Although I do not mean to suggest that all cultural critique is reducible to Foucault and his reception, it is just plain true that Foucault's much publicized emphasis on Man as a product of "discourse" and his "genealogical" approach to historical scholarship prepared the conditions for (1) an antifoundationalist theory of constitutive representation, and (2) a kind of reception historicism that accounts for the becoming dominant of certain representations over others (of sexuality, criminality, corporeal health, etc.). Extend Foucault's guiding assumption and method (that "identities" are representations and that all representations have dis/empowering histories) to categories such as ethnicity, gender, sexual preference, canons, and so on, display a love of detail in your research, and collapse the distinction between "ideology" and "discourse" in your critical procedures (sound familiar?), and you've got a bird's-eye view of the contemporary state of critical inquiry.

6. This will sound strange to readers, since buzzwords like *aesthetics—a* currently prohibited term—will set off a whole chain of capitalized critical

reflexes that will render the implication of Deleuze's thought taboo *before it is even thought*. The later Foucault's use of the word "aesthetics" can be aligned with Deleuze's emphasis on active and reactive "affects," but for us to be able to *hear* this we must overcome our own reactive affects—that is, *capitalized* academic affects that train us to hear the word *art* every time we hear the word *aesthetics*. Unless we learn to read Deleuze's philosophy as a materialist aesthetics that can overcome the reactive concept of art, critical capital will prohibit any attempt to associate aesthetics with immanent life by reducing any such attempt to "spontaneism" or "avante-gardism" (corporate life-as-art) or to "aestheticized" politics (political leadership as *artistry*).

7. For the received differences between "evaluative" and "analytic" approaches to culture see *Political Shakespeare* (Dollimore vii). See also Alexander Baumgarten's *Reflections on Poetry*, Walter Benjamin's "The Work of Art in the Age of Mechanical Reproduction," and Martin Jay's chapter on "'The Aesthetic Ideology' as Ideology" in *Force Fields*. The metonymic association of the word "aesthetics" with words like "art," "creativity," "beauty," and so on originates largely in Baumgarten's study of poetry and extends into twentieth-century formalism. Benjamin dismisses this metonymy as an "ideological" one while nonetheless recycling "art" and "aesthetics" as lexical equivalencies, whereas Jay argues that Benjamin's distinction between "politicized art" and "aestheticized politics" has *itself* become ideological through overuse.

From a Deleuzian perspective, however, these positions are not very different: they all maintain *some* archival investment in the metonymic association of "art" with "aesthetics," and consequently can only articulate the word "aesthetics" in "evaluative" cultural ways. In fact, Foucault at his most reactive also exchanges these terms by associating an "aesthetics of existence" with the activity of "creating oneself as a work of art" (see *The Foucault Reader* 350–51). It seems the stock exchange of the word *aesthetics* with the word *art* extends beyond Modernist formalism into the capitalized rhetorics of cultural critique itself. Academic bodies become the *affective site* where cultural capital and order-words enter into renewable relations of sense, marketing, and management. I suggest that these relations are at present more overdetermined than they need to be.

8. The Lefebvrian term *everyday life* is by now familiar and has been pertinent to the development of cultural studies as a whole. Deleuze, however, can introduce a postpsychological theory of affects to cultural discussions of everyday life (see Deleuze on Spinoza, as well as Elizabeth Grosz's and Michael Hardt's excellent readings of Deleuze).

9. The current "practical" emphasis in criticism has its impractical side. The present interest in reconstituting some form of agency after the poststructuralist critique of the subject is too secular. First, it returns us to human-centered notions of willful action—notions that, despite the best "activist" intentions of current criticism, coextend with the reactive individualist ethos at the unconscious heart of American racism, sexism, homophobia, class discrimination,

eco-destruction, and so forth. Second, while it perpetuates our humanist common sense in order to bring about effects of urgent social transformation, the binding element that constructs and coordinates this common sense is capital itself, and capital can continue to produce reactive bodies and desires in order to perpetuate its monopoly on consumer attention, even in a more "progressive" world. I suggest that we critics combine Marx's critique of capital with Deleuze's theory of affects in a way that can incorporate what is best in practical criticism with what is best in poststructuralism. If action is understood as affective capacity rather than agency, and capital is approached as that which makes and manages the reactive body, we have the theoretical basis for a practical criticism that can overcome the commodity status of all experiential humanism.

10. While I do not wish to suggest that anything can simply "resist" circulation through relations of commodification, things do pass through commodity circuits in different ways, producing different effects in general. The problem with fetishizing criticism is a particular one: the turnover of fashionable critical "styles" is too quick for any sustained critical attention of the world to take hold, yet academia's speed is the condition for its capitalized expansion and perpetuation. In the space of three decades American criticism has in effect demonstrated a short attention span. Doesn't the "quick" demand for new academic reputations risk reducing *any* type of criticism to a mere stage in the development of the Field, and might a lot of critical potential get lost in the process? This is precisely what the American reception of Foucault did to Derrida—Derrida became a thing "of the past" almost concurrently with his reception. If we do not align our engagement of *all* criticism with a critique of the academic capital that can coordinate our critical investments, the limits of what critics can think and do will always be shuffled about and manipulated by the demands of academic capital and not by the demands of life-at-large—and perhaps for a while in the novel name of Practice itself.

Works Cited

Arac, Jonathan. *Critical Genealogies: Historical Situations for Postmodern Literary Studies*. New York: Columbia UP, 1987.

Baumgarten, Alexander. *Reflections on Poetry*. Trans. Karl Aschenberger and William B. Holther. Los Angeles: U of California P, 1954.

Benjamin, Walter. "The Work of Art in the Age of Mechanical Reproduction." *Illuminations*. Trans Harry Zohn. New York: Schocken, 1969. 217–51.

Bové, Paul A. *Intellectuals in Power: A Genealogy of Critical Humanism*. New York: Columbia UP, 1986.

Deleuze, Gilles. "The Conditions of the Question: What Is Philosophy?" *Critical Inquiry* 17 (1991): 471–78.

———. *Expressionism in Philosophy: Spinoza*. Trans. Martin Joughlin. New York: Zone Books, 1990.

———. *Foucault*. Trans. Sean Hand. Minneapolis: U of Minnesota P, 1986.

———. *The Logic of Sense*. Trans. Mark Lester with Charles Stivale. New York: Columbia UP, 1990.

———. *Nietzsche and Philosophy*. Trans. Hugh Tomlinson. New York: Columbia UP. 1983.

———, and Claire Parnet. *Dialogues*. Trans. Hugh Tomlinson and Barbara Habberjam. New York: Columbia UP, 1987.

Dollimore, Jonathan, and Alan Sinfield, eds. *Political Shakespeare: New Essays in Cultural Materialism*. Ithaca: Cornell UP, 1985.

Eribon, Didier. *Michel Foucault*. Trans. Betsy Wing. Cambridge: Harvard UP, 1991.

Foster, Hal, ed. *The Anti-Aesthetic: Essays on Postmodern Culture*. Port Townsend: Bay P, 1983.

Foucault, Michel. *Discipline and Punish*. Trans. Alan Sheridan. New York: Pantheon, 1977.

———. *The History of Sexuality. Volume I: An Introduction*. Trans. Robert Hurley. New York: Pantheon, 1978.

———. "On the Genealogy of Ethics: An Overview of Work in Progress." *The Foucault Reader*. Ed. Paul Rabinow. New York: Pantheon, 1984.

Fraser, Nancy. *Unruly Practices: Power, Discourse, and Gender in Contemporary Social Theory*. Minneapolis: U of Minnesota P, 1989.

Grossberg, Lawrence, Cary Nelson, and Paula Triechler, eds. *Cultural Studies*. New York: Routledge, 1992.

Grosz, Elizabeth. *Volatile Bodies: Toward a Corporeal Feminism*. Bloomington: Indiana UP, 1994.

Hardt, Michael. *Gilles Deleuze: An Apprenticeship in Philosophy*. Minneapolis: U of Minnesota P, 1993.

Hoy, David Couzens, ed. *Foucault: A Critical Reader*. New York: Basil Blackwell, 1986.

Jay, Martin. *Force Fields: Between Intellectual History and Cultural Critique*. New York: Routledge, 1993.

Krauss, Rosalind. *The Originality of the Avant-Garde and Other Modernist Myths*. Cambridge: MIT P, 1985.

Laclau, Ernesto, and Chantal Mouffe. *Hegemony and Socialist Strategy: Toward a Radical Democratic Politics*. London: Verso, 1985.

Lentricchia, Frank. *After the New Criticism*. Chicago: U of Chicago P, 1980.

Martin, Bill. *Matrix and Line: Derrida and the Possibilities of Postmodern Social Theory*. Albany: SUNY P, 1992.

Miller, James. *The Passion of Michel Foucault*. New York: Simon & Schuster, 1993.

Newman, Michael. "Revising Modernism, Representing Postmodernism: Critical Discourses of the Arts." *Postmodernism: ICA Documents*. Ed. Lisa Appignanes. London: Free Association Books, 1989.

Rajchman, John. *Truth and Eros: Foucault, Lacan, and the Question of Ethics*. New York: Routledge, 1991.

Rice, Philip, and Waugh, Patricia, eds. *Modern Literary Theory: A Reader*. 2nd. ed. New York: Edward Arnold, 1993.

Rorty, Richard. *Essays on Heidegger and Others: Philosophical Papers*. Vol. 2. New York: Cambridge UP, 1991.

Said, Edward. *Beginnings: Intention and Method*. New York: Basic, 1975.

———. *Orientalism*. New York: Pantheon, 1979.

———. *The World, the Text, and the Critic*. Cambridge: Harvard UP, 1983.

Sartre, Jean-Paul. *Critique of Dialectical Reason I: Theory of Practical Ensembles*. Trans. Alan Sheridan-Smith. London: Verso, 1976.

Schor, Naomi. "Feminist and Gender Studies." *Introduction to Scholarship in Modern Languages and Modern Literatures*. 2nd ed. Ed. Joseph Gibaldi. New York: MLA, 1992. 262–87.

Varnedoe, Kurt, and Alan Gopnick. *High and Low*. New York: The Museum of Modern Art, 1990.

West, Cornel. *The American Evasion of Philosophy: A Genealogy of Pragmatism*. Madison: U of Wisconsin P, 1989.

Williams, Raymond. *Marxism and Literature*. Oxford: Oxford UP, 1977.

Chapter Four

This Feminism Which Is Not One: Women, Generations, Institutions

Devoney Looser

Because recent years have seen such widespread disagreements among feminists, trying to come to terms with the field of feminist studies today presents a daunting task.[1] Comparisons, juxtapositions, and mappings have been attempted, as feminisms have garnered a share of institutional cachet. To those just entering the fray, charting this territory may seem a never-ending task. Sorting through supposedly authoritative versions of second-wave feminist triumphs and setbacks frequently proves dizzying. There is more at stake in these versions than simply providing neophytes with much-needed summary. At issue in these classificatory negotiations is precisely "whose version of [feminist] history is going to be told to the next generation," as Jane Gallop notes (Gallop et al. 362). This is no small question. In the ongoing institutionalization of feminist studies, particularly in the humanities, generational conflict is one version of feminist history that is currently being drafted.

Who will be included in that next feminist generation (or if there will even be a next one) has been registered as an anxiety, especially among established feminist scholars. These speculations have led some feminists to conclude that "we" are now at an impasse (Fuss xii)—that "we" as feminists are dissolving (or have dissolved) as a "we." So-called third-wave feminists have been inundated with very particular versions of this alleged impasse. These versions usually seek to implicate our generation in the academy (whom I would identify as feminist graduate students and junior faculty) as the problem or as the solution. If consciousness of exclusion through naming is now acute, as Donna Haraway claims, so is consciousness of who or what will constitute "Feminists: The Next Generation" (155). In this essay, I consider the ways in which generations of feminists have been represented and what these models imply for those of us dubbed "young turks" ("Conference Call" 75).

Generational anxieties took hold in the guise of a theory versus feminism debate in the late 1980s. Young feminists practiced theory, so the stereotype went, and older feminists did not—nor would they want to. For instance, "feminist theorist" was written up as a contradiction in terms for Nina Baym. Baym writes that feminist theory succeeds only when it "ignores or dismisses the earlier paths of feminist literary study as 'naive' and grounds its own theories in those currently in vogue with the men who make theory" (45). Baym suggests that feminists who use theory wallow in male-identified esoteric luxury and ruin the sisterhood that she and other feminists created in the 1970s. There will be no future for a commonality of women, Baym claims, if we cannot "traverse the generations" (58). Baym suggests that she is a pluralist who laments the 'musts' and 'shoulds' of recent feminist criticism (59). Theorists, however, must and should be expelled from Baym's own sisterhood, it would appear. Such examples of feminists who would prefer to leave each other off the proverbial map during the late 1980s and early 1990s could be listed ad infinitum.

Feminist history has been described in other generational guises. In one version, political activism has been supplanted by a yuppiedom in which studying feminism is being "used" by graduate students. Annette Kolodny laments that "the seminar in feminist theory [has become] solely a means to professional advancement" (30). In an important article about the institutionalization and commodification of feminisms, Donna Landry similarly claims that sheis "unnerved" by "young feminist critics whose introduction to feminism has been a course in graduate school, usually one in 'French Feminist Theory'" (160). Unsympathetic readers might be tempted to ask about the absent professors introducing these unnerving young feminists to the field. Are not senior feminist faculty complicitous with the institutionalization of feminisms and feminist theory that they may (or may not) lament? In many of these versions of events the focus is not on tenured feminists but on academic daughters. It is the upstart daughters who have gone wrong, swayed by fashion, careerism, or political apathy. These monstrous offspring have either killed their mothers or loved their fathers to excess.

Blaming academic feminist "mothers" or "daughters" does little to further discussions of the so-called impasse, of course. To be sure, such blaming frames identities that skew the diversity within both groups. The linkage of youth with trendy or apathetic theories and age with dyed-in-the-wool activist feminisms is in itself a problem: there are theorists who were active in the feminist movements of the 1960s and 1970s and young feminists who do not do critical theory. There are even feminist theorists who are activists and nontheoretical feminists who do not do activism. The appropriateness of these assumed divisions is not what I would like to take issue with in this essay. The widespread assumption by many about the next generation of feminists is that we have been infected by theory.

In the last decade, theory/feminism antagonisms have continued to surface, although they seem to have been reconfigured into generational anxieties more generally. Even among those feminists who have aligned themselves—and not just males—with theory, generational speculations have come to the fore. In *Conflicts in Feminism* (1990), Marianne Hirsch claimed that feminists today have "somehow not been able to raise a generation that builds on what came before," and she lamented the passing of a feminist community in which it used to be a pleasure to work (Gallop et al. 365). Though Hirsch herself and many others have since questioned whether the community of seventies feminism was as unified and halcyon a sisterhood as has been claimed, nostalgia for early second-wave feminist practices has proliferated. Much of this nostalgia (and its subsequent generational implications) has circulated informally; I have seen it in countless conference question-and-answer sessions, for instance. Some of it can be documented in print as well.

Nancy K. Miller expresses such sentiments in her article "Decades" (1992). In her trademark style of personal criticism, Miller writes of the importance of constructing a feminist archives and collects anecdotes from her feminist coming-to-consciousness in the 1960s to the present. She concludes: "I confess: I look back wistfully to the 1970s . . . I miss the passion of community (what we took for community), and our belief that things would change" (80). Miller then links feminism's movement into middle age (characterized by retrospection and self-criticism) with what she calls the panic of her own aging. She asks, "Is there life for a female academic after the feminist plot of tenure and promotion?" Miller's article, in its adept mixing of personal, professional, political, and historical modes, raises many important issues for feminist histories.

However, some of the questions it raises are not necessarily the ones Miller would want asked. Job-seeking feminists might wonder whether or not tenure and promotion are worth excessive worry, as their plots wallow in the before section. Those of us who are not yet fully institutionalized might wonder whether or not we are even part of this middle aging of feminism. Must feminism's age be determined by the chronology of many second-wavers? To what age of feminism do twenty-something graduate students belong? To what age of feminism do graduate students and junior faculty who are now experiencing middle age belong?

In addition to the difficulties of feminist nostalgia and aging, troubling uses of the descriptor "passion" have become prevalent. A repeatedly invoked characterization of the next generation of feminists is that we may well be passionless where our predecessors were full of passion. Our dearth of passion has sometimes been linked to an abundance of theory. In "Passion and Politics in Women's Studies in the Nineties" (1991), Renate Klein argues that the early years of second-wave feminism were actually years of solidarity and inclusiveness and that seventies feminism wanted to, as she puts it, liberate *all* women (125). Many feminists of color, lesbians, and non-Western feminists have begged to differ, but these are not among those taken to task in Klein's article. Rather, poststructuralist feminisms in all of its guises are marked out as passionless, inorganic, unreal, and horrific.

Klein links these feminisms to what she concludes are parallel horrifying developments in reproductive and genetic technology. Klein's preferred politics, as she outlines them, would not highlight divisions but commonalities. Her conclusion shows what this would mean for the next generation:

> As we have a responsibility to pass on what has been created in the first twenty years of the women's studies movement to younger women, we need to work hard to maintain our continuity and continue our growth. We have the imagination, pragmatic shrewdness, and passion to turn "the margins" into the centre through using creative, wild, life-loving lateral thinking. (131)

This version of the feminist future contains its own horrors. Must we accept the process for continuity and growth that this platform imagines as productive? If so, does this leave supposedly young and poststructuralist feminists in some unimaginative, passionless margin, in need of a more true marginality? Might there be different ways of conceiving of feminist generational responsibilities?

In yet another example of documentable horrors, in *The Knowledge Explosion: Generations of Feminist Scholarship* (1992), Cheris Kramarae and Dale Spender suggest that their anthology contains a virtual absence of young feminists because there are so few. They write, "Another issue we would want to pursue now is, where are all the young women? They are virtually invisible in these pages" (15). Where, then, are the generations of their title? This dearth of young feminists may well be the case in larger circles.[2] It hardly seems to hold true in the academy, however, particularly in graduate study in the humanities and social sciences. For Kramarae and Spender, a supposed lack of young feminists is traced back to possibilities of ageism and, again, to difficulties facing established feminists trying to transmit information to the next generation.

Examples of feminists who would prefer to write up certain factions as more properly feminist than others might be listed ad infinitum as well. It is tempting to ask who is at fault when generations of feminists do not see eye to eye. At least part of the fault, however, is with the framing of the question itself. Blaming the impasse of feminisms on passionless graduate students who are, on the one hand, misbehaving children or bad daughters—or, on the other hand, on jealous or territorial mothers—proves dangerous and reductive. Such familial models keep feminist struggles from being viewed in larger contexts. If and how various ideas will "traverse the generations" involves social and institutional questions not limited to age- or role-bound understandings of either feminisms or generations.

Our field has seen a preponderance of feminist mapping of differences. In the face of such concentration on difference, many feminists have called for a truce. In part a response to the oft-cited backlash against feminism, we have heard many pleas to reforge a feminist community. Kolodny stated that it was important for us to tell our history so that others do not tell it for us, but she sought out a problematic "authentic intellectual [feminist] voice" to do so. She wanted to recover "the full diversity of our history as we lived it—and not as some cursory overview homogenized it" (36). Her wished-for harmony of feminist voices suggested that we could create a composite feminist picture if we only accumulated enough true stories. For Baym, it was not a matter of telling our own stories but of finding a way to enforce the retelling of an earlier story: feminists once got along well and now have fragmented, so we need to return to our beginnings. We must reradicalize or get back to feminist origins in order to "survive" (59), despite the fact that this origin has been called a legend by many who contend that "Feminists have been attacking feminists from the beginning" (Gallop et al. 365). These examples suggest that if feminisms do embrace a model for collectivity, it cannot be one that assumes or mandates agreement *in advance* (Shumway 115).

The very desirability of agreement and disagreement for feminisms could stand rethinking. This rethinking has been taking place in ways that go beyond filial piety models and mere nostalgia. The editors of the highly influential 1990 collection of essays, *Conflicts in Feminism*, state the hope that out of their book will emerge new models for preserving the dynamic possibilities of difference (5). Editors Hirsch and Evelyn Fox Keller register their complaint that schematic divisions among feminisms have grown stale (4). It would appear that here one might find new and promising tactics for approaching or engaging in conflict. In a dialogue about the state of criticizing in feminist criticism, Hirsch, Gallop, and Miller informally try to make sense of feminist struggles in the academy. The collective plea throughout the dialogue is to stop trashing among feminists and to keep up respectful criticism, using Gallop's tactics as a model. All three seem in agreement with Gallop's conclusion to the dialogue when she says: "We've had too much of this debate about whether we should or shouldn't criticize. What we need is an ethics of criticism" (368).

Earlier in the dialogue, Gallop points to Evelyn Fox Keller and Helene Moglen's widely cited article on competition among academic feminists, in which Keller and Moglen speculated that established feminists still see themselves as powerless and victimized and that graduate students resent this. Gallop notes that she feels vulnerable when attacked during a lecture, that she "forgets" that the person who is attacking her is a powerless graduate student. She points out that feminists do indeed have power in the world of academic literary criticism. It is important to link this aspect of Gallop's discussion to her conclusion to the dialogue. What does it mean that *these* are the feminists who are calling for an "ethics of criticism"? Halting feminist trashing seems more beneficial to those already in positions of power.

A groundbreaking 1990 "Conference Call" in *differences* raises similar questions. The written exchange among three so-called young turks of feminism and four established feminists is largely productive. The dialogue makes compelling points on the topic of women, generations, and institutions. Some of the "old guard" rightly criticize the family romance implications of feminist generational lore but go on to reject outright the term *generation*, calling it a false division. As is the case with an ethics of criticism, we should question whether it is easier to reject the very concept of a feminist generation from an established position. To call attention to the problematic ways that the term *generation* is currently constituted and circulated among feminists is one thing. To suggest that as a category "feminist generation" (like most divisions, at best incomplete and at worst false) need not require further scrutiny is quite another.

The *differences* "Conference Call" implicitly illustrates just how necessary a retheorization of generation, competition, and conflict among feminists is and should become. Some might suggest that less conflict and less competition—and not a retheorization of them—offer the answer. In her "Upping the Anti (sic) in Feminist Theory" Teresa De Lauretis problematizes simple feminism/theory divisions. She, like many, expresses exasperation with published feuds among feminist camps. De Lauretis derides Chris Weedon's attempt to "name a winner in the feminist theory contest" (258), suggesting that the answer is to eschew a feminist orthodoxy. De Lauretis outlines and then counts herself among yet another "new" camp, what she calls "non-denominational feminists" (260). These feminists, it would appear, are above and beyond the contest.

These sorts of conclusions rankle; on the face of it, many feminists are attempting inclusivity where others have sought divisiveness—trying to mend where others have practiced blatant one-upwomanship. Should these "inclusive" feminists be credited simply for trying to smooth the waters? The focus cannot be on good intentions. As Donna Landry has noted, "Feminism looks more homogeneous or heterogeneous depending on where one stands. And as with other commodities, only a committed user can fully experience the fiercer forms of brand loyalty which can make other positions, other brands, just disappear" (164). As this comment suggests, we might consider (1) how recent calls for feminist unity and calls for a halt to certain kinds of feminist contest and competition might make some of us "just disappear"; and (2) how to deal with this commodification in larger circles—how to ask different questions depending on where "we" stand.

There is a need for a healthy dose of skepticism about enforcing critical ethics. To be fair, most of the aforementioned critics do not pretend that problems facing feminists in the academy will be solved by a new-and-improved unity. But these unifying strategies beget further questions: will those who break hypothetical critical codes be relegated to the ground of nonfeminist or postfeminist? To what extent does an ethics of criticism comprise censorship rather than camaraderie? To what extent does the nondenominational monicker reinforce the already-empowered feminist institutional status quo? We should be skeptical about the "handing down" of feminist knowledge, as if it exists in a pure form and may not be altered in any way but negatively. At bottom these issues are about the desirability of feminist conflict. Such conflict—perhaps because of lingering nostalgia for an uncomplicated sisterhood or because of associations with "male" practices—has been largely devalued, though some have attempted to change this. Victoria Davion's article "Do Good Feminists Compete?" attempts to theorize feminist competition and conflict outside of a warlike model. More work in this vein is needed.[3] As bell hooks has written, "feminist solidarity rooted in a commitment to progressive politics must include a space for rigorous critique, for dissent, or we are doomed to reproduce in progressive communities the very forms of domination we seek to oppose" (4).

Additional issues that must figure into calls for feminist community are the simultaneous mainstreaming of feminism and the emergence of so-called postfeminism. When feminism is simplified and rewritten as monolithic (as it is in writings by Camille Paglia or Katie Roiphe), conflicts move from a question of degree to one of kind.[4] In such cases, the existence of feminist conflicts provides an answer as much as it does an impasse. Feminist outcry at the writings of Roiphe and Paglia illustrates that our conflicts provide a necessary corrective to simplistic accounts of who feminists are. Our conflicts in and of themselves provide proof against Paglia's claims that all feminists "embrace the feminine" and are "married to bookworm wimps" (A39). Feminist conflicts show that not all feminisms adhere to a victim model of identity politics, as Roiphe suggests. What has seemed damaging to our politics and praxis, then, also holds possibilities for redeployment as constructive strategy.

Seeing conflict as strategy, however, does nothing to address the issue of telling feminist history or histories. Are there ways to sort out competing definitions of feminisms and theories, to facilitate the would-be translation of feminisms between generations, or to intragenerationally traverse differences within feminisms? Are these even worthwhile goals? If feminist criticism is going to continue to make the enormous social impact during the next twenty years that it has made in the last twenty, as Linda Kauffman has argued, "it must constantly renegotiate its relationship to its own history . . . and to the dominant intellectual discourses of the present age" (3). For her part, Landry has concluded, "If we don't make academic feminism's uneven histories visible and accessible, no one else will. There can be no going back to a time before commodification, and it is up to us to articulate the historical differences between us, and their institutional effects, productively and not sancti- or acrimoniously"

(170). Taking these calls a step further, Mary Childers and bell hooks suggest that the way to deal with our differences is to reconceive of feminism itself. They provide important ways to continue this negotiation through viewing feminism as in motion—literally as movement—rather than as an always already established entity. This provides a promising beginning for dealing with feminist conflicts, within and across generations, though the emphasis cannot be on the singular movement. A notion of linear movement is an improvement over a model of stasis or of needed regression, but it too has shortcomings.

As part of the "feminism that is not one" in the academy, some of us in the next generation are painfully aware of the process of renegotiating relationships to our histories as feminists and to our espoused feminist histories. Our renegotiations are precisely what worry many senior faculty. How far will feminists new to the academy, working with seemingly unorthodox feminisms, stray from the last twenty years of work in our confrontations with other discourses, including those falling under the rubric theory? Who will determine and measure the point or points from which this supposed straying occurs? To deal with these questions most effectively, we must eschew versions of feminist history that posit a continuous line of heritage. There is no longer—there never was—an uncomplicated unity of feminist thought. As a result, strategies to forge (or reforge) a feminist community, to "get back to our roots" or to succeed in "transmitting" ideas, must be rendered suspect. To say this is not to deny the past and continuing importance of second-wave feminist work. Instead it is to attempt to open the term feminism to future possibilities, just as theorists Denise Riley and Judith Butler suggest we do with the category of women.

It is no easy task—no innocent task—to pronounce what it is time for emphasizing now, increased feminist collusion or continued differentiation. Haraway has argued that it is time for building coalitions, that at no other time was there greater need for unity to "confront the dominations of 'race,' 'gender,' 'sexuality,' and 'class' and that there has been no other time when this unity could have been possible" (157). Perhaps feminist strategies for integration and cooperation should become increasingly important. But perhaps some calls for unity, especially those seeking linear solutions or craving returns to bygone eras, provide little more than a way for empowered feminists to reign in the strays. Attempts to institutionalize a feminist community (whether through contesting contests, reforming bad feminist daughters, or returning to mythical origins) may ultimately constitute organized stifling by established feminists of emerging ones. Feminists of all stripes should be wary about making discord, discontinuity, and conflict taboo, especially when the intended or unintended result of such tactics is the silencing of new voices, whether appealing, strange, or dangerous.[5]

Notes

1. My thanks to those who have helped me grapple with feminisms and generations and whose valuable input helped this essay to take shape—especially Ann Bomberger, Antoinette Burton, Helen Cooper, Darlene Hantzis, George Justice, E. Ann Kaplan, Mona Narain, Sandy Sprows, Mary Sullivan, and Jeff Williams.

2. On young women and feminism, see Barbara Findlen's *Listen Up*; Darlene Hantzis and Devoney Looser, "Of Safe(r) Spaces and Right Speech"; Leslie Heywood and Jennifer Drake's *Third Wave Agenda*; Paula Kamen's *Feminist Fatale*; Devoney Looser and E. Ann Kaplan's *Generations*; Jean O'Barr and Mary Wyer's *Engaging Feminism*; and Rebecca Walker's *To Be Real*.

3. For further work on women and competition, see Garlick et al.'s *Stereotypes of Women in Power*; Longino and Miner's *Competition*; and Tracy's *The Secret Between Us*.

4. Two of the most visible academic feminists, Paglia and Roiphe, represent two generations—Paglia, a tenured Yale Ph.D., and Roiphe, a Princeton graduate student. Paglia and Roiphe share a castigation of victim models in feminism (often conflated to describe feminism as a whole) and offer individualist "bootstraps" feminisms instead.

5. It should be stressed that feminist work is a significant presence both inside and outside of the academy in the United States and internationally. The influx of international feminist work in the humanities during the last decade has been of crucial importance to the field. The disagreements outlined in this essay are only a part of—and certainly do not mean to ignore—the vital work on women and gender that continues to be produced.

Works Cited

Baym, Nina. "The Madwoman and Her Languages: Why I Don't Do Feminist Literary Theory." *Feminist Issues in Literary Scholarship*. Ed. Shari Benstock. Bloomington: Indiana UP, 1987. 45–61.

Butler, Judith. "Disorderly Woman." *Transition* 53 (1991): 86–95.

Childers, Mary, and bell hooks. "A Conversation about Race and Class." Hirsch and Keller, eds. 60–81.

"Conference Call." *differences* 2.3 (1990): 52–97.

Davison, Victoria. "Do Good Feminists Compete?" *Hypatia* 2.2 (1987): 55–63.

De Lauretis, Teresa. "Upping the Anti (sic) in Feminist Theory." Hirsch and Keller, eds. 255–70.

Findlen, Barbara. *Listen Up: Voices from the Next Feminist Generation*. Seattle: Seal, 1995.

Fuss, Diana. *Essentially Speaking: Feminism, Nature and Difference*. New York: Routledge, 1989.

Gallop, Jane, Marianne Hirsch, and Evelyn Fox Keller. "Criticizing Feminist Criticism." Hirsch and Keller, eds. 349–69.

Garlick, Barbara, Suzanne Dixon, and Pauline Allen, eds. *Stereotypes of Women in Power: Historical Perspectives and Revisionist Views*. Westport: Greenwood, 1992.

Hantzis, Darlene, and Devoney Looser. "Of Safe(r) Spaces and Right Speech: Feminist Histories, Loyalties, Theories, and the Dangers of Critique." *PC Wars: Politics and Theory in the Academy*. Ed. Jeffrey Williams. New York: Routledge, 1995. 222–49.

Haraway, Donna. "A Cyborg Manifesto: Science, Technology, and Socialist Feminism in the Late Twentieth Century." *Simians, Cyborgs and Women: The Reinvention of Nature*. New York: Routledge, 1991. 149–82.

Heywood, Leslie, and Jennifer Drake, eds. *Third Wave Agenda: Being Feminist, Doing Feminism*. Minneapolis: U of Minnesota P, 1997.

Hirsch, Marianne, and Evelyn Fox Keller. "Introduction: January 4, 1990." Hirsch and Keller, eds. 1–8.

———, eds. *Conflicts in Feminism*. New York: Routledge, 1990.

hooks, bell. "Thinking Past Censorship: Having the Courage to Criticize Our Allies." *On the Issues* XXV (1992): 4+.

Kamen, Paula. *Feminst Fatale: Voices From the "Twentysomething" Generation Explore the Future of the "Women's Movement"*. New York: Donald I. Fine, 1991.

Kauffman, Linda. Introduction. Kauffman, ed. 1–8.

———, ed. *Gender and Theory: Dialogues on Feminist Criticism*. Oxford: Basil Blackwell, 1989.

Keller, Evelyn Fox, and Helene Moglen. "Competition and Feminism: Conflicts for Academic Women." *Signs* 12.3 (1987): 493–511.

Klein, Renate. "Passion and Politics in Women's Studies in the Nineties." *Women's Studies International Forum* 14.3 (1991): 125–34.

Kolodny, Annettte. "Dancing Between Left and Right: Feminism and the Academic Minefield in the 1980s." *Language, Literature and Politics*. Athens: U of Georgia P, 1988. 27–38.

Kramarae, Cheris, and Dale Spender, eds. *The Knowledge Explosion: Generations of Feminist Scholarship*. New York: Teacher's College P, 1992.

Landry, Donna. "Commodity Feminism." *The Profession of Eighteenth-Century Literature: Reflections on an Institution*. Ed. Leo Damrosch. Madison: U of Wisconsin P, 1992. 154–74.

Longino, Helen E., and Valerie Miner, eds. *Competition: A Feminist Taboo?* New York: The Feminist Press, 1987.

Looser, Devoney, and E. Ann Kaplan, eds. *Generations: Academic Feminists in Dialogue*. Minneapolis: U of Minnesota P, 1998.

Miller, Nancy K. "Decades." *South Atlantic Quarterly* 91.1 (1992): 65–86.

O'Barr, Jean, and Mary Wyer, eds. *Engaging Feminism: Students Speak Up and Speak Out*. Charlottesville: U of Virginia P, 1992.

Paglia, Camille. "Madonna—Finally, A Real Feminist." *New York Times* 14 Dec. 1990: A39.

Riley, Denise. *"Am I That Name?" Feminism and the Category of "Women" in History*. Minneapolis: U of Minnesota P, 1988.

Roiphe, Katherine. *The Morning After: Fear, Sex, and Feminism on College Campuses*. Boston: Little, Brown, 1993.

Shumway, David. "Solidarity or Perspectivity." Kauffman, ed. 107–18.

Tracy, Laura. *The Secret Between Us: Competition Among Women*. Boston: Little, Brown, 1991.

Walker, Rebecca, ed. *To Be Real: Telling the Truth and Changing the Face of Feminism*. New York: Anchor, 1995.

Part II

The Question of Cultural Studies

Chapter Five

Cultural Studies: Literary Criticism's Alter Ego

Grant Farred

> As a result of developments in the new "social history," the humanist curriculum is increasingly open to popular histories and popular culture, while expanding its critical attention to cultural forms based on the experience of women, people of color, gays and lesbians. Pragmatic histories of the oppression, survival, and struggle for legitimation of marginal groups have begun to erode the massive cultural power generated by traditional idealist histories, histories which depict the moral struggles waged by heroic individuals in order to save Western civilization from successive "barbarisms."
>
> —Andrew Ross, *No Respect: Intellectuals and Popular Culture*

> While the Leavisite perspective engendered hostility to popular cultural formations and a generally anti-democratic ethos, it provided a method for analyzing cultural systems and products, and an emphasis on the importance of social transformation.
>
> —Michael Kenny, *The First New Left: British Intellectuals After Stalin*

From the very moment of its formation in the mid-1950s as the most dynamic intellectual articulation of the British New Left, cultural studies has always been ambiguously situated within the realm of both electoral politics and the academy. Politically and ideologically suspect to the Old (pre-1956) Left because of its apparent disregard for "real" issues of power (not least of which was its preparedness to complicate traditional modes of class conflict with new patterns of consumption), distrusted by the Oxbridge literary establishment because of its radical expansion of "culture" into the realm of the popular, the field occupied a position akin to that of New Lefters' relationship to the Labour Party. In the phrase of Stuart Hall, one of its founding members, the New Left was physically (and psychically) torn: it stood with "one foot in and one foot out" of the traditional party of the British left. Almost without exception, the New Left supported Labour electorally; ideologically it was at odds with the party on several issues, of which the condition and the future of the welfare state and the role of cultural politics were among the more contentious.

Within the academy, cultural studies' location has often tended to be less ambiguous (with a foot and a half out and a couple of toes in) than tangential, though invigoratingly so. Besides the much revered Birmingham Centre for Contemporary Cultural Studies moment (from the late 1960s through the end of the 1970s), an incarnation all too often uncritically celebrated, and a few experiments in the United States (of which the Carnegie Mellon program is among the most noteworthy), the field has never been formally institutionalized within the Anglo-American university. However, from within its marginal location in the university, cultural studies has crafted a rudimentary but intellectually vibrant home for itself. Through its impact on an assortment of disciplines, cultural studies (-inflected) courses have been taught in various language departments, the discipline of history, and other social sciences. From this amorphous and liminal site cultural studies has, over the past four decades, been able to impact and shape crucial debates about and within the "humanist curriculum." To state the case more strongly than Andrew Ross does in *No Respect*, cultural studies *opened* this curriculum to "popular histories and popular culture." The political struggle to change the shape, content, and pedagogical methodologies of liberal arts and social science courses could not have been envisaged, much less conducted, without the traditions of cultural studies. The commitment to remaking the humanist curriculum, no matter how incidental, tendentious, or fraught it may have been (and indeed continues to be), remains one of cultural studies' most important legacies to contemporary left scholars. It is a tradition of struggle that can be traced back to the earliest days of the New Left when

Hall, Raymond Williams, and Richard Hoggart were thinkers at once residually steeped in Leavisite criticism and attempting to produce a new form of cultural engagement in line with their political approach.

Although cultural studies has always been able to make history under conditions not of its own choosing (to colloquialize Marx), the contemporary conjuncture appears to be an especially challenging one. Cultural studies is at a crossroads, a juncture very different from the one outlined so spiritedly by Ross in the late 1980s. When *No Respect* was published, there was reason for optimism. However inequitably the resources were distributed both inside and outside the academy, the intensity of the "political correctness" wars led to (through both chance and political design) a series of gains by women, gays, lesbians, African Americans, and other traditionally disenfranchised constituencies. However, in an environment of academic (and larger sociopolitical) austerity, cutbacks, and the ever-receding possibility of tenure (the university's equivalent of retrenchment), cultural studies is now located at a crucial historical conjuncture. Increasingly represented by its opponents as a discipline of dubious intellectual merit, cultural studies finds itself more embattled than ever; the project is now waging a struggle for its political identity that will determine the shape and intellectual possibilities for its immediate future, and beyond. Cultural studies finds itself in an unfamiliar interregnum, precariously positioned between institutionalization and marginalization. On the one hand, after forty years of intellectual production, cultural studies is still far from entrenching itself in the academy; on the other hand, the efforts of these past decades have ensured that it does not quite retain the glamour and the inherent oppositionality of the periphery anymore either. Instead, it is in its New Left mode, a few toes inside the academic door and (more than) a foot and half outside that very same entryway, securing for itself a fragile and contradictory institutional space.

This essay examines the current conjuncture in cultural studies from the vantage point of its tussle with literature and criticism, a battle that has become increasingly contentious over the last few years. Contrary to the superficial premise that the struggle between literature and criticism and cultural studies is one between center and margin, this essay will demonstrate the expanse of common ground that links the two fields. As opposed to the antagonistic representation of their relationship, the two disciplines share uncommonly strong roots; in fact, one exerts a decidedly restrictive influence on the other. While the foundation of the dispute between literature/criticism and cultural studies is superficial, its consequences will nevertheless have real effects for how cultural studies situates itself within the academy. The links between the dominant traditional mode of close reading summarized under the label "New Criticism" (customarily applied to canonized literary texts) and cultural studies are closer, more intimate, and more intricate than we presume. "New Criticism" functions in this essay as a shorthand for Leavisite-inspired close reading, a practice in reality disbanded but not bankrupted by the theoretical developments of the 1970s. However, New Criticism's salient and most enduring feature, an insistently conservative text-centered approach, survived the innovative theories of the seventies; it remains a cornerstone of literary and cultural criticism. Its critical residues are crucial to those for whom cultural studies is the very nemesis of the cause of "Literature."

However, an exploration of the links between cultural studies and New Criticism will demonstrate how deeply they impact each other, particularly in terms of methodology. In *Literary Theory*, Terry Eagleton makes explicit the implications of the New Critical methodology of close reading: "To call for close reading, in fact, is to do more than insist on due attentiveness to the text. It inescapably suggests an attention to *this* rather than to something else: to the words on the page rather than to the contexts which produced and surround them. It implies a limiting as well as a focusing of concern" (44). The intellectual and institutional "focus of concern" in the debate between literature/criticism and cultural studies is an engaging one: Why is cultural studies under so much scrutiny, if not the target of vilification, at this particular moment? This is an inquiry which this essay will not answer fully, but it is a question that reveals several political agendas—not least of which, of course, is the political unconscious of the extant institution of Literature, as it were. Emanating from this issue is, however, a much more pressing set of concerns for cultural studies: How does the field use the space it has secured? Does it cede that territory? Can that space be expanded? What happens if cultural studies vacates, or is forced to abandon, the institutional space it now occupies?

Unlike Paul Smith, a prominent scholar in the field, who remarked in a recent interview that the "current state of cultural studies is actually bewilderingly diffuse and suffers because of that diffusion" (87), I would argue that the diversity of contemporary cultural studies is a healthy condition, though not unproblematically so. In the four decades of its existence, cultural studies has never been a single intellectual endeavor. Cultural studies is, as Graeme Turner puts it, a field characterized by "common elements" but it is by no means a "unified" project (11). While maintaining a singular political commitment to the experiences of excluded, marginalized and exploited communities, cultural studies has always shown itself capable of creativity, imagination, and flexibility—theoretically and ideologically, as well as in its object of study. Cultural studies takes as its object "traditional" literary texts as well as popular culture, a field with which it is sometimes—wrongly—conflated. The close relationship between cultural studies and popular culture has sharpened the issue about what constitutes the former practice, a matter which has long been subject to debate. However, for all its range, cultural studies has consistently shown itself capable of critical self-reflection and a keen awareness of its intellectual possibilities. For this reason alone, we should be loathe to police the field's breadth in the cause of resisting "diffusion." Any tendency toward disciplinary surveillance should be tempered by the plurality of its traditions. It is, after all, a field composed of "multiple discourses; it has a number of different histories" (Hall, "Theoretical Legacies" 279).

For all its reductiveness, the commonplace assumption that pits the study of literature diametrically against the study of culture is neither superficial nor anachronistic. Rather, it animates a long-standing dialogue over the legitimate field of study—a discussion that has attracted an illustrious list of scholars. As advocates of literature, culture (in its various manifestations), and criticism, Matthew Arnold, F. R. Leavis, Raymond Williams, to name but three, have over the last century or so formatively shaped this debate. The work of these three thinkers provides a map for the ways in which culture, literature, and criticism have impacted and reshaped each other—this trio's theories trace the trajectory from Literature to literature, from Culture to culture, from the discipline of English to that of cultural studies. In very different historical moments and in their distinct ways, the Victorian Arnold and the modernist Leavis were champions of bourgeois aesthetics. Arnold and Leavis offered definitions of culture commensurate with their (middle) class location: a vision which combined older traditions of Literature with the ambitions of their upwardly mobile socioeconomic constituencies. Ancient cultures were venerated as *the* Literary and intellectual model(s) and the standard by which all subsequent work was to be judged, almost always unfavorably. Arnold made this case most tersely in "Sweetness and Light," the opening chapter of *Culture and Anarchy*. In Victorian England, Arnold argued, culture was "valued out of sheer vanity and ignorance, or else as an engine of social and class distinction, separating its holder, like a badge or a title, from other people who have not got it" (43). Critical of a ruling class he regarded as lacking in scholastic rigor or ingenuity, Arnold derived his theory of criticism from older, more demanding, cultural traditions—Greek and Latin.

In turn Arnold subjected the existing Victorian literary canon and contemporary works to the standards he identified in these older models. Unlike Arnold, Leavis was less concerned with codifying Literature than with providing a methodology for the practice of criticism. Borrowing from Cambridge lecturer I. A. Richards's practical criticism, Leavis developed his text-centered approach to reading literature (especially poetry) in an effort to counter the theoretical and cultural malaise that characterized his intellectual milieu. Much of the work published in *Scrutiny*, a journal overseen by F. R. Leavis and his wife Q. D. Leavis, was to instill a tradition of rigor, through a reading of contemporary modernist writers (such as Auden, Caudwell, and Lawrence), into academic climate where little existed. "The rise of 'the moderns' in English literature," *Scrutiny* historian Francis Mulhern astutely reflects, "was expressed not so much in a flurry of aesthetic manifestoes as in a struggle for a new critical canon" (16). It was a signal, and often tendentious, conversation about 1930s culture that Leavis engaged from a strangely marginal institutional position. Excluded from the mainstream of Cambridge academic life because of his views, Leavis mounted a stinging critique of the literary standards espoused by the traditional intellectual ruling class—the "culturally homogenous milieu of England's public schools and older universities" (9). Schooled in the Leavisite moment, if not saturated by the Cambridge man's methodology, Raymond Williams explored the relationship between literary and philosophical production and historical context. In *Culture and Society*, a founding cultural studies text, Williams reviewed this process over a period of almost two centuries—1780 to 1950, from the Romantic poets through the nineteenth-century essayists to the modernists. In the course of his work, Williams came to assign ever greater significance to the routine and mundane quality of cultural production. He maintained, in one of his most memorable phrases, that "culture was ordinary."

Williams's claim engendered the rethinking of the relationship between literature of the Latin, Greek, or Romantic variety and the working class modes of expression (popular songs, ditties, political slogans) favored in postwar Britain. More than any other New Left intellectual, the Welsh Marxist was responsible for initiating conversations between texts traditionally studied in the university and those systematically excluded. Reflecting on Williams's role in the formation of cultural studies in his essay "The Emergence of Cultural Studies and the Crisis of the Humanities," Stuart Hall captures the essence of the Welshman's contribution. Williams's writings altered the way in which popular and working class cultures were received and engaged in the academy. Before Williams (and Hoggart and Thompson), Hall remarks, "Contemporary cultural forms did not constitute a serious object of contemplation in the academic world. And the political questions, the relationships, complex as they are, between culture and politics, were not a matter considered proper for study, especially by graduate students" (15). The efforts of the early New Left intellectuals such as Williams and Hall brought into question the very politics of canon-building and, we might add, its maintenance. In doing so these thinkers radically expanded the intellectual horizons of their peers and their academic and political successors, keeping in mind always their fraught but productive negotiations between their literary training and their left political impulses.

The stakes in this debate about literature and culture are, however, constantly changing. It is not incidental that the tension around the issue of literature versus cultural studies appears more acute at this particular juncture. Language departments, simultaneously bastions of literature and (somewhat less enthusiastically) proponents of new and groundbreaking scholarship, today find themselves in a tough bind—one that is only partly of their own making. Their enrollments continue to decline and these departments find themselves competing for undergraduates—and therefore faculty positions—who are more often lining up to pursue majors that are more tangibly marketable; that is, in the sciences or with an eye to going on to professional schools. In this environment cultural studies presents English departments, Comparative Literature departments and other language programs with an intriguing dilemma. Is cultural studies the dynamic, invigorating savior or is it the culturally diverse, insistently political Angel of Literary Death? By virtue of historical location and through almost no fault of its own, cultural studies has become a double-edged sword. Its first blade presents it as an anathema to a serious engagement with works of literature, its second glitters as a rare intellectual magnet—the initial lure to study Literature through the reading of (lesser) literatures.

It is, however, the first edge that provides the dominant perception of the project. After all, despite the fact that the project took its cue in the 1930s and 1940s from Leavis and the *Scrutiny* group's commitment to historically contextualizing the production of literatures and to provide a rigorous standard for a critical engagement with literary texts, cultural studies is perceived to have rapidly abandoned that program by the mid-1950s. Under the early influence of Williams, E. P. Thompson, and Richard Hoggart, quickly assisted by the likes of Stuart Hall and other *New Left Review* scholars (such as Perry Anderson, Tom Nairn, and Paddy Whannel), cultural studies expanded its field of reference far beyond traditional literatures; the project has derived its relevance from many other issues. Over the course of the ensuing decades and with different emphases, cultural studies has introduced into the academy the politics of working class culture, the issue of marginality, the experience of ethnic minorities in metropolitan centers, sexuality, and the reading of popular cultural texts such as movies, music, contemporary fashion, and the strategies for representing the bodies of blacks, youths, and postcolonial subjects. The project has transformed these modes of cultural production into objects of serious critical reflection. Despite the gains the field has made, however, these are all issues that continue to struggle to secure a place within the halls of academe.

The flip side of the cultural studies coin is, of course, nothing but the same side gilded with a different finish. The aspects of the field that offend and render it of questionable value are precisely the qualities that make it a lure for students, graduate and undergraduate alike. It engages the kinds of cultural products that has immediate relevance to the everyday experiences of these students, thereby threatening to take precedence—as indicated by the popularity of course enrollments—over the traditional literary curriculum. Cultural studies has also secured a certain critical reputation and institutional cachet: it is a methodological approach that is theoretically sophisticated and cutting edge because it invokes a timely critique of politics, gender, ideology, and economics. Stuart Hall outlines these radical possibilities:

> Both in the British and the American context, cultural studies has drawn attention to itself, not just because of its sometimes dazzling internal theoretical development, but because it holds theoretical and political questions in an ever irresolvable but permanent tension. It constantly allows one to irritate, bother, and disturb the other, without insisting on some final theoretical closure. ("Theoretical Legacies" 284)

It is a rich and productive tension, a dialogue between the visions of theory and the limitations of political activism. Rooted in the immediacy of our postmodern and postindustrial moment, it arbitrates among the plethora of cultural developments with which we are confronted daily. Scholars in the field determine what is culturally relevant (which TV program should be watched, which newspaper or journal should be read), account for the phenomenon (what is significant about a particular fashion trend; how is it marketed), and explain its sociopolitical importance. Cultural studies' very hipness, then, derives from what is perceived as its nonliterariness.

It is this, cultural studies' second blade, which its detractors point to as the tyranny of hip—to coin a phrase. The trendiness of cultural studies is tantamount to a lack of academic seriousness. The scholarship is suspect for a variety of reasons: the subject matter is transitory and nontraditional, it is of little aesthetic merit, the issues have a short shelf life, they represent a preoccupation with the new at the expense of the established canons, and the objects of study are deemed trivial. However, more than anything, cultural studies has broken down the link between literatures that are popularly consumed and literatures that are read within more revered intellectual confines. Cultural studies is a practice that refuses to acknowledge the divisions between the traditional and the popular or operate within the dominant literary paradigms. Instead, it explores the links between these different texts and their varying modes of expression. Furthermore, cultural studies attempts to account for the canonization of certain works and critiques the hierarchization of literatures. In its most incisive approach, cultural studies is not so much concerned with flattening the aesthetic distinctions as with historicizing and investigating them more fully. Why were some texts esteemed and others not? How did those judgments reflect the intellectual and ideological tenor of the times? What was required to rethink the construction of these literary and critical canons? Should literary canons simply be expanded to make room for nontraditional texts or should the very notion of an esteemed set of books be dismissed? How, if at all, would the inclusion of popular texts and theories of working-class cultures reconfigure this literary alignment?

Conducting these inquiries has been among the salient features of cultural studies. One of the signal achievements of cultural studies is that it has been able to, along with African-American and Ethnic Studies departments and programs, create a space in which scholars can do new and sometimes groundbreaking work. Although the institutional accommodation that cultural studies has secured is often small and frequently besieged, it has (again in conjunction with some of the aforementioned communities) validated the experiences of the constituencies from which some of these scholars originate by making it the focus of rigorous intellectual work. By creating a new space for those narratives, cultural studies has challenged and redefined how the academy conceptualizes both itself and its relation to communities it has historically excluded. In its more radical moments it has engaged those communities and their particular experiences. The very trajectory of the project, of course, is borne out of a distinct political and intellectual struggle. Cultural studies' formation depends on taking the production of nontraditional texts seriously and subjecting them to the same intellectual scrutiny, if not always through employing the same critical methods, as accepted literary works.

However, this second (and potentially redemptive) blade of the two-edged sword is not without its own dangers. Cultural studies—and here some of its practitioners, such as Andrew Ross,[1] have been singled out more than others—is currently being subjected to intense criticism both from outside and inside its own ranks. Two of those critiques spring immediately to mind. The first, and the more substantiated and researched of these appraisals, is that resistance is everywhere omnivore. The argument goes that cultural studies, borrowing from theories of resistance developed by anthropologists such as James C. Scott, theorists such as Homi Bhabha, and innovative historians such as Robin D. G. Kelley, has expanded the definition of opposition to problematic lengths. The work of these (and other) scholars is said to see working class and marginal communities' resistance in every aspect of their lives. So much so, in fact, that the field is able to identify challenge by oppressed groups in places that are at best unlikely or at worst, implausible. While many of the criticisms are unwarranted, it is nevertheless an important reminder to those who study the experiences of "subaltern" life. Ross, in a recent essay on the West Indian intellectual C. L. R. James, cautioned against this tendency, commenting on James's insights on political opposition that: "As far as theories of popular culture go, it is quite original, and manages to avoid the 'resistance is everywhere omnivore' which is the stereotypical target of critics of modern cultural studies" ("Civilization" 79).

The second "target of critics of modern cultural studies" is the field's deficiency in addressing class, an issue that is just starting to gain ground. As it has taken up issues of gender, ethnicity, the national-popular, sexual orientation, and race, cultural studies seems to have less attended to class as a grounding category of social investigation or a vehicle for effecting political transformations. The ideological trend has been moving, to borrow the title of cultural studies historian David Harris's book, "from class struggle to the politics of pleasure"—a process accelerated and complicated by a range of 1960s and post-1960s politics. However, in making this argument we always have to be careful of not retreating to the earlier Marxist position where class predominated at the expense of all other political categories. Cultural studies has consistently worked to redress this situation, reconceptualizing class as a political category: class was no longer overdetermined by Marxist economics (or party political affiliation) but reinscribed as an experience inflected and complicated by issues of race, identity, sexual orientation, and gender. Moreover, as that assiduous cultural (and American) studies scholar Michael Denning recently reminded us so insightfully, we occupy an ideological moment where we are confronted less with a "'turn' from class . . . than the remaking of the working class." This is an ongoing process and one that currently demands that we attend to the rapid transformation of the global "working class" into the class of the unemployed and the unemployable. The working class, furthermore, is now "made" by race, gender, sexual orientation, identity, and ethnicity as much as it is by economic location.

In no way, of course, does this writing of class undermine its status as the constitutive category for cultural studies from its inception. The experience of working-class life was especially vital for the initial wave of British New Left members, those thinkers who gave the field its earliest shape and themes in the late 1950s and 1960s. Many of this first generation of cultural studies scholars, of whom Raymond Williams is the most prominent example, came from working-class backgrounds, and this experience was central to their work. They directed their energies toward redressing a primary lack in British academic life: the programmatic exclusion of the experiences of the nation's laboring class. They challenged the representations of a hegemonic British culture which disregarded it as a matter of rote. In David Harris's terms, the nation's mainstream acted as if "there was simply no working-class culture, or at best a sadly deficient one, a mere 'otherness,' best forgotten and hidden under a continual attempt to police the speech, manners, diet, modes of dress, leisure pursuits and ambitions of working-class students" (xiv).

Williams belonged to a generation of working-class students educated in the 1930s whose ranks were greatly supplemented by the university graduates of the postwar period. Both these generations of working-class scholars took as their ideological brief the public articulation of their cultural histories. This collection of intellectuals undertook the task of recording the political centrality of their cultural practices and the impact it had on the everyday life of the British working class. This project was aided by the fact that cultural studies' radical trajectory coincided with major demographic and ideological shifts in British civic life. In the 1960s metropolitan Britain was reconstituted by the large-scale arrival (and settlement) of black immigrants from the Caribbean, the Asian subcontinent, and Africa. This materially strapped and ideologically embattled new constituency quickly found itself in conflict with the native working class into whose declining inner-city neighborhoods they moved and with whom they competed for jobs after the postwar boom collapsed. Black immigration made race a domestic political issue in British society from the late 1950s onward when the race riots of 1958, which originated with an altercation between a black and white man in a grungy pub in the Midlands city of Nottingham, caused a bloody upheaval in London's Notting Hill district. New Lefters such as Hall played pivotal roles in opposing the anti-immigrant mood from the late 1950s on. During the mid- to late 1970s, in his position as director at Birmingham, Hall was later to prove formative in the training of the first generation of British-born black cultural studies intellectuals such as Paul Gilroy and Hazel Carby. In the intervening years, Hall and his fellow–New Lefters had to counter the rhetoric of Enoch Powell (and his like) and later outbreaks of the anti-immigration virus.

In less spectacular fashion, but of no less significant political impact, the feminist movement of the 1960s transformed gender into a pivotal social category. In the 1970s race and gender would coincide and find dynamic expression in the work of Hazel Carby. In *The Empire Strikes Back: Race and Racism in 70s Britain*, Carby and her colleagues, among them Gilroy and Pratibha Parmar, members of the first generation of native-born Afro-Saxons, provided their retort to their structural exclusion from metropolitan society. In the opening lines of "White Woman Listen! Black Feminism and the Boundaries of Sisterhood," Carby made her critique of racism and patriarchy most emphatically:

> The black women's critique of *his*tory has not only involved us coming to terms with 'absences'; we have also been outraged by the ways in which it has made us visible, when it has chosen to see us. *His*tory has constructed our sexuality and our femininity as deviating from those qualities with which white women, as the prize objects of the Western world, have been endowed. . . . Our continuing struggle with *his*tory began with its 'discovery' of us. (212)

Refracted through the lens of race and gender (it would take until the 1980s before sexual orientation registered as a political presence), class became a more fractured category; a form of political community that was lacking in ideological uniformity, even if there were not discernible differences in the various constituencies' separation from the means of production. Class as a category had to be rethought, working-class history had to be remade from a position which took into account colonialism, postcolonialism, the politics of urban devastation, postmodernity, patriarchy, as well as economic alienation and disenfranchisement.

In cultural studies' current incarnation on both sides of the Atlantic, class is now a critical approach that has been nuanced with great adroitness. Class has been transformed from a singular, fundamental political category to a paradigm reconfigured through a series of ideological issues that have gained unexpected precedence over the past two decades. So much so that it ranks as secondary when read through the prism of our historical moment: a postindustrial malaise overwritten by a variegated politics of identity. "The move away from the singularities of 'class' or gender as primary conceptual and organizational categories," Homi Bhabha argues, "has resulted in an awareness of the subject positions—of race, gender, institutional location, geopolitical locale, sexual orientation—that inhabit any claim to identity in the modern world" (1). As can be gleaned from Bhabha's repetition (and telling resituation) of "gender," it is clear that class is really the "conceptual category" that has been reconstituted by a new range of "subject positions"—a list to which we might add ethnicity. The complication of class, which some read as its ideological "relegation," is a process that has been accelerated since the late 1970s by consecutive victories of Margaret Thatcher and Ronald Reagan over parties that were traditionally seen as sympathetic to (if not fully conversant with) the cause of workers.

The multiple election defeats suffered by the British Labour Party and the U.S.'s Democrats (the former being of greater ideological consequence than the latter) rendered the trans-Atlantic Anglophone Left's class-based analysis vacuous and ineffective in the face of the Right's appeals to the idealized, homogeneous "nation." Displaced by a legacy of defeat, class has found itself ideologically superseded by the politics of identity and subsequently reduced to a political gesture. Class has become underutilized as a theoretical tool. It is a condition of neglect, theoretical and political, to which cultural studies will have to attend—how do we rethink class? Michael Denning, a thinker shaped by his connection with the Centre for Contemporary Cultural Studies at Birmingham, has thus far made the most compelling contribution to this debate. Concerned about the ways in which class is being deployed, Denning nevertheless urges us to reflect on why class has been recast so significantly. Arguing in a

Gramsci-Hallian mode, Denning insists that we think class in its historical locale: "class analysis in the account of specific historical conjunctures requires not a static sense of the 'working class' or the 'middle class' but an account of the making and remaking of specific historical blocs, and an attention to 'class generations' and what Pierre Bourdieu calls 'class trajectories.'" Class formations are, much like capitalism, social organisms infinitely capable of rapid ideological and political mutation. It responds to changes in the material conditions as much as it is able to produce alterations in the social formation it occupies. It has been one of cultural studies' strengths that it has responded to the "specific historical conjunctures" and that it has mapped the multifarious ways in which "classes" align themselves to different historical blocs. It is in this regard that Denning's point about the complications of (class) identity and (class) location provides an effective counter to critiques that cultural studies has abandoned class as a political category. With Denning's cautions in mind, we are equipped to inquire not as to how do we make class efficacious, but rather: What kind of political vehicle is class in our conjuncture? What are its limits? How do we deploy it efficaciously?

However overt or concealed cultural studies' mode of class analysis, it has always been founded on unrelenting social critique. Conversely, the intellectual discipline with which it is seen to be in conflict, traditional literary criticism, was until just two generations ago struggling to acknowledge its own ideological basis. Despite the fact that cultural studies may at times be, in my view, just lit crit business as usual, its explicit commitment to questions of politics has always made it vulnerable within the academy. However, it is necessary to inquire why cultural studies has become at this conjuncture such a target for all kinds of intellectual attacks. What kind of academic climate facilitates such an attack? What political and ideological anxieties underwrite these intellectual sorties? What is it that cultural studies represents that is so offensive or so threatening? Why is it that a field which has, despite its short but distinguished history, secured only an embattled space in the academy elicited such antagonism? At least part of the answer lies, as was suggested earlier, in the ambivalences of the numbers game. For all its (lucrative) popularity, cultural studies diverts attention from traditional texts. Nor should we forget that cultural studies' rise to institutional prominence (if that is the appropriate phrase) coincided with the achievement of multicultural curricula, the establishment and consolidation of African-American, Latino, gay and lesbian, and women's studies programs. In the era of institutional downsizing, these intellectual centers have been the most vulnerable institutional targets. A classic case of the use of the post-Fordist rhetoric of scarcity to execute that age-old (racist) economic practice: last hired, first fired. Because of (though some might argue despite) its precarious location within language departments, cultural studies has become a principal target. It has none of the protection of institutionally recognized programs so that it has to rely on the ideological tenor of its always already reluctant (and possibly even resentful) host.

As Literature departments find themselves in a double bind, so does cultural studies. The field is hemmed in on both flanks. If it does not expand the space it has garnered (in conditions that are becoming increasingly hostile), it will not be able to accomplish much except to act as a vulnerable (and unwilling) stormtrooper. It is theoretically and politically resourceful, but unable to secure, let alone claim, much territory. On the one hand, by not creating more room for itself it will authorize its own marginality, even if it alters the shape and content of that position from time to time. On the other hand, if it cedes that space, it is highly likely in a moment of reactionary backlash that the resources at its disposal and the academic space it has carved out—modest though they both may be—will be appropriated by more conservative intellectual enterprises. Cultural studies' ambivalent position is reinscribed: it is both ideological vanguard and academic buffer. It has little room to maneuver and very little room for error. Cultural studies has to make history under conditions clearly not of its own choosing, but also in circumstances that constrict intellectual vision.

What is arguably the most interesting aspect of this moment is the fact that cultural studies is being assailed at the very moment that it exhibits its closest ties yet to some of the fundamental ways literary criticism is practiced. Articulated as they are at this conjuncture, cultural studies and the study of literature are frequently depicted as polarized academic practices: one reads Literature or one studies contemporary cultural practices. To state the case more schematically (and perhaps reductively), one is grounded in tradition or preoccupied with the trends (or trendiness) of the present. The assumption that girds this view is that since the two fields take radically different subject matter as the focus of their study, they share no common intellectual and methodological ground. However, simply because cultural studies' subject matter is nonliterary, it does not necessarily follow that it is nonliterary in its method or critical approach. In fact, from its earliest moments cultural studies has been rooted in and closely affiliated to English departments. Cultural studies' first practitioners, Williams, Hoggart, and Hall (Thompson and his Yorkshire-based *New Reasoner* group provided the historians), were all trained as language scholars. Many of the current crop of cultural studies come from the same literary background. Even if they are not products of a strictly literary training, as is the case with Birmingham graduates Carby and Gilroy (who is a lecturer in sociology), they were often schooled in this ethos and currently teach in language departments or American studies programs (Carby, Denning, and Ross); furthermore, they are regularly in intellectual conversation with these fields—as cultural studies scholars are in dialogue, in this moment of interdisciplinarity, with sociology, political philosophy, and anthropology (Hall, e.g., is professor of Sociology at the Open University in London and has been at the forefront of cultural studies' conversations with other fields). The substantive literary basis of cultural studies equipped its graduates to teach in English or Comparative Literature departments, continuing the tradition of engagement with and immersion in Literature even as the (largely unsuccessful) struggle to secure an independent institutional space was being conducted. Located within its halls, literature departments have been able to assimilate cultural studies and exert an as yet unexamined influence on a discipline with which it is ostensibly in conflict.

Of course this trend in no way undermines the influence cultural studies has exerted on literary studies. Cultural studies introduced the issues of working class literatures and cultural practices, looked at conditions of literary production, and was crucial to making race, gender, and sexual orientation a focus of literary reading. Cultural studies and literary studies have thus, despite both their superficial and more deep-seated differences, shown themselves to be inextricably if uncomfortably joined. Nowhere is this link between the two fields more clearly demonstrated than in cultural studies' increasing tendency to appropriate literary criticism in its approach to popular culture. And this form of literary criticism, theoretically grounded in a long established literary practice, is neither particularly interesting nor challenging. Rather, it is conservative, adopting a mode that is firmly embedded in the traditional study of literatures. While retaining its commitment to engaging the popular and the marginal, cultural studies seems to be assuming a formation that is primarily occupied with the practice of close reading. The texts, films, music videos, popular television programs, and popular cultural figures are unfamiliar but the methodology is eminently recognizable. These texts are being analyzed frame by frame or line by line in ways all too reminiscent of the New Critic's approach to poetry or drama. And therein lies the rub. Cultural studies has taken the most salient feature of New Criticism and applied it to bodies of work for which it was not originally intended and with which it has not been identified.

Cultural studies' turn to close reading—a cornerstone of literary criticism—marks a return to a mode of literary scholarship that the field has for so long opposed and against which it has defined itself. Because language departments have so successfully resisted the institutionalization of cultural studies, in part by housing and absorbing (and thereby disciplining its development) the project within its own domain, literary criticism has been able to exercise a formative influence on the field. The real issue for cultural studies may very well have become a furtive one: How can the field function effectively under conditions of restricted institutional autonomy without becoming a cultural studies of the New Critical variety?

Note

1. See, for example, the unsympathetic representation of Ross and his American Studies project at New York University in an article entitled "Yo, Professor" (Mead).

Works Cited

Arnold, Matthew. *Culture and Anarchy*. Ed. J. Dover Wilson. Cambridge: Cambridge UP, 1988.

Bhabha, Homi. *The Location of Culture*. New York: Routledge, 1994.

Carby, Hazel V. "White Women Listen! Black Feminism and the Boundaries of Sisterhood." *The Empire Strikes Back: Race and Racism in 70s Britain*. New York: Routledge, 1982. 212–35.

Denning, Michael. "Does Cultural Studies Neglect Class?" American Studies Association Convention, Nov. 1995.

Eagleton, Terry. *Literary Theory: An Introduction*. Minneapolis: U of Minnesota P, 1983.

Hall, Stuart. "Cultural Studies and Its Theoretical Legacies." *Cultural Studies*, Ed. Lawrence Grossberg, Cary Nelson, and Paula A. Treichler. New York: Routledge, 1992. 277–86.

———. "The Emergence of Cultural Studies and the Crisis of the Humanities." October 53 (1990): 11–30.

Harris, David. *From Class Struggle to the Politics of Pleasure: The Effects of Gramscianism on Cultural Studies*. New York: Routledge, 1992.

Kenny, Michael. *The First New Left: British Intellectuals after Stalin*. London: Lawrence and Wishart, 1995.

Mead, Rebecca. "Yo, Professor." *New York Magazine* 14 Nov. 1994: 48–53.

Mulhern, Francis. *The Moment of 'Scrutiny.'* London: New Left Books, 1979.

Ross, Andrew. "Civilization in One Country? The American James." *Rethinking C. L. R. James*. Ed. Grant Farred. Cambridge, MA: Blackwell, 1996.

———. *No Respect: Intellectuals and Popular Culture*. New York: Routledge, 1989.

Smith, Paul. "Questioning Cultural Studies: An Interview with Paul Smith." With Jeffrey Williams. *the minnesota review* ns 43–44 (1995): 84–98.

Turner, Graeme. *British Cultural Studies: An Introduction*. New York: Routledge, 1992.

Williams, Raymond. *Culture and Society, 1780–1950*. New York: Anchor, 1960.

Chapter Six

Peer Pressure: Literary and Cultural Studies in the Bear Market

Michael Bérubé

It is a wondrous fact in American culture that a literary critic could write a book insisting that (alas) literature has no socially redeeming value, no "utility" at all, and have gotten glowing reviews from practically every major English-language newspaper on either side of the North Atlantic. The idea of "the aesthetic" may have been under assault in the groves of academe, but in the general culture arguing for the autonomy of the aesthetic and against the School of Resentment netted a best-seller and an advance of over half a million dollars. The moral is clear: whatever "aesthetic value" may be, it is definitely convertible into a big pile of cash.

I am talking, of course, about Harold Bloom's *The Western Canon*. Part of Bloom's success stemmed not merely from his status *as* Bloom, and not merely from his considerable talent at coming up with sound-bites as "provocative" as anything Stanley Fish, Andrew Ross, or Bloom-protégé Camille Paglia can offer the media, but also from the sheer certainty of his determinations of value. Here is someone who knows what great literature is, and is not afraid to say so. It does not matter whether anyone *agrees* with Bloom's determinations; no one human can. The point is that he has made them—like E. D. Hirsch, Jr., in a handy back-of-the-book compilation—and thus afforded every literate person an endless supply of what Northrop Frye once called "the literary chit-chat which makes the reputations of poets boom and crash in an imaginary stock exchange" (18). One might say that Harold Bloom has brought to the discussion of American letters some of the thrill of the NCAA basketball and football seasons: Could Penn State have beaten Nebraska? Was James Jones really faster than James Baldwin in the 40-yard dash? Is the Big East (Whitman, Dickinson, Williams) a better poetry conference than the Mississippi Valley (Eliot, Ransom, Tate)?

These are the central questions for criticism, the determinations of value that separate the men from the boys, the thrill of victory from the *agon* of defeat. Indeed, Bloom was fortuitously joined by a host of values-hawkers ready and willing to tell us the difference between a four-star poet and a C+ movie. William Henry III, the late drama critic for *Time*, made an impassioned case that some things are just *better* than others, dammit, and so too are cultures that go to the moon superior to cultures that push bones through their noses. "I find the blues irresistible," wrote Henry; "I have always liked square dancing. But these are lesser forms of art than, say, oil painting and opera and ballet, because the techniques are less arduous and less demanding of long learning, the underlying symbolic language is less complicated, the range of expression is less profound, and the worship of beauty is muddied by the lower aims of community fellowship" (176). For similar reasons, Henry called for the closing of community colleges (165) and—a nice touch in a book titled *In Defense of Elitism*—"massive layoffs of faculty" (166). The redoubtable Thomas Sowell put the screws to cultural relativism as well, writing that some cultures are "*better* in some respects than others" (4) just as "Arabic numerals are not merely *different* from Roman numerals; they are *superior* to Roman numerals" (5)—a principle few would contest, unless it were stripped of its qualifying clause, "in some respects," and extrapolated to cover moon shots and nose bones. And they were joined by a whole host of Cal Thomases, Bill Bennetts, Dan Quayles, and Rush Limbaughs, wise and learned people who know what virtue is and why they have it and we don't. As a result, the tide of liberal PC relativism was finally turned, and America's quota queens and welfare cheats were hurled from their positions of national power.

Although it would not be hard to imagine a future book entitled *The Western Canon the Way It Ought to Be*, Bloomian authoritarianism may not have anything more than an analogical relation to Limbaughian authoritarianism. Nevertheless, I do want to suggest that his success, like William Henry's, should be understood as a negative symptom of the general, if fitful, academic consensus that value is contingent and constructed: both Bloom and Henry spare no term of opprobrium in abusing academic literary critics, and this too is part of their appeal to the "common reader." Since this academic consensus is widely (mis)understood to entail the doctrine of cultural relativism, under which one book is as meritorious as any other, it would seem that the return of the Arbiter of Aesthetic Value—he who knows what is good and why, and can place every form of cultural expression in its natural order—speaks to a widespread popular desire for clear-cut determinations of value. If I am right about this, there is a real audience out there for the juridical form of literary criticism that unself-consciously participates in the culture's general obsession with rankings.

I am writing, however, to register something rather more critical than mere bemusement at Bloom's commercial success. Literary and cultural studies are indeed experiencing a crisis of evaluation, not just a "perceived" crisis; this is, in other words, a matter of intradisciplinary uncertainty as well as a question of public relations. And because we are uncertain, in ways Bloom is not, about what counts as good literary, critical, and theoretical work, it sometimes appears that the only criteria of evaluation we have are mercantile criteria: what's hot, what's selling, what's the newest latest. Or so says David Bromwich, in a remarkable passage in *Politics by Other Means* where, in rendering a detailed fictional account of a sham tenure meeting, he explains how vacuous are the criteria by which we promote professors in nonfields like "Postmodernism and Cultural Studies" (177). The tenure candidate is named "Jonathan Craigie," and he is a hotshot:

> The author of two books and editor of three collections of essays and interviews, the candidate in the last five years has delivered 30 papers at professional conferences—many of them deft and wide-ranging in the interdisciplinary way. His undergraduate courses are popular. They deal entirely with special subjects; for, armed with a counter-offer, Craigie negotiated early to sever his obligation to teach the department's bread-and-butter surveys. . . . The only recorded exception to the consensus occurred a year ago, when a pair of history students dropped [a graduate] seminar at midterm—because, they said, Craigie did not know the facts of the period implied by his title, "Postmodern Politics and American Culture, 1945–1990." (177)

Craigie's a poseur, that much is clear. But then things get worse: Since Craigie's work is so posteverything (his next book "is a double biography of Madonna and 'a post-gendered novelist still to be named'" [178]), the tenure meeting turns entirely on the letters of his referees—as it must, writes Bromwich, because no one in the department can judge Craigie's work: "None had a language to describe or judge, let alone to praise or blame adequately, work that came in so curious a shape" (178).

And here is where Bromwich really goes to town, exposing not merely his fictional Craigie but every similar intellectual fraud perpetrated on the profession under the cover of professionalism:

> Of the six letters received, none came from a scholar who had done first-hand work on similar subjects; four, however, were written by eminences of theory, who could imply without quite asserting a meta-competence in several historical periods. (And, it was urged, what is postmodernism if not the theorist's topic par excellence?). . . . These carefully placed accolades were the fruit of assiduous networking: the cultivation, without ulterior intellectual aim, of influential cronies who are pledged to serve the advancement of one's career. Since Craigie had once devoted half a semester of a graduate seminar to the topic of networking, it was natural for this to form the first topic of an unusually frank and speculative tenure review. (178–79)

The crucial moment of the review comes when someone at last speaks up for traditional scholarly standards—the kind that prevailed in the pretheory days, when tenure reviews were truly rigorous—and is stifled by one of the Eminences of Theory. The subject is Craigie's article on "Alger Hiss Remediated: America's Left/Right, Vertical/Horizontal Control," and only one person in the room has the courage to say the essay is not wearing any clothes:

> "This thing doesn't even have much information; I don't see any evidence that he reads the work he cites. In the Hiss article, he bases the whole thesis of 'image-consolidation' on a single discredited work of cultural history. He doesn't seem to have read any political history. He didn't look at the transcript of the congressional hearings or the trial. He didn't read *Witness* or *In the Court of Public Opinion*—nothing!"
>
> A brief silence falls. Then—quietly, significantly—are heard the following grave words from the front of the room. The speaker is a recent high-profile recruit to the department:
>
> "A couple of you people talk as if you were opposed to anything new." (180)

Craigie is eventually given tenure on the grounds that "if we turn him down lots of people will be asking why" (179) and "in a year or two, he'll have a great offer from Duke or Emory, and he'll leave" (180).

Part of what makes Bromwich's account so breathtaking is what I call the Gerontion Effect: the young neotraditionalist trying on the voice of the old man in a dry month. When first I read this account I could not help but think, in outrage, of the staid, solid scholars I have known who have run into trouble with incompetent tenure committees because their work was "too feminist" or had run afoul of one Gray Eminence or another (not a Theory Eminence, either). I thought of my three years as Illinois's placement director, watching one Ph.D. candidate after another fail to find full-time employment despite a terrific teaching record and a capable dissertation on a topic even Bromwich would recognize as legitimate. But once I managed to recover my breath, I realized I too had been taken in by Gerontion: for Bromwich's account had, in effect, asked me to compare Craigie's worthlessness (a worthlessness that can only be glimpsed from the privileged vantage point of disciplines with real standards, like history) with other contemporary scholars in English. And in so doing, Bromwich had briefly made me forget that in the golden pretheoretical age he alludes to earlier, when lectures were not mere entertainment but learned addresses to "an audience of peers, who [were] relied on to know the material as well as the lecturer" (174), English professors basically got tenure if they could sign their names or prove they were carbon-based. Moreover, he had also made me forget that those worthy people, tenured in the 1960s when times were flush, were now sitting in judgment of junior faculty and Ph.D. candidates who had published and taught more just to get a job than most senior faculty had done to earn lifetime tenure 30 years ago.

Bromwich's shortsightedness is all the clearer if we contrast his book with a brief essay by George Levine that shares some of Bromwich's misgivings about the profession: "At the moment, the profession doesn't know or even want to know what it is," writes Levine. "[M]any of the best-known in our field are professionally interested in things that are only marginally related to English or literature," such as "cultural studies, film, gender, psychology, sex, pop culture, multiculturalism" (43). By contrast to Bromwich, Levine is, on the whole, sanguine about the field: "English is a far more exciting and interesting, if qualitatively uneven, discipline than it seemed to be back then [when he entered it], and its current troubles have come about largely because it takes more risks, makes bigger mistakes, reaches out farther, welcomes more diversity, does better by women and minorities, and confronts its own assumptions more directly and perhaps even with greater sophistication" (43). But, he cautions, our health and our public support depend on our commitment to a principle many in the profession do not in fact support: "We must examine the value of the literary and the aesthetic (even if only in the terms that Eagleton offers in *The Ideology of the Aesthetic*) if English, as a profession sustained by publicly and privately endowed institutions, is to survive" (43–44). What makes Levine's account both more plausible and more trustworthy than Bromwich's, I suggest, is that where Bromwich can only practice a form of ventriloquism, adopting the voice of the senior sage whose eyes have seen better days, Levine actually knows whereof he speaks: "When I got my degree from the University of Minnesota" in the 1950s, he writes, "almost all my colleagues, no matter how dumb they were, got at least three job offers" (43).

But then there was a third moment to my reading of Bromwich's tale of peer review gone wrong—the moment when I realized that Bromwich has a sound premise even though his account bespeaks his poor sense of disciplinary history (a nice paradox, since he exposes Craigie precisely for his fraudulent historical sense) and a truly odd sense of disenfranchisement (it is not every day that someone is appointed to head the Whitney Humanities Center at the age of 40 and responds with a tirade about how such professional rewards usually go only to shallow networkers). Bromwich's caricature of tenure review may be outrageous, but it speaks to entirely legitimate concerns; and I myself would not want to bet the car on the proposition that a real-life Craigie could never win tenure. For we *don't* have a scale of values that can measure the work of people doing postgender studies of Barbie dolls in the same terms as the work of people doing pregender studies of Hopkins's experiments in prosody. Nor can we plausibly compare *those* projects with books in writing studies or recent Australian film—and yet we are routinely asked to do precisely this, for tenure reviews, fellowship applications, article submissions, and salary determinations.

I think it is true, then, that our professional evaluations do sometimes depend more on our sense of "currency" and "market value" than on our assessments of scholarly merit, and I think that in a bear market such as this one, when there are so few decent jobs for so many worthy candidates, the indefiniteness of our standards of merit warrants further discussion. The reason I will not echo the self-serving conclusion Bromwich draws from this, however, is that we need to remember (as Bromwich does not) that when our professional standards are uncertain, the appeal to "what's hot" can—and is—used to dismiss new work as often as it is used to praise it: *This has a certain flair*, one hears, *but it's insufferably trendy*. Or: *I suppose this is what's fashionable at Duke or Berkeley, but we needn't encourage it here*. Those who believe that peer reviews no longer contain such phrases are, I am afraid, woefully mistaken. Indeed, because of the explosion of the field and the contraction of the market, the very idea of "peer review" has become increasingly problematic: on the one hand, the books of younger scholars are being judged by people who never wrote a book, and on the other, cultural studies work on Australian film is being judged by people who still do not like seeing the word "gaze" in film criticism (just as worthy "traditional" work is being judged by people who do not like *not* seeing the word "gaze" in film criticism). One way of phrasing this peerless paradox, as W. J. T. Mitchell pointed out nearly a decade ago, is to say that the discipline's official forms of pluralism are always bumping up against institutional limits on their operation. Asking "Who is qualified to testify on the merits" of various scholars in the profession, Mitchell writes:

> With theory, feminist criticism, or Marxist criticism, the decision is much more difficult [than with eighteenth-century studies]. Chances are we have no senior person in the field, and that the very existence of the "field" as a respectable discipline is in doubt. If the existence of the field is granted, chances are that there is deep suspicion about the experts and standards to be consulted. The result is that everyone in a department feels qualified to judge persons in these fields, while in fact no one is really qualified. Chances are that no such appointment will be made, or that, once made, it will be more difficult to achieve tenure in the marginal, problematic field. (501)

Like Levine and Mitchell, I have no illusions that things were better in the days imagined by Bromwich, when everyone could be "relied on to know the material," because, for one thing, I have found from perusing past MLA programs that in all our professional gatherings from 1883 to 1963, only one paper was delivered on a black writer (Blyden Jackson gave a paper entitled "The Dilemma of the Negro Novelist" in 1953). More generally, unlike Bromwich, I would not want to purchase disciplinary consensus on our protocols of evaluation at the price of getting rid of all the writers, theorists, and intellectual movements that have done so much to problematize "value" in the past few decades. Until only a decade ago, for instance, our major professional journal would not accept essays on "minor" writers; the official policy of *PMLA* was that it would consider essays that took on "a broad subject or theme," "a major author or work," or "a minor author or work in such a way as to bring insight to a major author, work, genre, or critical method." And there is no advantage, it seems to me, in trying to return to some kind of disciplinary consensus that would bar "minor" writers from *PMLA* essays until they had been magically elevated to "major" status by critical work published elsewhere.

But what has impelled me to agree that our professional protocols of evaluation *are* in crisis, curiously enough, are the variously bitter and cynical accounts of the profession I have seen from people who have nothing much in common with Bromwich. Take, for example, this telling moment from a recent review essay on the Routledge *Cultural Studies* volume edited by Larry Grossberg, Cary Nelson, and Paula Triechler:

> The list of contributors on this book's cover is equally familiar, although precisely at odds with the kind of "collaborative" work it might herald in another economy—the economy this book keeps claiming, while it so successfully continues to operate within capitalism. Routledge's "Press Release" emphasizing the "prominent cultural theorists" writing in this book, and their winnowing of the list of names on the cover to headline the eight most prominent, makes clear the logic of advertising here: these are the celebrities, the *big* names who can draw an audience to a conference or readers to a book. (Langbauer 470)

Leaving aside the question of whether *all* the contributors to *Cultural Studies* were truly already "familiar" to everyone in 1992, let me suggest that this passage shares Bromwich's assumptions about the profession almost completely. These guys and gals in pomo and cultural studies are not really scholars, they are just celebrities; indeed, the essay is titled "The Celebrity Economy of Cultural Studies," and in it, Victorianist critic Laurie Langbauer penetrates to the empty core at the heart of the cultural studies enterprise, its dependence on (blindness to, reinforcement of, inscription within, etc.) precisely the forms of commodity capitalism it seeks to critique. "The marks of the celebrity economy in *Cultural Studies* may initially seem unremarkable," admits Langbauer, "because they are part of the customary economy of marketing under capitalism" (469–70). Ay, but there's the rub:

> All books do this. The problem is that the editors of this book treat "legitimate" cultural studies as if it did not. They indeed recognize

> the "significant investment opportunities" revolving around cultural studies in "academic institutions—presses, journals, hiring committees, conferences, university curricula" (1). Yet they ignore that it is within capitalism too that their own conference is funded and their book published, and it is capitalism's laws that govern its marketing. (470)[1]

My guess is that one could not write such an essay unless one were profoundly unsure of the intellectual merits of the book: for if we had some measure of confidence that the work of these celebrities actually *merited* their professional recognition (granting this even in the case of the eight "winnowed" superstars, whoever they were), we wouldn't be spending an entire review commenting on the relationship between a book's marketing and its self-representation rather than on its contents. We would think that the value of these critics' work merited their marketing, instead of supposing that their marketing constituted their value. Once again, that is not to say that we should want to return to the days when everybody knew that a study of Christian imagery in the work of a major author like Dryden was "intrinsically" more important than a study of gender relations in the work of an unknown like Hurston (and therefore no one wrote the latter). But it is to say that there is an extraordinary level of cynicism in the industry these days, partly because our old criteria of value have disappeared and we are not sure whether the new ones have arrived yet, and partly because most new Ph.D.s' hopes of full-time employment have disappeared as well, leaving us a cantankerous profession with eight superstars drawing people to conferences and eight thousand adjunct instructors teaching bread-and-butter surveys.

Langbauer's essay is not unique, nor is its seemingly gritty exposure of professional "celebrity" applicable only to the nonfield of cultural studies. On the contrary, the profession of whatever it is we do has recently given birth to a new subgenre of such essays, wherein prominent critics such as Donald Morton and Daniel O'Hara remorselessly critique the celebrity economy by which other critics have become "superstar 'free agents'" (O'Hara 43), construing lesser-known faculty and students, in Morton's more-cynical-than-thou locution, as "celebrities-in-waiting" (144). What is driving these essays, however, is not merely the intradisciplinary explosion that has made it all but impossible for us to judge the relative worth of a new close reading of Robert Frost, a new theoretical wrinkle in Writing Studies, and a new critique of the suturing of the subject in the political imaginary of the post(techno)logical sublime. Rather, as O'Hara's, Langbauer's, and Morton's essays variously make clear, it is our intradisciplinary explosion *in tandem with* the collapse of the job market. What is happening to our professional protocols of value is that they are being squeezed by a system whose ideal image of itself promotes theoretically sophisticated, interdisciplinary work in extraliterary studies but whose material base is shrinking as fast as its superstructure is expanding. To put this impasse in historical perspective (since it no doubt will be counterargued that the job market has been awful before), it was roughly 20 years ago that Richard Ohmann pointed out, in *English in America*, that the profession of English studies thought of itself as doing criticism and theory but was in actuality devoting half its courses to introductory composition. In the 1990s, by contrast, the profession devotes *more* than half its courses to composition, faces a rising number of Ph.D.s together with a declining number of tenure-track (or even full-time nontenurable) positions, and thinks of itself as doing everything from recent French philosophy to analyses of popular music to new editions of the C-text of *Piers Plowman*.[2]

I would have no difficulty with this profusion of material for study—nor, I wager, would many of my un-Bromwichian colleagues—if it were not coincident with the collapse of the job market. It is not that I believe the job market would improve if we would all agree to stick to reading *Piers Plowman* and leave the hip-hop to writers for glossy magazines; the market works by variables that have nothing to do with the profession's intellectual interests. On the contrary, the profession's intellectual interests can often be the dependent variable (dependent, that is, on the market)—and that is the problem, particularly for our graduate students: the discipline thinks it is going from literary to cultural studies, and the market tells us we are going from literature to technical writing.

One effect of this conundrum is that students have little idea how to value (or how to gauge whether the profession will value) a dissertation on slasher films vis-à-vis a dissertation on sprung rhythm vis-à-vis a dissertation on penal codes in nineteenth-century Australia vis-à-vis the ability to teach four sections of comp, the History of the English Language, and maybe a Shakespeare course every other year. They suspect, correctly, that a truly singular dissertation on slasher films *and* Australian penal codes will win them more "attention" from search committees and publishers than a careful reading of Hopkins's prosody—but then again, they also suspect that because there are only two jobs in the country for writers of such dissertations, they are going to wind up doing piecework comp courses for the local community college at $900 per while they try to send the book off to Routledge. But even should they publish that book with Routledge or anywhere else, they still have little reason, often enough, to expect full-time employment; and when a good teaching record and a published book cannot get you hired at a university—in a system where indifferent teaching and a published book was once sufficient for tenure and sometimes even for promotion to full professor—it is no surprise to find widespread professional confusion and cynicism about what the profession professes to value.

The recent experience of one of my students is perhaps a leading indicator of what the coming years will look like: having published two essays in important journals while temping at a variety of small colleges, the student finally got a book manuscript accepted by a prestigious university press, only to be told—*after* completing nine months of revisions—that the marketing department had nixed the book on the grounds that it would not sell widely enough. Had the book been accepted, the student might have had a chance at landing a new kind of job offered by a nearby college: a 4/4 instructorship leading (for the worthy candidate) to tenure *without* promotion. In other words, a lifetime instructorship without hope of advancement, regardless of the quality of one's teaching or scholarship. Without a book in hand, however, the student had a poor chance of competing against the rest of the applicant pool for this rotten job, since so many of the other applicants, according to the search committee, had already published one book or more.

Before we congratulate ourselves for moving from literary to cultural studies, therefore, we should at the very least ask how this new *Selbstverständnis* meshes or conflicts with the brutal realities of the job market; it may be plausible, for instance, to think (as people like James Berlin—or, in a different vein, Henry Giroux—have done) of cultural studies in English more in terms of its relation to rhetoric, pedagogy, and composition classes than as a competitor with "literary studies" for already-scarce disciplinary resources. Conversely, it may be possible to envision an American cultural studies as an inter- and antidisciplinary field of endeavor by practicing it in nondepartmental units, such as Humanities Institutes and African-American Studies Programs; this option would allow students and young faculty in cultural studies to attempt *real* interdisciplinarity rather than the interdisciplinary waterskiing that is all most ordinary graduate students have time for, but the likelihood of realizing this possibility will depend simply on whether universities will want to hire students so trained. In any case, the "success" of our disciplinary shift from literature to culture is not something that will be decided by journal articles or essays like this one, but largely by the availability of jobs, which in concert with the dissemination of cultural studies will in turn determine the extent to which English departments will remain places that study and value "literature" as most of the literate culture understands it.

Two conclusions follow from this line of argument, one of which has to do with English's formal protocols of value as they are perceived outside English, and the other of which has to do with the future of literary study. For as long as I have been involved in the profession—beginning with my entrance to graduate school in 1983—I have thought of, and experienced, English's heterogeneity as something admirable, exciting, and valuable. Indeed, it is for that reason that I never understood "disciplinarity" as the dirty word it is sometimes taken for (as in Ellen Rooney's article on cultural studies, "Discipline and Vanish"), since I had the good fortune to be working in a discipline notable for its vigorous interdisciplinary importation and exportation of methodologies. But the flexibility of English is as often ridiculed as admired by scholars in other disciplines, and the more an outside observer values disciplinary stability, consensus, and "performativity" (in Lyotard's sense), the more of a liability English will seem to him or her. Indeed, to judge by a recent book that defends the American university partly by distancing its authors from the "dangerous" loonies in English, some of our fellow humanists construe our disciplinary messiness as a sign that English should (or does) not exist. In *Up the University*, Robert and Jon Solomon write:

> "English" is not a natural subject, but a dangerous amalgam of functional service courses (teaching two of the basic "three Rs"), an arbitrarily truncated literature program (which seems to include only writing that does not require knowledge of a foreign language), and an often arrogant collection of literary theorists, who are typically at war with each other as well as with their more down-to-earth colleagues. They make their reputation by attacking and alienating everyone else in the department. There is a very real question why and whether the university should continue to have an English department at all, but for now, we want to make a much more modest claim—that the university is not the English department, and the embarrassments and anecdotes of a few notorious departments should not be taken as the nature of the university itself. (296)

It may seem odd that we be faulted for our disciplinary disorganization (not to mention our constitutional arrogance) at the same time we are faulted for not teaching literature in languages other than English, but perhaps this passage is motivated more by fiscal than by intellectual concerns: whatever else they are doing, the Solomons are basically proposing that English take the first and deepest cuts when the college budget is on the block. It is important for this reason that these criticisms come not from Kimball, Sykes, Cheney, and Co. but from colleagues across the quad, housed in departments of philosophy and classics. My point, obviously, is that should arguments like this carry the day with deans, donors, trustees, and local legislatures, the scarce resources for work in English could get still scarcer. Again, I am not suggesting we give in and stick to *Piers Plowman* in the hope that the dean and the trustees will look kindly on English and return to us all the faculty lines they have "absorbed" in the last few years. The point is to *contest* these accounts of the field, and at the very least to come up with convincing rationales—that is, rationales that will not only convince *us* of the value of what we do with literature (though we do need these) but will also be intelligible outside the discipline—as to why it is that English values its disciplinary heterogeneity, and how it is that the value we place on heterogeneity does not so preclude us from making determinations of scholarly value that we are forced, like Bromwich's fictional tenure committee, to rely simply on scholarly commodity fetishism as a substitute for "value."

I said that my second point had to do with the future of literary study. The turn from literary to cultural studies unfortunately comes at a time when American universities are seeking to divest themselves of "unproductive" fields of study and modes of inquiry. As English is increasingly compelled to "instrumentalize," that is, to devote ever more of its course offerings to basic writing instruction, literary study will indeed be found vestigial if we do not contrive convincing justifications for it. In recent years it has sometimes seemed to us sufficient to point out that most of the claims made for literature can be made for "extraliterary" works as well, just as it has seemed satisfactory to note that the ancient study of rhetoric was much more capacious than the New Critical study of "literariness," and that "literature" has come to mean "belles lettres" only in the past two or three centuries. These arguments are right, I think, and they have done salutary work in unravelling the brief but powerful (and powerfully deceptive) disciplinary consensus of the 1940s and 1950s that literature was an object for study unlike any other object of study. Yet even the most narrowly "literary" works really can defamiliarize the familiar and renew perception; compel readers to imaginative sympathy, disgust, ecstasy, terror; train young adults to attend to the subtleties of language, the rhythmic variations of verse, and the power of rhetorical hermeneutics; lengthen children's attention spans to the point at which they can understand how Frank Churchill's letter finally exposes Emma Woodhouse's inability to read *Emma's* multiple subtleties of language; and, in rare cases, make undergraduates curious enough to keep reading after they graduate. And when critics on the cultural left point out that none of this is necessarily inconsistent with the project of giving students mere ideological obfuscation or training them in quietism, my impulse is to agree—and then to suggest in return that if one desires guarantees that one's teaching and writing can never be put in the service of ideological obfuscation or quietism, one would be better off not wasting time with the humanities in the first place.

Besides, if these formalist rationales are not enough to justify the discipline, you can always come across one of those literary texts that so trouble the Right, whose author may in fact have been more savvy about gender, power, empire, hegemony, or sexuality than your average associate professor in the Midwest. For that matter, those critics who are engaged in "archival" work with the neglected writers of the past or "advocacy" work with the underread writers of the present have an important stake not merely in maintaining but in expanding literary study *as* literary study: neither such critics nor their client-authors will be well served by a disciplinary regime that jettisons "literature" as a spent vehicle no longer able to assist in cultural study's further expansion.

For all his commercial success, Harold Bloom managed only to offer the claim that aesthetic contemplation of the beautiful is an end in itself; perhaps we theory-addled multiculturalists, we whom Bloom calls "displaced social workers," can do better. At the very least, we should not allow Bloom's solipsistic defense of the field stand as the only one in public view. Whenever we are castigated as politicos and philistines intruding on the purity of the aesthetic experience, we need to remind our accusers that—as one theorist once put it—literature not only delights but instructs, at least every once in a while. It is a shame that arguments such as these are now more prevalent among cultural reactionaries, embittered aesthetes, and right-wing flacks than among the leading figures in departments of English; reactionaries and flacks have done much to make these arguments suspect, and Bloom himself has done more than anyone to discredit the idea that value judgments in the field of English can be something other than expressions of idiosyncratic predilections.

As for my own predilections, I can say that whenever I read a professional reactionary like Robert Brustein maligning the "victim art" of choreographer Bill T. Jones on the grounds "that reality without artistic transcendence turns us all into voyeurs, that the visionary gleam rather than any narcissistic glitter is what redeems American art" (10), I want to run screaming from any discussion of "aesthetics" or "transcendence." But we should not let the hypocrisy of flacks or the arrogance of Blooms deter us from making the case for the value of literary study *and* the forms of literary scholarship that have so broadened—and troubled—the field. It is time we took up the challenge to offer evaluative criteria that will answer, rather than merely denounce, those of our detractors; and we need not devise Top Ten lists or declare the inviolability of the aesthetic in order to make the case that the power and pleasure of imaginative literature should be among the things our discipline values most highly.

Notes

1. I am indirectly implicated by Langbauer's argument, since I also reviewed *Cultural Studies* (for the *Village Voice Literary Supplement* in April 1992), thus helping to commodify the book still further. To explain some of the circumstances, in March 1992 the *VLS* ran a preview of its April issue, closing it with a tag line on *Cultural Studies*: "If you plan to continue living in America, read this book." Routledge used this line in promotions for the book, run together with a passage from the closing paragraph of my essay, where I wrote that cultural studies would be contested terrain in the 1990s and that *Cultural Studies* will be "the most capacious text in the fray." I have since been accused of making the reading of *Cultural Studies* into a residency requirement for U.S. citizens, and I want to make it known that I never wrote any such thing. I merely said the book was really big, and that no serious or curious reader should ignore it. Looking back on the review some years later, I find neither proposition especially questionable.

2. The extent to which Levine's argument is an update of Ohmann's can be gauged by the following: "The two functions of English departments that institutions and the culture as a whole endorse, and pay us for, are perhaps the two to which we as research faculty members are least committed. One is the teaching of writing as a basic skill that all educated people need to acquire, and the other is the teaching of literature as it is widely understood by those who don't make the study of it their profession" (44). Likewise, at the end of the essay, Levine comes to the sound, Ohmannian conclusion that "we must learn to build departments whose interests and objectives are less at odds with their immediate public responsibilities" (45).

Works Cited

Bloom, Harold. *The Western Canon: The Books and School of the Ages*. New York: Oxford UP, 1995.

Bromwich, David. *Politics by Other Means: Higher Education and Group Thinking*. New Haven: Yale UP, 1992.

Brustein, Robert. Letter. *The New Yorker* 30 Jan. 1995: 10.

Frye, Northrop. *Anatomy of Criticism*. Princeton: Princeton UP, 1957.

Henry, William III. *In Defense of Elitism*. New York: Doubleday, 1994.

Langbauer, Laurie. "The Celebrity Economy of Cultural Studies." *Victorian Studies* 36.4 (1993): 466–72.

Levine, George. "The Real Trouble." *Profession* 93 (1993): 43–45.

Mitchell, W. J. T. "Pluralism as Dogmatism." *Critical Inquiry* 12.3 (1986): 494–502.

Morton, Donald. "The Politics of Queer Theory in the (Post)Modern Moment." *Genders* 17 (1993): 121–150.

O'Hara, Daniel T. "Lentricchia's Frankness." *boundary 2* 21.2 (1994): 40–62.

Ohmann, Richard. *English in America: A Radical View of the Profession*. New York: Oxford UP, 1976.

Rooney, Ellen. "Discipline and Vanish: Feminism, the Resistance to Theory, and the Politics of Cultural Studies." *differences* 2.3 (1990): 14–28.

Solomon, Robert, and Jon Solomon. *Up the University: Re-Creating Higher Education in America*. Reading, MA: Addison-Wesley, 1993.

Sowell, Thomas. *Race and Culture: A World View*. New York: Basic Books, 1994.

Chapter Seven

The Work of Cultural Studies in the Age of Transnational Production*

Crystal Bartolovich

> "Fifty years ago, a slip of the tongue passed more or less unnoticed. . . ."
>
> —Walter Benjamin, "The Work of Art in the Age of Mechanical Reproduction"

The rather grandiose title of this essay begs a polemical question: What *is* the work of "cultural studies" in a world increasingly dominated by a transnational capitalism that brings into constant contradiction "national" and "global" spatial logics?[1] Both title and question assume what may be rather doubtful propositions to many readers: (1) that cultural studies *is* "in the world," and (2) that it plays a role in negotiating transnational relations. However, once we recognize that the academy, in any given site, is not an entirely autonomous sphere of knowledge production, our next task is to consider its complex articulations with social, political, economic, and cultural forces often considered to be "beyond" its walls without either under- or overestimating the agency of the academics situated there. Taking up such a task, Tony Bennett has been advocating the participation of cultural theorists in the "practical" work of policy debate, Michael Bérubé has called for a more dispersed and populist cultural analysis, and Fredric Jameson (among others) has defined cultural studies as the potential site for a coalition politics of the "new social movements." Each of these critics demands the opening up of cultural studies to certain kinds of engagement with a world "outside" of the academy, and an articulation with struggles presumably situated elsewhere. While all of these roles for the cultural theorist and analyst are important ones, they assume a "closure" to the university that I would like to call into question.

I contend alternatively in the following pages that academia in general and cultural studies in particular are already in the world in a far broader sense than many of its practitioners seem to be aware or able to admit. From the local vantage point of a humanities lecturer, paper-grader, book-orderer, committee-participant, and researcher, the relationship between the academy and the world may seem to be so mediated as to be practically nonexistent, but there are nonetheless—sometimes quite direct—articulations. It is one of the burdens of *Capital*, after all, to point out that the actual relationship of the worker to the capitalist, and the situation of each within a broader set of social relations, does not immediately announce itself as such in the commodity produced, rendering misrecognition not only possible, but also typical.[2] Knowledge producers ("symbolic analysts" to Robert Reich) are not immune to such misrecognition. Hence, Gayatri Spivak has argued that persistently "questioning the separation between the world of action and the world of the disciplines" is a crucial task for the university-based intellectual even if "there is a great deal in the way" ("Reading" 95). Such a gesture is difficult in any case, but all the more so in an academy preoccupied with protecting disciplinary boundaries and refusing to recognize its own participation in dispersed power/knowledge networks.

Left cultural studies has always (at least in theory) resisted a view of knowledge production as transcending everyday life and local conditions of emergence. Nevertheless, for university-based practitioners it often becomes largely an academic matter: syllabized, indexed, published, and examined into recognizably curricular and professional forms. So while it has been preoccupied with addressing—through materialist readings of social as well as verbal texts—questions of power and the various means by which it is contested on an uneven field, these analyses rarely find their way into practical struggles. However, unless left cultural studies engages in this materialist reading practice not only to talk about the world, but also as a necessary moment in any attempt to change it for the better (what Gramsci calls "analysis of situations") it has little to recommend it over its disciplinary neighbors. To the extent that it *has* managed to hone the tools of, and engage in, the "analysis of situations," left cultural studies is very much in the world—even if its direct effectivity is relatively small.

A left-oriented analysis of situations is, however, by no means the only, or even the most pervasive, form of cultural studies at work in the world. The problem with assuming an academic insularity for "cultural studies" was brought home to me when, while browsing through journals one afternoon, I came across this sentence: "The attraction of cultural analysis is that it encourages us to question our assumptions." Then, a little later (the words emphasized with larger type): "I try to get people to be less ethnocentric by helping them understand the nature of culture." If I had been reading, say, *Social Text* or *Cultural Studies*, these sentences would not have called attention to themselves, except perhaps for their banality. However, since I discovered the first passage in the *International Journal of Strategic Management* and the second in *Personnel Journal*, I took notice (see Morgan 117; Forsberg 84). More hours in the business periodicals room revealed that such views are by no means atypical in these forums. Increasingly businesses, especially transnational corporations, seem to expect—and are hiring staff to ensure—that their employees are trained in their own version of "cultural studies." Since 1981, when the pressures of globalizing capital and "workplace diversity" had apparently asserted themselves to the point that recognition of cultural difference became a significant corporate concern, this trend has generated enough commentary to necessitate a separate heading in the *Business Index* for "cross-cultural studies."[3] What corporate "cultural studies" should remind us of, at least in part, is how the polysemic resonance of signs themselves, as "cultural studies" in this case, can indicate sites of larger, extremely complex, social struggles.

Perhaps because cultural theorists and critics spend so much of their time fighting (important) battles against, or being consumed by the demands of, traditional disciplines on matters such as syllabus reform, they have not heretofore appreciated the extent and impact of corporate cultural studies (CCS).[4] Even if few university-based intellectuals are in the corporate forest to hear it, however, theoretical trees that we may think of as of little interest to others are currently being logged by "human resources" and other managers as they construct their own cultural agenda. Their use of theories and concepts familiar to us (albeit often in unfamiliar ways) indicates how much "cultural studies" is "in the world" and participating in the negotiation of transnational relations. Capitalizing on corporate demand for "cultural studies," consultants and "educational" institutions both small and large are positioning themselves as experts in "global" culture. While these efforts may in some ways seem salutary if the alternative is a crass cultural imperialism-as-usual, they are suspect from a left perspective as long as their fundamental goal is furthering corporate profit rather than ending exploitation.

An advertisement in *Business Week* for the "American School of International Management" ("Thunderbird"), for example, tells us that "it takes a global citizen to understand a global Market" and explains that "through superior business skills, multilingual abilities and cultural sensitivity [Thunderbird graduates] are able to see borders as opportunities rather than barriers" (10). The accompanying graphics display a small (but gleaming) globe tucked between the halves of a smart corporate briefcase. A job candidate from Thunderbird, the ad implies, will be ready to work anywhere, and be in as much control of a dispersed and flexible corporate network as he is in control of his paperwork. To produce such a flexible subject, transnational capital sees itself as needing to refocus the identity-politics of its employees and direct them to unlearn at least the *inefficient* forms of their "cultural" insensitivity.[5] Many contemporary corporations have thus emphasized their "cultural" educative function to an unprecedented degree. So deeply have these ideas pervaded the corporate workplace that professors of corporate cultural studies do not rely on traditional schools alone as ideological apparatuses, but often form their own schools, such as Motorola University, the education complex of the electronics conglomerate, to train managers to shoulder the burden of globalizing capital. For these corporations, all the world has become not only (ideally) a single marketplace, but also a school.[6]

At such a moment, it behooves academics to reassess the "boundaries" that ostensibly separate the university from the rest of the world. It is with this thought in mind that I picked up a recent MLA-"commissioned" publication with the promising title *Redrawing the Boundaries*.[7] Edited by Stephen Greenblatt and Giles Gunn, the volume promises a discussion of "the transformation of English and American Literary Studies" (its subtitle). This claim calls for a semantic aside: "Transformation: 1. The action of changing form, shape, or appearance; metamorphosis. 2. A complete change in character, condition, etc." (OED). However, in spite of the dramatic insistence of the title, the changes actually described in the volume are not really so very extreme. With a few notable exceptions, *Redrawing* chronicles more of a reorientation than a transformation, a shift in emphasis and direction rather than a wholesale becoming-other. The boundaries the title refers to are primarily "the parameters of individual historical fields" and their "specialties and subspecialties"

(2). Only intermittently (as in the chapters on gender criticism and deconstruction) does a sustained consideration of the relationship of such study with *current* "nonacademic" matters come to the fore in the book's various chapters, which offer a survey of "literary studies" (as traditionally categorized) from "Medieval" to "Postmodernist," along with a guide to critical "approaches" from "Feminist" to "Postcolonial." Almost nowhere is a global context considered. In the chapters devoted to the literary periods, history is relegated primarily to a context for the reading of literature, not itself a system of relations to be read—and certainly not a site in which to question why we bother reading literature at all, and what social work it performs in the present. While all of the contributors provide more or less competent narratives of the history of criticism in their respective fields, often pointing out the ways in which literature participated in the politics of past moments, they are far less likely to discuss the politics of the university now. No exploited adjuncts and unemployed graduate students inhabit these pages (though they do make a cameo appearance in Richard Marius's essay on "Composition Studies"); nor does a discussion of where literary study might fit into a "whole way of struggle" in the modern world beyond the university. None of the writers on the periods hazard an explanation of why so much critical ink has been spilled, and why we should continue to do so. "Reason not the need!" is one possible response, but it is not an entirely satisfactory one for a critical practice that may do harm by not paying careful attention to what it does do.

One problem with this failure to consider the current politics of the institution of English emerges in that the very attempt to separate out a distinctive "literary studies" goes against the grain of many of the theoretical trends of the late twentieth century, as John Carlos Rowe points out in his discussion of "Postmodernist Studies." While the editors (and most of the contributors) seem to be well aware of this, they largely choose to examine narrowly professional dilemmas of marking out the "literary" and the various subfields of its study rather than the broader cultural politics at work in such gestures. Hence, the editors observe:

> criticism . . . possesses written and unwritten treaties—subject, as all treaties are, to challenge, rupture, and abrogation but for a while at least understood as binding. The sense of solidarity that builds up around something like deconstruction, the new historicism, or cultural criticism, or around early modern, eighteenth-century, or modernist studies, is largely an illusion. Yet the illusory feeling is important, even if it is the result not of natural limits—there are

> none—but only of arbitrary regulations that have become naturalized in the imagination. (8)

Because they choose to focus on the relations among these "fields" and "critical approaches," many questions about the position of "English" in the university and "the world" in which we live and work now go unanswered (although occasionally raised). This matters because—while the boundaries of "eighteenth-century studies" may indeed be "arbitrary"—there is nothing at all "arbitrary" about the boundaries of the university itself, especially of the "elite" universities, nor about the continued separating out of the "national" literatures. Such boundaries protect specific interests, which need the most careful elaboration and (in my opinion) "transformation."

Redrawing's assumption of academic isolationism would be disappointing in any case, but is all the more so because the editors provocatively *analogize* the university to the world without suggesting that literary studies are *in* the world in any but the most distantly mediated way. Echoing cold war rhetoric, the editors contend that "each branch of literary study is inherently ambitious, eager to extend its sphere of influence" (6). This image seems to offer the promise of potential "extension" beyond even the university itself, but nothing in the editors' discussion suggests that the "ambition" they refer to means anything more than skirmishes between academics over which "literary" works to study or how to approach them. While seventeenth- and eighteenth-century studies battle away within the university over who gets, say, *Oroonoko*, however, corporate "culture" deploys itself in a wider field as it seeks to transform "borders into opportunities." It is my contention in this essay that university-based intellectuals must interrogate this division of labor, and "literary" studies needs to see its place in the world—the whole world—not just in the U.S. university.

One place to begin this interrogation is with Homi Bhabha's discussion of "postcolonial criticism" in *Redrawing the Boundaries*. For Bhabha, "literary study" is a far broader category than it is to many of the volume's other contributors. For him it suggests a study of "letters" in the broadest possible sense, and he calls on scholars to direct their considerable reading skills toward an understanding of textual relations beyond the U.S. library and classroom as well as in them. Bhabha (as does Henry Louis Gates, Jr., in his *Redrawing* essay) questions spatial and other categories in which we tend to think, critiques binary logic, and insists that postcolonial criticism "bears witness to the unequal and uneven forces of cultural representation involved in the contest for political and social authority within the modern world order" (437). Compared to the world historical conflicts underwriting the "geopolitical divisions of east and west, north and south" invoked by Bhabha, the territorial squabbles among practitioners of seventeenth- and eighteenth-century studies, for example, or pitched battles between Marxist and New Historicist literary (in the narrow sense) critics seem trivial and embarrassing. One need not be an advocate of an unreflective and superficial "activism" in order to hope that these energies might be more fruitfully directed. It is precisely because I think that literary studies can train students so well that I want them to be able to use their skills to understand how racism in the United States as well as in *Othello* "works," and to be able to use such readings to imagine and carry out social "transformations" on a larger scale than *Redrawing the Boundaries* (on the whole) proposes.

Early cultural studies was emphatically preoccupied with such shifts in reading practice. In *Mythologies*, which is, in this respect, paradigmatic, Roland Barthes describes his project: "while concerning myself with phenomena apparently most unlike literature (a wrestling match, an elaborate dish, a plastics exhibition), I did not feel I was leaving the field of this general semiology of our bourgeois world, the literary aspect of which I had begun to study in earlier essays" (11). Taking over what had been a high-cultural, largely aestheticist set of strategies toward the study of "literary" texts and turning them to the study of social practices and forms not previously (or now) likely to be understood as either "high" or "literary" in the ordinary sense of the term, has been "transformative." "Literary" studies could not engage in such a task while proceeding as usual; new strategies were needed—not just new objects of study—for Barthes to show how imperialist and capitalist views of the world were naturalized in everyday life in France. Building on Marxist critiques of specialization in the university, and the way in which such specialization works to help keep academics from addressing important questions about the relationship among, say, cultural, economic and political forces, left cultural studies, as Anne Balsamo notes, "might best be regarded not as disciplinary or multidisciplinary but rather as postdisciplinary, no longer able, in other words, to fully recover its source disciplines and, indeed, no longer interested in doing so" (50). As long as "English" or "literary studies" maintains its interest in reproducing its own boundaries ("literary," "national," and institutional), it is not a hospitable environment for the development of a cultural studies whose project is, in Balsamo's terms, "post-disciplinary."[8] Nor, is it, I should add, a likely site to stage an effective resistance to corporate cultural studies.

I foreground this particular example because many practitioners of cultural studies find themselves housed in English departments in U.S. universities; hence, the pronouncements of a publication sponsored by the main professional organization of university English teachers might help us see to what extent an alliance with English (as currently constituted) limits its practice. Through a brief tour of *Redrawing the Boundaries*, especially the editors' introduction, I want to foreground its resistance to the project of "cultural studies" as a Gramscian analysis of situations, and consider the implications of this resistance, especially its attenuating effect on an explicitly "worldly" cultural studies. We might then be in a better position to assess how English would need to be "transformed" in order for it to be a site for the practice of left cultural studies.

Greenblatt and Gunn are explicit in providing soothing words for traditionalists who wish to preserve a privileged site for the study of "English and American" literature within the university. Taking stock of the turn to "theory," the collection declares itself to be directed to the "many members of our profession . . . [who] find themselves situated uncertainly between condemnation and celebration convinced neither that [changes in the profession indicate that] some rough beast is slouching toward Bethlehem to be born, nor that we are witnessing again the rise of a Phoenix" (1). They situate this middle somewhere to the left of Allan Bloom (!)—whose legacy has been Fukuyama's *End of History*—and to the right of an unspecified progressivism: "For some readers, as the favorable response to a book like Allan Bloom's *Closing of the American Mind* revealed, these changes [in literary studies] have seemed to pose a threat to humanistic education. For others, they have been welcomed as evidence of a profession in the process of renewing itself" (1). Although they do not take a definitive position, the editors seem particularly sympathetic to middle-of-the-road readers who "find themselves vacillating uneasily between the belief that received opinions and procedures have for too long gone unchallenged and the view that much revisionist activity may be motivated more by modishness or political posturing than by critical insight" (1). Much complexity is swept away in this formulation.

Indeed, the suspect narrowness of the category of "critical insight" in this passage is brought to the fore in the ensuing claim that "older members of the profession now often lament that their brightest students are more interested in becoming theoretically sophisticated than widely read" (2). This charge implies, of course, that one can only be "widely read" in "literature"; attention to theory or cultural forms other than "literature" apparently do not count as "real" reading. With its view of proper reading practice as opposed to "political posturing," this position also reveals what one might call an "*a*political posturing," the staking of a profoundly politicized position that must dissemble itself as "disinterested," or "just the way things are," in an attempt to preserve the status quo. Indicating to students the metrical patterns in *Paradise Lost* and possibly even exploring its links to Revolutionary and Restoration politics (safely located in the long ago) would apparently evade political posturing, but reading Derrida, or deconstructing a speech made by George Bush, is somehow more likely to be suspect. In *Redrawing the Boundaries*, the main strategy for defense against "political posturing" is drawing firm boundaries (albeit with controlled permeability) to define the "literary" profession and exclude the *explicitly* political from it. As the editors put it: "there are for literary critical studies at any given moment distinct boundaries" (6). These "distinct boundaries" are policed by the "institutional structures of the profession" which, according to Greenblatt and Gunn provide the "analogue" of a "passport" to its members (7). The disciplines and professional specialties of universities are accorded here the (analogical) status of nation-states, directing our attention to how these units operate as a world unto themselves, rather than how they function as part of actually existing nation-states. By analogizing the university to the universe, the editors sidestep the problem of how it interacts with the universe with which it is analogized.

This protected space of literary-humanist transcendence of what Stuart Hall has called the "dirtiness" of the worldly and political is defended by the editors with an astonishing use of metaphor ("Legacies" 278). Drawing on the work of the historian Peter Sahlins—who claims that national "frontiers" are neither an effort of "interest" or "ideology" but rather of "belief . . . in an imagined space" (1425)—the editors claim of literature that it "is not entirely separable from either interest or ideology, but it is not reducible to those either. Indeed, in certain circumstances literature may pull quite sharply against both interest and ideology, may even function precisely as their opposite" (6). What that "opposite" is, however, Greenblatt and Gunn leave unspecified. Goodness? Truth? Beauty? By giving no answer, they can leave a space for a vague transcendent aestheticism without making too strong a case. Ideology is not "omnipresent" for them as for Althusser, since "literature" can elude it, pushing back beyond its own "frontier" (cf. Althusser 161).

However, it is difficult to read a word like "frontier" in the U.S. context and *not* call to mind the ideology of "manifest destiny," the extermination of native peoples and other unsavory historical matters. Although this does not seem to occur to Greenblatt and Gunn, their use of "frontier" nonetheless helps naturalize dominative—even crudely colonialist—gestures by assuring readers that when we think of the protective boundaries for literature (or its subfields) we think of "frontiers," or the "line of advance against an adversary" (11). Such a view can hardly be considered neutral or innocent when the literature spoken of is "English" and "American." Referring to Sahlin's citation of an atlas compiler from the time of Richelieu, who described the "natural boundaries" (e.g., mountain ranges or rivers) of a realm as the limits of the prince's ambition, Greenblatt and Gunn draw an analogy to literary studies. Each branch of literary studies, they claim, attempts to enlarge its territory until it recognizes at some point that "the advantage of expanding the sphere of influence would be outweighed by the cost" to them (6). This colonizing mentality, presented uncritically and as "inherent" is troubling, especially since it seems to echo appreciatively a long tradition of colonialist theory. The "other" is not only called on to consolidate the (disciplinary) self, but also to offer itself up to mastery.

One is reminded by these metaphors of Gayatri Spivak's critique of Foucault in "Can the Subaltern Speak?" In that essay she points out that "to buy a self-contained version of the West is to ignore its production by the imperialist project" (291). While Foucault traces the workings of Power in the European scene of writing, the examples he produces operate as "screen-allegories that foreclose a reading of the broader narratives of imperialism" (291). Greenblatt and Gunn's "analogues" can be subjected to a similar critique; by positing a certain kind of closure to the university and literary study (however provisional or "imaginary"), they too "foreclose" certain questions by directing our attention primarily to the "internal" relations of the profession rather than the "external" ones. More significantly, "English" and "American" remain largely uninterrogated, encouraging Greenblatt and Gunn's metaphors of disciplinary imperialism to serve as screen allegories of the corporate and national variety.

Let us follow this chain of metaphors a bit further. Greenblatt and Gunn contend that the "notion of limit [to ambition] can be set against the quite different implication of frontier," which they point out is, for Sahlins, the place where one "'stood face to face with . . . an enemy'" (6). The military image is quite elaborately developed: "Now what lies beyond the existing boundary is an enemy—whose forces are feared, whose territory is regarded with a hostile gaze. That gaze may have within it desire, envy, the wish to appropriate or, alternatively, the wish to eradicate, tear down, reconstruct on a better pattern" (6). This passage is qualified with a quite astonishing note: "A military frontier implies hostility to difference, though we can imagine other attitudes. For example, the forces of one territory may wish to occupy the other, without substantially challenging or eradicating its otherness," which is the editors' way of justifying the appropriation to literary studies of whatever its practitioners find interesting in other (sub)fields without becoming other (11). While this observation might seem to be addressing the troubling issue of negotiating a relation of nonmastery between self and other, Greenblatt and Gunn have a different agenda. They point out: "we are still dealing with hostile foes . . . but the other may in some sense survive the occupation, either through the policy of the occupying force or though the ruses of the occupied" (11). Their example is of alternative interpenetrations of history and literary studies: "There may be powerful, if obscure, currents of literary criticism running through a work of history, while the assumptions that govern history writing may shape a work of formalist literary criticism ostensibly indifferent to history" (11). The "frontier" analogy may (although even this is doubtful) seem to work for "literary criticism" and "history," narrowly construed, as in the previous example, but only because the stakes appear to be so low. Let us raise them and evaluate the effect: Would it be likely for Arab residents of Israeli-occupied parts of the West Bank to feel "unchallenged" by Israelis even if no shots are fired? And is it possible to imagine such disputes take place entirely outside of cultural domains, outside, for example, how we tell the stories of history and if and how we read the cultural texts of the disputants? Beyond media representation and the social texts of racism and orientalism?

It is necessary to ask such questions because Greenblatt and Gunn drop all pretense of uncontentious cohabitation by the end of the essay. Not only is "occupation" praised, but it is also presented as determinate, natural—and precisely as subsuming "otherness": "the power of literature, and of literary study lies in its ability to infiltrate any speech and writing, transforming what seems outside itself into something else, into its own odd being" (11). From threatened nation, literary studies is transformed into a global empire. So much for limits to ambition! Difference will simply disappear before the "infiltration" of "literature" and "literary study." All "otherness" becomes, then, the same. In a world where the meaning of social texts is disputed not only within the university but between (and within) cultures, such "transforming" can hardly elude broad social and political effects. Should we not be asking, then, what such a claim as Greenblatt and Gunn's means in a global context, not just in the narrow dispute between a history department and "English"? A global perspective cannot simply be exiled to Postcolonial Studies since the categories "English" and "American" produce and are an effect of particular world relations, not essential attributes of "English" and "American" peoples writ large.

The problem is not that Greenblatt and Gunn imagine the university and literary studies rife with contention; it is. Rather, the problem is that such contention is divorced from broader social conflict and contention at both the local and especially the global level, not just by Greenblatt and Gunn but by many of the contributors to the volume. For example, in setting out his views of a "politics of reading" characteristic of the New Historicisms, Louis Montrose observes that "the merely academic phenomenon of new historicism is incommensurable with the worldwide social movement articulated by feminist, Marxist, postcolonial and gay and lesbian discourses" (408). Presumably, he is attempting to obviate the facile assumption that classroom politics are sufficient to effect social change—an unexceptionable view. However, this does not mean that there is *no* space for the new social movements in the university simply because it is an *insufficient* space for a broad-based politics. Such a view situates New Historicism (not surprisingly) as distant from a political cultural studies, which, in Fredric Jameson's recent description, is the site in the university where the very movements Montrose sees as "incommensurable" with the work of New Historicism are welcomed and encouraged.

Although Montrose suggests that there is no "necessary" (409) antagonism in New Historicism to politically committed analysis (he mentions feminism in particular), he is quite clear that much work actually produced under the New Historicist label is ambiguous, at best, in its politics and that political commitment is certainly not necessary to New Historicism: "American male academics producing New Historicist work in Renaissance studies during the past decade tended to displace and contain the cultural politics of their own practice by at once foregrounding relations of power and confining them to the English past that was presently under study" (406). He contrasts this retreat into the past with the practice of the Cultural Materialists in Britain

> where class barriers remain more clearly articulated than in the United States; where, too, radical politics enjoy stronger traditions; and where the coercive pressure of the state on centralized

> educational institutions and practices has for some time been direct and intense—[so] there has been a polemical emphasis . . . on the uses to which a historical present puts its versions of the national past. (406)

Class markers, such as accent, may indeed be more pronounced in Britain, but "barriers" between classes are not necessarily any greater there if we examine, for example, the gaps between the richest and poorest members of the populations. According to the 1995 *Human Development Report*, there is only a one-percentage point difference between the share of income accruing to the poorest 40 percent of the population in the United States (15.7%) and in Britain (14.6%); in *both* countries the income gap between the wealthiest and poorest is large and increasing, suggesting that class "barriers" are "clearly articulated" materially in each site, even if there are discrepancies in the recognition of, or attitudes toward, this gap.

Similarly, the United States does *not* lack a strong radical tradition: it lacks a strong historical memory of it. This distinction is crucial. Even a ten-minute browse through a widely available volume such as Zinn's *People's History of the U.S.* (or even Cohen's or Stimpson's essays, limited as they are, in *Redrawing*), if not more specialist studies, should be enough to disabuse readers of Professor Montrose's misleading (if common) assessment of U.S. history. Students in my classes are often truly shocked when I show them archival footage of private corporate militias shooting strikers, or the police beating civil rights protesters, and photos of suffragettes being restrained and force-fed during hunger strikes. There certainly has been a strong "radical tradition" in the United States—but it has often been successfully marginalized politically and expunged historically, as the "history of victors" always attempts to do.

C. L. R. James once observed that U.S. intellectuals are more likely than other intellectuals to fail to see the remarkable accomplishments of labor, antiracist, and feminist radicals, apparently assuming that all good things come from the benevolence of the state and corporate capital, rather than long and hard struggles by the men and women who were beaten, shot at, killed, imprisoned, harassed, and reviled in the pursuit of something like equality and justice in the United States. Pointing in particular to the struggles to establish the CIO in 1935–37, James observes: "It is evidence of the general backwardness of American social thought that this great movement is not firmly established as a part of American History and American consciousness" (124). He, too, makes a contrast between Britain and the United States in this respect, but it is a quite different one from Montrose's: "The corresponding movement in England, the strike of the dock workers and match girls in 1889, though not anything near the range and power of the C.I.O. movement, is an established part of the British people, not only of the working class. But of all socialist minded intellectuals . . . the American intellectuals . . . are the most backward" (124). That New Historicists help perpetuate this backwardness through silent collaboration with the status quo in the present is most unfortunate, though not surprising. Montrose's analysis fits well within the boundaries drawn by Greenblatt and Gunn, who want to make sure that it is possible to place "literature" on one side of the fence and mere "ideology" and "interest"—politics—on the other.

Let me be precise about what I mean by "politics" here. In Greenblatt and Gunn's imaginary, to affirm literary boundaries is to participate in a system in which, "without . . . signs of identity and right, you are not allowed to pass; indeed, you risk being shot" (7). It is disturbing to find the turf wars of the current U.S. academy equated with territorial struggles such as those in Bosnia or the Middle East in which real bullets find their way into real bodies and render real people dead. However, the analogy is inappropriate for a more important reason than its excess in relation to "merely academic phenomena" as such (Sedgwick's essay in *Redrawing* refers to this as a problem of "condensation"). The more troublesome aspect of this analogy is that it suggests in its very use of great things to describe small that "merely academic phenomena" have no bearing on scenes of actual violence. A more appropriate gesture than this simultaneous aggrandizing (within a narrow sphere) and discounting (within a larger) of "literary" studies would be to show how they have helped consolidate the boundaries (most notably "national" ones) and the hierarchies which help underwrite the firing of guns (see Said, *Culture and Imperialism*; Gilroy). Benjamin's reminder that there is no document of civilization that is not at the same time a document of barbarism might be invoked here. The ways in which "literary" studies are irreducibly bound up with the political is in the realm of meaning production, of symbolic value. Cultural studies has attempted to pursue the articulations of such meaning production with economic and political forces without assuming that any one subsumes the others.

In spite of this, it is precisely on the issue of (presumed) subsumption of the "literary" by the "material" that cultural studies is often attacked. A *Redrawing the Boundaries* contributor, Anne Middleton, in her chapter on Medieval studies, makes this perceived threat explicit when she remarks that "recent work suggests further opportunities for differentiating a specifically literary history and criticism of medieval texts from the practices and goals of cultural studies, into which literary scholarship in general has lately been widely subsumed" (26). Her concern that literary studies is somehow being "subsumed" by cultural studies is astonishing given the fact that while this may be the case in a few pockets here and there, and in the cutting-edge journals, it is hardly the case in the profession as a whole, which remains very much grounded in a narrowly literary—and disciplinary—past (as *Redrawing the Boundaries* suggests). The most recent MLA survey of English curricula indicates strikingly little change in authors studied, or even in approaches used, thirty years ago.[9]

Nonetheless, let us take Middleton at her word and see what it is that is so troubling about "cultural studies" to a "literary" scholar:

> the focus of a revised literary history would be the formal factors and cognitive practices that make human beings, individually and in groups, intervene in their societies by defining themselves as makers, users and possessors of texts, to examine how such formal concerns generate conflict rather than merely serve as a displacement for conflicts supposedly produced elsewhere, in 'material' interests. (27)

Cultural studies folk, in her charge, are so worried about "material interests" that their readings all end up sounding the same, whereas talking about "textual and generic forms" (35) offers more variety.[10] Reading such a charge, I can only conclude that Professor Middleton has not read widely in cultural studies, which emerged precisely as a critique of "economism," the crudely reductive attribution of "vulgar material" causes to cultural forms understood merely as effects.

Raymond Williams, one of its early exponents in the British context, describes his methodology in *The Country and the City* as follows:

> the witnesses we have summoned here raise questions of historical fact and perspective, but they raise questions, also, of literary fact and perspective. The things they are saying are not all in the same mode. They range, as facts, from a speech in a play and a passage in a novel to an argument in any essay and a note in a journal. When the facts are poems, they are also, and perhaps crucially, poems of different kinds. We can only analyze these important structures of feeling if we make, from the beginning, these crucial discriminations . . . a persistent problem of form. (12)

Now it is true, of course, that a practitioner of cultural studies would want to examine the relations of these cultural forms to economic and political "interests" and not privilege the cultural form any more than the older Marxist methods tended to privilege the "material interests." Middleton, on the other hand, quite clearly wants the cultural form to be the primary concern of the "literary" scholar, leaving the "social historian" and the cultural critic to tend to the "material interests." This division of labor was precisely the one that cultural studies was developed to overcome, by observing that such divisions tend to impoverish analyses on both sides of—to borrow Greenblatt and Gunn's vocabulary—the "frontier" they produce.[11]

In addition, the emphasis on "frontiers" in *Redrawing the Boundaries* gives an odd and troublesome valence to, among other things, the complex politics of "multiculturalism" both "in" and "beyond" the university. Since the far right has attacked academia on this issue for so long, it is extremely easy to fall into the trap of thinking that expanding the "frontiers" of the canon somehow eludes the power/knowledge relations of all other disciplinary activity. However, teaching Harriet Jacobs or Amy Tan is not, *of itself*, necessarily a radical gesture in the current conjuncture in the absence of a thorough and ongoing critique of the power relations in which the university itself participates, including issues of access and "merit," as well as the function of "literature" in subject formation. Some of the contributors to *Redrawing the Boundaries*, nevertheless, congratulate themselves simply for "expanding" the canon. The editors note, for example, that "as American [sic] higher education has become more accessible to people of different backgrounds—ethnic, racial, social, cultural, sexual, and religious—teachers of literature have found that the traditional humanistic curriculum seems less representative. The perception has aroused interest in revising and expanding the literary canon" (3). This assessment overlooks (or at least deemphasizes) the struggle of *students* to force reluctant administrations (and sometimes faculty as well) to make such changes (this is mentioned in Gates' essay). It also subordinates *how* students read to *which* books are taught. The editors divert our attention away, thus, from developing materialist reading practices that would help students evaluate the world in which canons are formed as well as the items in any given canon.

The essays in *Redrawing* echo and reinforce Greenblatt and Gunn's position in this respect more often than not, either by sidestepping the issue, or repeating their claims in a variety of guises. Philip Fisher, for example, traces the historical process of the segregation of U.S. intellectuals as academics in the university, where he leaves them, and then offers this remarkable observation in his chapter on "American [sic] Literary and Cultural Studies Since the Civil War":

> Analysis within American studies will always be of sectors of a diverse culture characterized by the absence of a monopoly of power. These studies will always be historical and not anthropological, because of the commitment of the culture itself to a rapid building up, wearing out, and replacement of systems of all kinds by new arrays of persons and forces. The updraft is strong, the door of immigration both to and within the country is open, the exhaustion of control is always imminent and control itself is porous. Because America had no experience of monarchy, it has a permanent democratic core working against not only the centralization of power but, more important, its inheritance or preservation over time. (247)

Leaving aside here obvious objections to Fisher's claims about "open" immigration and the "democratic core"—to which recent events from the passage of Proposition 187 to congressional resistance to "single-payer" health care bills give the lie—I want to point out how very closely passages such as these fit in with the concerns of a corporate cultural studies which seeks to "help companies cope with an increasingly diverse domestic work force and find ways to benefit from diversity" (Carlsen 4).

If we recognize that corporations have such interests, we might be able to see that efforts in the academy toward, as Catharine Stimpson puts it in her essay in *Redrawing the Boundaries*, "the recognition of differences, [and] a movement into pluralism" (251)—*in the absence of a specific critique of corporate (and other) interests in such gestures*—are readily transferable into the disciplining of a new "tolerant" workforce (which is also one of the key goals of corporate cultural studies). Such "tolerance" is not without its secondary gains for members of groups who have not previously (or at least not recently) attracted this level of assimilative attention from employers; however, we need to keep in mind that these gains are inscribed primarily in the interests of capital, not those of the working population.[12] Also, if we fail to recognize that we are all now participating in an international labor market, willy-nilly—both as consumers and workers—we will also fail to see how conditions at "home" are affected by, and have effects on, a global system.

Tom Moylan has warned that we "need to understand recent tendencies toward the commodification and co-optation of cultural studies by corporate interests as one reason for its flourishing status in the university" (35). The flip side of this coin is, of course, that programs which are less amenable to corporate takeovers may well be less likely to be "flourishing." Left cultural studies has had to respond to attacks on numerous fronts: right-wing critics of "political correctness," human development advocates of corporate views of "culture," critics of interdisciplinary work from a variety of fields. These groups have quite different agendas, and therefore different strategies of attack. At the same time as right-wing attacks on "multiculturalism" and radical studies of difference in U.S. universities and colleges have attracted lots of media attention, and caused a backlash against the most progressive aspects of many university curriculums,[13] corporations, and business schools have been quietly establishing a cultural studies suited to their own needs, with language training, a "sensitivity" to the customs, manners, and traditions of "other" places, and a translation of cultural processes into discrete bits of learnable and manageable "information" highest on their agendas. Thus we find situations such as broad corporate support for "diversity workshops" of the kind that the far right rejects.[14] It is important to recognize that transnational corporate agendas actually often *conflict with* the efforts of far right opponents of "multiculturalism." We often think of the "right" as against a "progressive" study of "culture" in the university, but the right is by no means homogeneous on this issue.

Nevertheless, it is not difficult to see that the profusion of discourses and practices that have manifested themselves, often contestedly, under the rubric of "cultural studies" in humanities and social science journals, conferences, and classrooms are profoundly different from both Corporate Cultural Studies and "literary studies" as Greenblatt and Gunn delimit it. Richard Johnson attempted to describe the necessarily indeterminate disciplinary (and "worldly") formation of cultural studies by pointing out some of its main, left-oriented assumptions:

> First . . . that cultural processes are intimately connected with social relations, especially with class relations and class formations, with sexual divisions, with the racial structuring of social relations and with age oppressions as a form of dependency. . . . Second . . . that culture involves power and helps to produce asymmetries in the abilities of individuals and social groups to define and realize their needs. And . . . third . . . that culture is neither an autonomous nor an externally determined field, but a site of social differences and struggles. (39)

CCS, on the contrary, being influenced heavily by empiricist social science and directed toward practical application in (capitalist) offices and markets, puts little emphasis on contestation and struggle, more on "synergy" and how corporations can *use* "culture" (or at least not let it get in the way) in meeting marketing and public relations goals. Its textbooks have titles such as *Managing Cultural Differences* (the 1979 classic of the field, now in its third edition) and *International Public Relations* (which includes the chapter "Recognizing and Handling Cultural Differences"). These books indicate the broad sphere of influence, instrumental rationality, and reified definition of culture assumed by their authors; for them, culture is just one thing among many to be managed by a well-trained organizational agent, a position which evades potentially troubling questions about power relations and their effects.

Redrawing the Boundaries, while (ostensibly) operating in a far narrower sphere, also argues for a instrumental relation between "criticism" and the domain of culture appropriate to it. Although Greenblatt and Gunn concede that there are a few "intellectual enterprises" (!) that should not be "reduced" to tools "for interrogating individual works of literature," the very establishing of exceptions suggests that most "intellectual enterprises" are so reducible (10). In addition, the editors note that the map of the field they propose in the chapter headings "could easily have been drawn some other way" but it is a drawing that in all the examples they provide, respects the professionalized practices of literary scholars within the boundaries of the university and subordinates all "intellectual enterprises" to them. Even the "intellectual enterprises" that (for Greenblatt and Gunn) exceed a literary critical function do so only in order to exert a force on *other critical discourses* as they "resituate all the interrogatory operations of criticism within new constellations of force and tension" (10). Hence, deconstruction ("most notably") and "feminist studies" ("above all") get singled out *not* for engagement in actual political struggles but rather for their tendency to discuss other *theoretical* matters as well as literature; "postcolonial studies" is also mentioned in this regard—in a footnote, relegating the theorization of (neo)colonial "otherness" precisely to the margins of the introduction. In a book that uncritically privileges "English and American" literary studies this is, perhaps, precisely where one would expect to find it. *Redrawing the Boundaries* takes the boundaries of nation-states for granted, while those between disciplines are interrogated (but preserved).

British Cultural Studies, on the other hand, has been obliged to call into question the national boundaries with which the study of cultures has often been assumed to coincide. Critiques of the construction of "Englishness" have been produced "internally" (Gilroy, Hall) and "externally" (Ang, Turner). The "external" critiques have called into question false universals in the development of "cultural studies," such that "British" or "U.S." culture purports to stand in for all culture without marking out its specificity. From this perspective, *Redrawing the Boundaries* might be seen as theoretically sophisticated in its explicit description of its purview as "English and American" literary studies (as opposed to literary studies in general). However, uninterrogated "particularisms" of this kind lead to problems of their own, as the "internal" critiques of so-called "British" Cultural Studies have emphasized. As Hall puts it:

> Initially cultural studies was very much locked into an argument about British culture, British literature, etc. Those are just not what the questions are anymore, or rather, the question of "Britishness" can only even be framed in relation to its "others" within the global cultural system . . . processes which no longer belong to, or can be settled within the framework of any one national culture. ("Internationalization" 399)

Not only does "Britain" as a construct occlude, for example, "Wales" and the influence of postcolonial diaspora on the construction of "British" identity, but assuming that a nation "ceaselessly gives birth to itself" from within, as Gilroy puts it, looks increasingly oversimplified and ethnocentric from recent perspectives, which urge the development of more flexible spatial and cultural analysis than "national(ist)" paradigms permit (14).

"English" (and Cultural Studies) in the United States need to come to understand the "global cultural system" Hall refers to more fully. Greenblatt and Gunn see "English" as a construct, but not a "global" one in Hall's sense. For them, English and American literary studies is an effect of "treaties" among members of a profession divided into separate camps by critical and period affiliations. Together they produce boundaries from "arbitrary regulations that have become naturalized in the imagination" (8). "English" and "American" literary studies in this description are forged from within the university by the scholars who perform the studies: their practices are the significant elements of the construct. However, in the global context to which Hall draws our attention, boundaries determined in this way are anything but "arbitrary" or reducible to university professionals. They take place in a set of irreducibly global relations and help produce and police power differences based on specific interests and agendas, to which *Redrawing the Boundaries* remains indifferent, as it describes what purports to be an entirely academic imperialism.

Strikingly similar to this "imperial" attitude of English (although on a vastly different scale—and certainly without suggesting that the corporation is distinct from "the world"), corporate classroom "culture" indicates that it and an expansionistic, territorializing vision for capital, have become synonymous. This passage from *Multicultural Management* (1993) is typical:

> Because of the significant social and political changes that are currently underway, there is real opportunity for world traders and entrepreneurs, free of ideologies, to engage in peaceful commerce for the benefit of humankind. The globalization of the mass media has shown many people the possibilities available within modern society, and has made them desire improvements in their quality of life. Such market needs can only be met on a global scale when a new class of managers and professionals come prepared with multicultural skills. (Farid and Harris 1)

Of course, capitalism has long harped on the string of its benefit to human kind, but this passage moves in new directions with the reference to "global scale" and in its emphasis on "multicultural skills." The play of passive and active voice in this passage is also significant. "Social and political changes" and "the globalization of the mass media" are agentless events that simply "are currently underway" and have provided a mission for "world traders and entrepreneurs" to undertake: the meeting of "market needs" of global consumers. With (ostensibly) no ties to the "social," the "political" or even "the media," the corporate fulfillers-of-needs can hone their "multicultural skills" while distancing themselves from "ideologies" (which, we might recall, Greenblatt and Gunn claim "literature" can do as well). Naturalizing the ways in which transnational capital helps produce the very conditions (consumer desires, a workforce disciplined to sell its labor) it then seeks to meet as "market needs," the discourses of corporate cultural studies project their own "benefit" onto "humankind," and then attempt to consolidate mass perception of this "benefit" as general. When one reads, however, that "in our society [U.S], poverty is considered a handicap and a condition to be overcome; whereas in other parts of the world poverty is taken for granted, or even is seen by some as a special blessing," one can see not only "ideology," but also a justification for global exploitation, in the making (Harris and Morgan 205–06).

This passage from the 1991 *Managing Cultural Differences* is unusual and provincial—but not in its ideological positions. Rather, it is idiosyncratic in assuming a U.S. reader. More "transnationally" oriented volumes regularly shift "national" points of view since they are destined for use in training managers from many different geographical origins in what is increasingly described as a "borderless world." Above all, the texts strive to assure that cultural difference will not impede the free flow of capital—or hinder profits. As one analyst puts it, bluntly: "a cross-cultural blunder is . . . a decision affecting the foreign operations of a firm that results in a greater than necessary cost *to the firm*" (Maddox 19, emphasis added). The costs to injured parties does not matter in such a formulation. As long as a "blunder" costs the firm nothing, there is no need to take account of it.

Thus it is only in the interests of profit that conflicts must be smoothed over, and "synergy," the corporate buzzword for apparently struggle-free "cooperation," attained:

> it is ineffective when one entity simply tries to impose its culture on another. It is more productive to seek a cultural synergy between and among the systems involved. . . . Nowhere is multicultural management more desirable than in the formation of a consortium made up of several corporations, or of representatives from industry, government and universities. (Farid and Harris 3)

A useful critical gesture to deploy when faced with such a passage is to remove the mystifying term "synergy" and replace it with "hegemony" which invites a certain line of questioning that "synergy" attempts to head off—and also indicates that a mere dismissive demonization of global capital will not suffice as critique.[15] Where consent to capital is secured in a slow process of negotiation and discipline through schools, advertising, the workplace, the media and shopping malls—the whole ideological network promoting the "American Way of Life"—a more nuanced approach is needed. Spenser's *View of the Present State of Ireland* chillingly and too matter-of-factly observed long ago in the early stages of European colonialism: "to the willing there is no harm done." Given the politics of "willingness," one might doubt this then—and now—but one would still have to tease out the complex conditions of possibility for the "willingness."

With Spenser's observation (which is pertinent to current neocolonial as well as colonial politics) in mind, we can pursue the possibility that the industry-government-university bloc proposed in the above quotation from *Multicultural Management* insists on the continuing pertinence of Gramsci's concept of hegemony, which, in pointing out the limits of "economism," emphasizes the need to unravel the complex system of forces through which dominant groups achieve and maintain broad "consent" to a particular set of socio-politico-economic conditions. Such forces can be regressive or progressive, and can only be analyzed by taking account of how "the dominant group is coordinated concretely with the general interests of the subordinate groups" (182). Such a complex analysis forces us to remember that perceived "benefit" (in Spenser's lexicon, "willingness") is an effect of a situated—and perhaps even contradictory—calculus on the part of so-called benefactors and beneficiaries alike.

The "benefit" of attempting to etch out a pure space for the humanities betrays its contradictions when we recall how deeply implicated the traditional academy has already become in forming the "consortiums" advocated by transnational corporations. Indeed, the day-to-day budgetary decisions of the U.S. academic institutions many of us inhabit are entangled with the very economic forces those of us in left cultural studies spend a considerable amount of our time critiquing (see Feldman; Soley; Watkins, *Work Time*). At least one speaker at a 1988 conference at Virginia Tech on "University Spin-off Companies" argued that the initiatives of this kind currently underway at the university level even needed to be replicated at "all levels of education from kindergarten through twelfth grade to the large research universities," a task that calls for "substantial cultural reawakening" (Cantlon and Koenig 10). A translation of this "reawakening" into Gramsci's terms would be the organizing and maintenance of "consent" to it.

Already Virginians are being urged to answer this wake-up call; advertisements in *Business Week* for the Fairfax County school system (designed to attract corporate investment to the area) depict a Japanese man writing Japanese characters on a blackboard for a group of children (two white boys, two white girls, and one black boy). The ad assures parents and potential corporate sponsors that

> to build the country's best educated workforce, you have to start at the beginning. If you want to compete in the twenty-first century, you're going to have to know the language. And the language won't always be English. That's why the public school system in Fairfax County offers language immersion programs in Japanese, Spanish, and French. The goal is to make students fluent

> by junior high. And by adulthood, more competitive in world trade. (11)

This explicit linking of the educational ideological apparatus with corporate concerns is perhaps not so surprising given the pervasiveness of "better-educated workforce" discourses, but the shift away from even a rhetorical privileging of U.S. "culture(s)" is notable. Such deprivileging—with a reprivileging at another level (via "Fairfax")—of the "U.S." in "world trade" marks a reworking at the local level of transnational corporate interests at a time when legislation such as NAFTA and the Canada Accords, which primarily benefit transnationals, have unsettled economic agendas in which state and national-corporate policies converge. Only in a very restricted sense is the United States reprivileged in this move: through a metonymic displacement onto "Fairfax," which is a high-tech corridor locale, a node in the transnational corporate network.[16]

While the gap between rich and poor widens in the United States and throughout the globe, it is important to remember that such regional economic boons do not affect all members of the local population alike, nor are they equally distributed on the face of the globe.[17] "American" (and "English") cease to signify in quite the same way in such a situation; "globalization" has implications for culture as well as corporations. Not only does the legacy of imperialism oblige us to interrogate "English" and "American" literature and the cost of assuming their integrity, but also the radically different spatial politics of the present demand we consider alternative understandings of the ways parts of the globe interact (see Appadurai; Sklair). Since the "consent" of educators is specifically appealed to in the corporate bid for hegemony for its view of culture, left cultural studies can directly intervene by resisting attempts of corporations to naturalize their activity and to organize broad consent for it.

If left cultural studies is to do this, it needs to strategize with more awareness of the agendas of CCS in mind while continuing its more local struggles. Moving in this direction, Bruce Robbins and Gerald Graff's chapter on "cultural criticism" in *Redrawing* at least views the forging of alliances "with the new social movements outside the university" (435) as a desirable (and possible) task for university intellectuals, but even their essay is limited by the frame of the book as a whole. Specifically, presumably because *Redrawing the Boundaries* is focused on "English and American Literary Studies," Robbins and Graff write a story whose telos is "cultural studies" as if it grew out of "cultural criticism" of literature in England and the U.S. alone—views that recent work in cultural studies, as I've detailed, has taken pains to refute. Robbins and Graff rightly point out that the emergence of national literature departments coincides with that of nationalism and an attempt to "keep an expanding immigrant population under control," and that a literary counterculture develops in resistance to such efforts at homogenization (422). However, they imply that this story explains "cultural studies" as well as "cultural criticism," as if the former grew directly out of the latter.[18] They also fail to examine the "external" as well as "internal" conflicts through which nations are produced (e.g., not just the attempt to control immigration "inside" a country by differentiation and "assimilation," but imperialism, trade, debt, etc. produce "nation-effects"). In addition, while they make the extremely important point (obscured by the right's attacks on the so-called politicization of the universities), that cultural criticism (of the Arnold and Howe variety) has always been "political"—sometimes even explicitly so—they seem to suggest that all that the world needs to cure its ills is better communications skills and the opportunity to use them: "Cultural Studies suggests that the aim of cultural criticism is something more than preserving, transmitting, and interpreting culture or cultures. Rather, the aim is to bring together, in a common democratic space of discussion, diversities that had remained unequal largely because they had remained apart" (435). The cultural studies that I know suggests something rather different: that peoples have remained unequal because of "conquest, theft, political intrigue, courtiership, extortion and the power of money" (Williams 50). No amount of "discussion" or (ostensibly) "neutral" presentation of "the conflicts" will adequately defend against or redress the damage done by such forces.

What is to be done? It seems to me that left cultural studies needs to focus its attention on corporate developments in a direct and systematic way, and resist these with the whole arsenal at our disposal: discussion certainly, but also the encouragement of unionization (including the forging of transnational alliances of unions), strikes, boycotts, legislation, creation of alternatives to for-profit enterprises (such as community run co-ops), marches, and demonstrations—whatever is necessary. Heretofore, our attention has been engaged in more local battles which derive from our attempts to define ourselves as a disciplinary formation "in" the academy, battles that often take the form of attempts to resist assimilation into traditional disciplinary forms.[19] Such battles take on tremendous importance at that local level having to do with curriculum, resource distribution, and the diverse departmental politics that take up so much of our energy in everyday academic life. However, these struggles, when directed toward the "traditional" disciplines alone, are also distracting us from combating an even more potent enemy: corporate cultural studies. We must make the time to resist the "friendly fascism" of transnational corporate cultural studies.[20]

Concretely: in the classroom we can provide an alternative educational practice to corporate cultural studies by refusing liberal and conservative attempts to act as if the classroom is a "neutral" space, even as they further their own political agendas in the name of neutrality and objectivity. We can teach our students to "analyze situations" in Gramscian fashion wherever they may find themselves. In addition, we might work on practicing what we preach in our own houses: deal with the difficult problems of un- and underemployment of Ph.D.s in English, with the attendant waste of promise and desire; the hyperexploitation of adjunct labor; the seduction of careerism at the cost of our radical practice; the protection of freedoms of speech for the most vulnerable members of universities (including "support staff" and other "nonacademic" employees as well as the junior faculty and graduate students); the establishment of workplace democracy. These "material interests" do not seem to fall within the boundaries redrawn by Greenblatt and Gunn.

So if we are to take them up in a meaningful way, we may also need to keep our agendas clear and distinct from the English departments where many of us are housed if they are not willing to undergo a "transformation" more extensive than the one *Redrawing the Boundaries* describes.[21] Cultural Studies' own attempts to describe itself have generated a great deal of uneasiness, but it is precisely this uneasiness, when accompanied by a recognition of it in cultural studies work, that is its strength. Because it is not "defined" by reference to a specific "object" (such as literature), it can more flexibly rework its suppositions and commitments. The introduction to the influential Illinois *Cultural Studies* volume puts it this way:

> a scholarly discipline, like literature, cannot begin to do cultural studies simply by expanding its dominion to encompass specific cultural forms (western novels, say, or TV sitcoms, or rock and roll), social groups (working class youth, for example, or communities 'on the margins,' or women's rugby teams), practices (wilding, quilting, hacking), or periods (contemporary culture, for example, as opposed to historical work). Cultural studies involves how and why such work is done, not just its content. (Grossberg et al. 11)

Stuart Hall emphasizes that such work can never be undertaken with a sense of certitude about methodological or theoretical adequacy to a given situation: "It is a project that is always open to that which it doesn't yet know, to that which it can't yet name" ("Legacies" 278). Cultural theorists must always engage in a self-criticism, assume that their conclusions are incomplete and provisional, and ask themselves questions such as: Why are we studying this text (by no means limited to print materials)? What are the implications of this study? How might this project be thought otherwise? What must we exclude in order to undertake this project? What are the effects of this exclusion? And, more important, if we are to get past narrowly disciplinary concerns, we must also ask: How do our practices articulate with other institutional practices elsewhere? What relations of power do they help produce and maintain? In other words, how are our practices "worldly" and "worlding"?

These are not questions available to the disciplinary formation of "literary studies" generated by Greenblatt and Gunn in their introduction, or—as an effect of their framing, in spite of dissident chapters—in their volume as a whole.[22] Indeed, although there have been many calls in recent years for a radical reorganization of the disciplinary structure of the humanities by practitioners of cultural studies,[23] *Redrawing the Boundaries* is a book unable or unwilling to imagine the "transformation" of the English department except as a movement from one kind of narrowly construed "English and American *literary* studies" to another (emphasis mine). The volume fetishizes "literature" and clings to an organizational structure—periodization—which Gerald Graff himself has shown us in *Professing Literature* has been familiar in one form or another since the turn of the century when "English" succeeded in its struggle to overturn the ascendancy of classics in U.S. colleges. Most problematically, the nation remains largely uninterrogated as an organizing principle for the fields under discussion. This is not the site from which cultural studies is likely to be able to position itself against transnational corporate cultural studies in any meaningful way.

Greenblatt and Gunn justify the boundaries of a literary studies whose emphasis is more on the page than in the world by noting that "one of the ways in which historical claims of territory are established is through continuous possession, inheritance, ancient titles" (7). The example they give is of "rhyme," which they claim has been taken up by "literature" and therefore belongs to it by right of "continuous possession." However, as soon as we introduce questions of power, this analogy cannot be pushed very far—not even when dealing with narrowly literary, or academic, matters: if, for example, white men have had "continuous possession" of the canon, and the upper-departmental ranks, should they, by virtue of simply having always been in those positions, continue to do so? As Raymond Williams has pointed out:

> There is no innocence in the established proprietors, at any particular point in time, unless we ourselves choose to put it there. Very few titles to property could bear humane investigation, in the long process of conquest, theft, political intrigue, courtiership, extortion and the power of money. It is a deep and persistent illusion to suppose that time confers on these familiar processes of acquisition an innocence which can be contrasted with the ruthlessness of subsequent stages of the same essential drives . . . the ancient stocks to which we are sentimentally referred, are ordinarily only those families who had been pressing and exploiting their neighbors rather longer. (50)

If we replace "families" with "departments" we can strategically analogize Williams's analysis of class relations in the countryside to relations within the university.

Leah Marcus, in her chapter on "Renaissance/Early Modern Studies," suggests at least one reason why such an analogy is unlikely to be willingly endorsed by scholars comfortably situated in literary studies. While discussing the "contradiction" of using geographic metaphors in the course of critiquing early forms of European colonialism (a hot topic in Early Modern Studies), she writes:

> The goal of our quest to explore and map new worlds out of the past is intellectual stimulation, of course, but also, increasingly, financial well-being and prestige: professorships at major universities in the United States have become more remunerative than at any time before, or at least within living memory, and much of the largesse has gone to scholars in the area of Renaissance/early modern studies. Renaissance dreams of glory still haunt us as we open up vast new territories for conquest within the early modern. (61)

This moment of frank discussion of the material conditions of scholarly enterprise, and the desire to preserve the "turf" that seems to support it, is significant. The extent of Marcus's capacity for professional self-criticism is refreshing, and subversive of the project of the book, although earlier in the essay she diligently provided an overview of "Renaissance/

early modern [literary] studies" similar to the other "period" chapters in the volume. This emergence of material interests in her essay nevertheless makes the vague unquestioned celebration of "literary" study elsewhere in the text suspect. "Continual refashioning," Greenblatt and Gunn tell us, "is at the center of the profession of literary study: it is both a characteristic of the texts we study and a crucial means to keep our critical practice from exhaustion and sterility" (5). We must entertain the possibility in the face of such a claim that an area of intellectual inquiry which can produce no better reason for "refashioning" than its reproduction (therefore, anything will do), may already be exhausted. Why "literary study" should be engaged at all is the crucial question left unanswered by this volume. I myself think it is important enough to deserve an answer.

My point here, however, is not only to call for a critical perspective toward "literature" as an institution, but also to argue that cultural studies has often problematically critiqued the "ancient stocks" without taking account of the fact that it, too, often lives off the income of the same land. Inhabiting the traditional departments—and the universities—will necessarily be contradictory for left cultural studies at the current conjuncture. How one inhabits such a space, however, is—at least a little—negotiable. In *Discipline and Punish*, Foucault argues that "in the first instance, discipline proceeds from the distribution of individuals in space" (141). Following him in this case, I would argue, as *Redrawing the Boundaries* indicates, disciplines proceed from the distribution of their practitioners in conceptual-metaphorical space—by establishing limits to thought, discourse, and practice. Already subject to misrecognition of itself as isolated from a larger public by the segregation of the university from quotidian politics in the interest of providing a space of ostensibly disinterested knowledge production (an "isolation" imposed on humanities faculties, rather than their colleagues in the sciences with less-conflicted usefulness to corporations and the military), academics who currently inhabit English departments are further enjoined by *Redrawing the Boundaries* to keep their minds contained within a narrowly defined category of the "literary." This containment helps make possible the continued effacement of the ways in which the university is always already in the world and thus interests can dissimulate themselves as "disinterest."

Discovering a pedagogical commitment in business publications for "cultural studies" (of all things!) forced me to question the possibility of such disinterest and ask: What work does (a by no mean homogeneous) cultural studies perform? in what sites? why? Setting out to address these questions, I invoked Benjamin at the beginning of this essay because I want to assert an affinity in my project; when he saw discourses of "art" manipulated by Nazi propagandists, he responded by attempting to produce a theory of art which he hoped would be "useless for the purposes of Fascism" (218). In a related oppositional gesture, I want to claim a specificity for a cultural studies whose primary task is to resist the reproduction of capitalist relations even though it must continue—necessarily—to operate within capital's pores at the current conjuncture. My hope is that by asserting a critical difference, left cultural studies might evade becoming—in, say, 50 years—a mere slip of the tongue of corporate cultural studies, a repressed set of discourses and practices which, its frames of reference effaced, will not even be recognized.

Of course it is possible that (as one of my critics has noted) if left cultural studies did disappear "most people would say 'so what?'" I refer such cynics to the quotation from Benjamin with which I began this essay. "Fifty years ago, a slip of the tongue passed more or less unnoticed" reminds us that frames of reference and conceptual categories *matter*; they police the boundaries between the thinkable and the unthinkable, what will be "noticed" and what will not. In a world in which capitalism continues to ensure that the gaps between the material conditions of existence of the wealthiest and the poorest populations remain so wide—and continue to widen—the transnational corporate study of culture can hardly be considered a matter of little consequence. Its "ways of seeing" have effects that bear on us all, though not all alike. It seems imperative, then, to direct attention to corporate appropriation and representation of "culture" as part of left cultural studies. To do so, cultural studies cannot see itself as *a* "position" but must, rather, engage in a "war of position" in Gramsci's sense—a many-fronted and continuous mode of resistance to capital's hegemony—in which "corporate cultural studies" is playing a supporting role. It has been the burden of this essay to suggest that this resistance is impeded while we are contained within traditional disciplinary structures which divert our attention from the ways in which "cultural studies" is already very much "in the world." Thus it is not so much a question of taking cultural studies into the streets, but learning to use, and providing alternatives to, the forms of cultural studies that are already there. We should also keep in mind, however—to *detourne* a line from an ad in *Business Week* I discussed above—that the "language will not always be English," and thus we have listening to do as well.[24]

Notes

*An earlier version of this essay appeared in *minnesota review* 45–46; I have revised some parts of it for clarity and intensification. The basic argument remains the same. I am grateful to the several scholars—especially Dick Ohmann—who wrote to comment on the piece after it came out in *mr.* I would also like to thank the participants in the Summer Institute on Culture and Society, June 1993, and the Cultural Studies Colloquium, May 1994, both at Carnegie Mellon, for their many helpful comments on earlier versions of this paper. I am especially grateful to Keya Ganguly, Eric Clark, Michael West, Lisa Frank, Paula Geyh, Mike Hill, and Michael Bérubé who read more recent drafts and helped me work over trouble spots. Finally: if Jeff Williams had not suggested I take a look at *Redrawing the Boundaries* this paper would never have been written. I am grateful for his suggestion, among many other things.

1. Stuart Hall, following Wallerstein, puts it this way: "Tension between the tendency of capitalism to develop the nation-state and national cultures and its transnational imperatives is a contradiction at the heart of modernity" ("Culture" 353). He points out that "the present intensified phase of globalization has favoured the tendencies pushing nation-states towards supra-national integration" and "a slow, if uneven, erosion of the 'centred' nationalisms of the Western-European nation-state . . . opening up local and regional economies both to new dislocations and to new relationships" (354).

2. "The mysterious character of the commodity-form consists therefore simply in the fact that the commodity reflects men's own labour as objective characteristics of the products of labour themselves, as the socio-natural properties of these things" (Marx 165).

3. One business journalist puts it this way: "By evaluating the values a person brings with a cultural background, multiculturalists are able to understand the barriers that exist between people. Then they use . . . research to develop methods to reduce them. . . . [Claude] Schnier, who has a background in cultural anthropology, has worked in Spain for several years to help multinational companies overcome cultural differences. . . . Since returning to the United States, [he] has worked as a consultant to Bay Area companies to improve communications within multicultural work forces. . . . Companies with large international operations have long recognized the importance of orientation for workers going overseas, and many have expanded that training into broad multicultural training programs" (Carlsen A4).

4. The work of Evan Watkins and a few other cultural critics being exceptions. See *Social Text* 44 (1995) for several essays on this topic.

5. Some of the adjustments in management style that accompany the changes in workforce and production practices have been discussed by Clarke and Newman. They write: "the stress on managing culture combines the emphasis on enterprising selves with a recognition that changing organizational

forms (towards greater devolution, decentralization and divisionalization) make traditional modes of corporate strategic management even less likely to succeed than before" (430). I am grateful to Larry Grossberg for bringing this article—one of the few to deal with business "culture" directly in cultural studies journals—to my attention. As Clarke and Newman themselves note: "The missing component in cultural studies is the disappearance of economic relations and work cultures as objects of enquiry, such that cultural studies has become increasingly focused on the texts and practices of 'free time' with the realm of the economy appearing only as a backdrop to the real action. The absence would be significant in its own right, but it is juxtaposed with the discovery of culture in managerial discourses as a domain of working life which needs to be actively managed" (427).

6. This "education" involves not only the staff of corporations, but their potential customers, including the school-aged population: "Recognizing the importance of capturing consumers early, many companies are starting with the very young. . . . Among the first reaching out for children are A&P stores (with little shopping carts), Delta Airlines (Fantastic Flyers Club), Hyatt Hotels (Camp Hyatt and accompanying newsletters), Sears' Discover credit card (the Extra Credit personal finance education program in Scholastic magazines), and Apple Computer (school computer donations and discounts)" (Davidow and Malone 230).

7. In her contribution to *Redrawing the Boundaries*, Deborah Esch notes that it was "commissioned by the Modern Language Association's Committee on Research and Publication to outline the transformation in literary studies in English over the past quarter century" (384).

8. It should be noted that Greenblatt and Gunn are rather fuzzy and contradictory on the "nationality" issue. When they cite Sahlins on the frontier, they note that while for him the "belief" in frontiers gives rise to an "imagined national space, bounded and unified," literary frontiers are not necessarily either "unified" nor "national" (6). One wonders then why they go to such trouble to distinguish the "literary studies" in their volume as specifically "English and American." One also wonders, of course, about the use of the term "American" at all in a book restricted to a discussion of literature in English. At least one of the contributors, Cecilia Tichi, observes that the deployment of "American" in this way is problematic, although without, apparently, thinking it necessary (or convincing the editors) to revise the title or text of *Redrawing* to address the problem: "'American' in those years [pre-1960s] seemed synonymous with "United States," and teachers and students were in the main untroubled by conceptual problems implied in a body of literature representing a developing nation-state but claiming the whole of two continents as its purview. . . . [However, to] a post-1960s generation of scholars and editors . . . the term American began to seem hegemonic and inaccurately univocal" (209). Of course in spite of Tichi's suggestion that the 1960s somehow brought on the first glimmer that there were problems in the use of "American" in the manner she

describes, there were inhabitants of North and South America who were already "troubled" by the "conceptual" and "other" problems that only later occurred to a critical mass of academic intellectuals.

9. "MLA Survey Casts Light on Canon Debate" indicates that there has been relatively little change in the works covered in university classroom, or how they are read; a more recent report argues that "the MLA survey actually exaggerates the extent to which new literary texts and approaches are being used" because assistant professors were overrepresented in the sample. See Wilson.

10. Stanley Fish also attempts to keep "literary study" and "politics" distinct in *Professional Correctness*, another recent book that describes an English Department structurally and irreducibly hostile to the practice of left cultural studies.

11. In order to stave off the impression that literary studies is a static field, Greenblatt and Gunn take pains to distinguish between "limits" and "frontiers." A limit, they claim, is a "fixed line" while the frontier is a site of activity, the place of "bellicose expansion and zonal defense" (6). As they clarify in an endnote: "frontier . . . is not something in the ground, as it were; it is the line of advance against an adversary." When "frontier" turns up later in the collection, it is Frederick Jackson Turner's "myth" of the frontier in the chapter on post–Civil War "American Literary and Cultural Studies" (233–4). Critiques of "manifest destiny" enter neither the chapter on American Literature, in which Turner is cited, nor the editor's introduction. The "adversary" of literary studies also remains unnamed.

12. As Ellen Wood has put it: "new modes of organization [in capitalist firms] are conceived not as new forms of democracy, making the organization more accountable to its workers, or to the community at large, but on the contrary, as means of making the workers more responsive to the economic needs of the organization" (291). For a somewhat more positive perspective, see Evan Watkins' essay in this volume.

13. William Bennett's *To Reclaim a Legacy* set the tone for what has now been a decade of concerted attacks in popular publications from the *New York Times* to the *Atlantic*.

14. For example, an advertising supplement to the *New York Times* featured "The Diversity Challenge" (23 Oct. 1994). Corporations, universities, hospitals and other organizations declared their interest in "tapping the talents of tomorrow's work force." R. R. Donnelley Financial announces that "Knowledge is Power. Diversity is Strength." Kidder, Peabody tells us that their "ability to compete and succeed in [a global] marketplace will be based solely on the talents and abilities of a diverse workforce." Similar claims fill the rest of the 32 pages of the supplement. Because capital is predicated on preserving inequalities (e.g., between owners and nonowners of capital), we must wonder if such corporate declarations of investment in "diversity" describe a situation recently discussed by Étienne Balibar, in which "neo-racism" asserts itself in the very discourses

and practices that ostensibly provide the remedies for past racisms: "It is a racism whose dominant theme is not biological heredity but the insurmountability of cultural differences, a racism which, at first sight, does not postulate the superiority of certain groups or peoples in relation to others but 'only' the harmfulness of abolishing frontiers, the incompatibility of life-styles and traditions" (21).

15. However, we must keep in mind that the concept of hegemony is not universally applicable, and that in certain local situations, domination is the more useful concept. See Guha.

16. For a discussion of the trend toward regionalization from a (celebratory) business perspective, see Ohmae.

17. As even liberal bourgeois commentators, such as Robert Reich, emphasize.

18. The New Left and the solving of specific problems in Marxism (unmentioned in Robbins and Graff's account) were far more significant for the development of Cultural Studies in Britain than problems in literary criticism. See, for example, Michael Kenny's *The First New Left* and Graeme Turner's *British Cultural Studies*. Also, Stuart Hall's account of CCCS's uneasy relationship to literature study—and to the English Department at Birmingham—suggests that British Cultural Studies, especially in its formative moment, found it impossible to negotiate the tensions with literary studies as a disciplinary formation (see "Cultural Studies and the Centre").

19. There are, of course, other possible reasons for the neglect of corporate cultural studies: a political agenda that focuses on subaltern groups; lack of interest in, or at least familiarity with, business periodicals; an emphasis on the rhythms of "everyday life" outside the workplace, and so on. In any case, such an important omission from cultural studies is "overdetermined." My point, here, however, is that if we are often caught up in traditional "disciplinary" concerns that these will certainly *not* lead us to (or reward us for) the consideration of corporate cultural studies, which I think that it is crucial for us to undertake.

20. In a 1980 book, Bertram Gross described contemporary state-corporation alliances as forms of "friendly fascism" characterized by "manipulative use and control of democratic machinery, parties and human rights" rather than "open subversion" of democratic values (170). Gross calls attention here to a global system in which the "colossal transnational corporations and complexes that help knit together a 'Free World' . . . are elements of the new despotism" which is, if anything, more in need of exposure and resistance today than when he wrote his book.

21. For example, at Carnegie Mellon, where I used to teach, the Cultural Studies group periodically received requests from the University administration to "make our courses more recognizable" [i.e., "traditional"]. In *Against Literature*, John Beverley describes a similar situation at the University of Pittsburgh: "The conversion of cultural studies from a form of radical opposition

to the avant-garde of bourgeois hegemony will be driven by three major concerns: (1) making cultural studies acceptable to faculty, administrators and trustees rather than to students . . . ; (2) diluting its potential to become a form of ideological-epistemological agency of the social groups and movements outside the university whose subalternity it is precisely concerned with theorizing; (3) keeping cultural studies separate from the natural sciences and the sphere of technology and the professional schools. . . . The code words of this project will be 'pluralism' and 'interdisciplinarity,' but the end effect will be depoliticization. (This is in fact more or less what, after seven years of operation, has happened to the graduate program in cultural studies . . . at the University of Pittsburgh.)" (21).

22. Although Greenblatt and Gunn claim that they asked their contributors to consider "How are significant changes in literary study generated? Where and how have these changes met resistance either within the institutions of literary study in America or in wider society? Which alterations have produced (and continue to produce) the most resistance and conflict?" these questions become ultimately a matter of "literary professionalism," which limits them (9). The chapters on the literary periods rarely take up these questions, or do so mostly to discuss past politics or context. On the other hand, the "criticism" chapters, which often do consider wider social processes, sometimes fail to discuss literature at all, or only incidentally (Esch, Sedgwick). Anne Middleton draws a connection between the rise of the New Criticism and the birth of Medieval Studies in U.S. universities to "the coming of age of the United States as a world power and as a producer of world-historical signification" (21), but neither develops this observation at any length, nor makes claims of this kind in her discussion of more recent developments in Medieval Studies. William Kerrigan's account of seventeenth-century studies is entirely academically insular, a decontextualized itinerary of ideas which travel from one scholar to another without any apparent structuring influence beyond the books themselves. Marjorie Perloff manages to discuss "modernism" with barely a glance at problems of "modernity." These essays, and others like them, fit very tidily into the boundaries drawn by Greenblatt and Gunn. Even the more subersive essays in "criticism" are contained by the framing of the editors, which narrows political projects into "criticism" and produces a national, academic and literary space into which they are easily (although, of course, not necessarily) recuperated, however far they may attempt to stray.

23. Compare, for example, this description of how contemporary businessmen operate to Greenblatt and Gunn's preferred metaphors: "Today, your international businessmen are really the equivalents of conquering armies of several hundred years ago. . . . When you talk about flying around the world and doing business in different time zones, it requires people who are extremely fit, smart, skillful and extremely motivated. They are fighting competitors and conceiving strategies to win market share. These entrepreneurs are the modern economic equivalents of what we used to do with mercenary armies in the

middle ages. In our modern-day society, we need to have a greater realization of the importance of these types of people and help in their development" (Millard and Buss 57).

24. On "detournement," see Sadie Plant: "The closest English translation of *detournement* lies somewhere between 'diversion' and 'subversion.' It is a turning around and a reclamation of lost meaning: a way of putting the stasis of the spectacle in motion. It is plagiaristic, because its materials are those which already appear within the spectacle, subversive, since its tactics are those of the 'reversal of perspective,' a challenge to meaning aimed at the context in which it arises" (86).

Works Cited

Althusser, Louis. *Lenin and Philosophy and Other Essays*. Trans. Ben Brewster. New York and London: Monthly Review, 1971.

Ang, Ien. "Dismantling 'cultural studies'?" *Cultural Studies* 6.3 (1992).

Appadurai, Arjun. *Modernity at Large: Cultural Dimensions of Globalization*. Minneapolis: U of Minnesota P, 1996.

Balibar, Étienne. *Race, Nation, Class*. Trans. Chris Turner. New York: Verso, 1991.

Balsamo, Anne. "Feminism and Cultural Studies." *Journal of the Midwest Modern Language Association* 24.1 (1991): 50–73.

Barthes, Roland. *Mythologies*. Trans. Annette Lavers. New York: Hill and Wang, 1975.

Benjamin, Walter. *Illuminations*. Trans. Harry Zohn. Ed. Hannah Arendt. New York: Schocken, 1969.

Bennett, Tony. "Useful Culture." *Cultural Studies* 6.3 (1992): 395–407.

Bennett, William. *To Reclaim a Legacy*. Washington: NEH, 1984.

Bérubé, Michael. "Bite Size Theory: Popularizing Academic Criticism." *Social Text* 36 (1993): 84–97.

Beverley, John. *Against Literature*. Minneapolis: U of Minnesota P, 1993.

Cantlon, John E., and Herman E. Koenig. "Global Economic Competitiveness and the Land-Grant University." *University Spin-off Companies: Eco-*

nomic Development, Faculty Entrepreneurs, and Technology Transfer. Ed. Alister M. Brett, David V. Gibson, and Raymond W. Smilor. Savage: Rowman and Littlefield, 1991.

Carlsen, Clifford. "New Business Forms to Bridge Cultural Chasms." *San Francisco Business Times* 10 Apr. 1992: A4.

Clarke, John, and Janet Newman. "The Right to Manage: A Second Managerial Revolution." *Cultural Studies* 7.3 (1993): 427–41.

Davidow, William H., and Michael Malone. *The Virtual Corporation*. New York: HarperCollins, 1992.

Farid, Elashmawi, and Philip R. Harris. *Multicultural Management: New Skills for Global Success*. Houston: Gulf Publishing, 1993.

Feldman, Jonathan. *Universities in the Business of Repression*. Boston: South End, 1989.

Fish, Stanley. *Professional Correctness*. Oxford: Clarendon P, 1995.

Forsberg, Marcia. "Cultural Training Improves Relations with Asian Clients." *Personnel Journal* 72.5 (1993): 79–89.

Foucault, Michel. *Discipline and Punish: The Birth of the Prison*. Trans. Alan Sheridan. New York: Vintage, 1979.

Gilroy, Paul. *The Black Atlantic: Modernity and Double Consciousness*. Cambridge, MA: Harvard UP, 1993.

Graff, Gerald. *Professing Literature: An Institutional History*. Chicago: U of Chicago P, 1987.

Gramsci, Antonio. *Selections from the Prison Notebooks*. Trans. and ed. Quintin Hoare and Geoffrey Nowell Smith. New York: International Publishers, 1971.

Greenblatt, Stephen, and Giles Gunn, eds. *Redrawing the Boundaries*. New York: Modern Language Association, 1992.

Gross, Bertram. *Friendly Fascism*. New York: M. Evans, 1980.

Grossberg, Lawrence, Cary Nelson, and Paula Treichler, eds. *Cultural Studies*. New York: Routledge, 1992.

Guha, Ranajit. "Dominance without Hegemony and Its Historiography." *Subaltern Studies* (1989): 210–309.

Hall, Stuart. "Cultural Studies and Its Theoretical Legacies." Grossberg et al. 277–86.

———. "Cultural Studies and the Centre: Some Problematics and Problems." *Culture, Media, Language: Working Papers in Cultural Studies*. Ed. Stuart Hall, et al. London: Hutchinson, 1980. 15–48.

———. "Cultural Studies and the Politics of Internationalization." *Stuart Hall: Critical Dialogues in Cultural Studies*. Ed. David Morley and Kuan Hsing Chen. London: Routledge, 1996. 392–408.

———. "Culture, Community, Nation." *Cultural Studies* 7.3 (1993): 349–63.

Harris, Philip R., and Robert T. Morgan. *Managing Cultural Differences*. 3rd ed. Houston: Gulf Publishing, 1991.

Human Development Report. United Nations Development Program. New York: Oxford UP, 1995.

James, C. L. R. *Spheres of Existence*. Westport: Lawrence Hill, 1980.

Jameson, Fredric. "On Cultural Studies." *Social Text* 34 (1993): 17–52.

Johnson, Richard. "What Is Cultural Studies Anyway?" *Social Text* 6 (1986/87): 38–90.

Kenny, Michael. *The First New Left: British Intellectuals after Stalin*. London: Lawrence and Wishart, 1995.

Maddox, Robert C. *Cross-Cultural Problems in International Business: The Role of the Cultural Integration Function*. Westport: Quorum, 1993.

Marx, Karl. *Capital I*. Trans. Ben Fowkes. London: Penguin, 1990.

Millard, Pete, and Dale Buss. "Patience and Passion: The Most Challenging International-Trade Obstacles Are Developing Global Entrepreneurs and a Willingness to Follow New Rules of Engagement." *Corporate Report Wisconsin* May 1993, sec. 1: 57.

"MLA Survey Casts Light on Canon Debate." *MLA Newsletter* Winter 1991: 12–14.

Morgan, Malcolm J. "How Corporate Structure Drives Strategy." *International Journal of Strategic Management* 26.2 (1993).

Moylan, Tom. "Response to Money, Space and Culture Symposium." *Mediations* 17. 2 (1993): 35–40.

Ohmae, Kinichi. "Putting Global Logic First." *Harvard Business Review* 73.1 (1995): 119–25.

Plant, Sadie. *The Most Radical Gesture: The Situationist International in a Postmodern Age*. New York: Routledge, 1992.

Reich, Robert. *The Work of Nations*. New York: Vintage, 1992.

Said, Edward. *Culture and Imperialism*. New York: Knopf, 1993.

Sahlins, Peter. "Natural Frontiers Revisited: France's Boundaries since the Seventeenth Century." *American Historical Review* 95 (1990): 1423–51.

Sklair, Leslie. *Sociology and the Global System*. Baltimore: Johns Hopkins UP, 1991.

Soley, Lawrence. *Leasing the Ivory Tower*. Boston: South End, 1995.

Spenser, Edmund. *View of the Present State of Ireland*. Oxford: Clarendon P, 1970.

Spivak, Gayatri Chakravorty. "Can the Subaltern Speak?" *Marxism and the Interpretation of Culture*. Ed. Cary Nelson and Lawrence Grossberg. Urbana: U of Illinois P, 1988. 271-313.

———. "Reading the World." *In Other Worlds: Essays in Cultural Politics*. New York: Methuen, 1987. 95–102.

Turner, Graeme. *British Cultural Studies*. London: Routledge, 1992.

Watkins, Evan. *Work Time: English Departments and the Circulation of Cultural Value*. Stanford: Stanford UP, 1989.

Williams, Raymond. *The Country and the City*. New York: Oxford UP, 1973.

Wilson, John K. "The MLA's 'Deceptive' Survey." *Democratic Culture* 2.2 (1993): 15–17.

Wood, Ellen. *Democracy Against Capitalism*. Cambridge: Cambridge UP, 1995.

Part III

Professional Channels

Chapter Eight

Dancing in the Dark: A Manifesto against Professional Organizations

Lennard J. Davis

It is a sign of the times that the stolid sets of institutions of English have stood fast against the whirlwinds of left politics and postmodern theory. These institutions seem impervious to change despite the fact that much of contemporary criticism has a radical agenda as its goal. Indeed, proponents of leftist critique, deconstructive analysis, feminist interpretation, and the other thousand discourses came of age during and since the sixties when mistrust of institutions was a *cri du coeur*. It has been argued, and probably rightly so, that the tenured and untenured radicals, who only recently seemed about to bring down the house of Western wisdom, sharpened their home-wrecking tools on the anti-institutional student revolutions of the sixties. Despite the radical agenda of many current thinkers, the institutions of professional scholarship groan on with a superannuated immortality, as if no one had ever said the words "ideology," "aporia," or "hegemony." This institutional resistance to change whispers that theory may only be a shimmer moving over the surface, a sea change, which of course only changes the appearance of the sea not the fact of it. As we have learned from Marx, Foucault, Bourdieu, Habermas, and others, institutions endure because they function to guard powerful interests.

Professional organizations are rooms in the institution full of old echoes; they bespeak the verities of bourgeois systems of thought and assumptions about knowledge and life that radicals might seek to discredit. In academia and in the field of cultural studies, we have come to accept this radical critique of institutions as self-evident, but we have not turned the critique on ourselves to any profound degree. While we talk about self-policing, the gaze, state and ideological cultural apparatuses, and the panopticon, we continue to attend megacorporate gatherings like the annual Modern Language Association convention, belong to periodicized professional organizations, read their journals, and engage in activities of the profession. In short, we participate willingly in self-policing, the gaze, and the panopticon, but because the institutions are our own, we see them as part of the background of life in academia. What has brought us to this sorry state of intellectual hypocrisy in our reliance on professional organizations?

I ask this question since the obvious thing about professional organizations in general is how well they dovetail with institutional agendas. By and large, professional organizations are traditional, conservative, and controlled by those professors who are more advanced in their careers and therefore more professionalized. In a world of little capital, professional organizations normalize the unequal distribution of intellectual capital. Bourdieu notes,

> Paradoxically, it is precisely because there exist relatively autonomous fields, functioning in accordance with rigorous mechanisms capable of imposing their necessity on the agents, that those who are in a position to command these mechanisms and to appropriate the material and/or symbolic profits accruing from their functioning are able to *dispense with* strategies aimed *expressly* . . . and directly . . . at the domination of individuals, a domination which in this case is the condition of the appropriation of the material and symbolic profits of their labour. (184)

Rather than resorting to a crude toolbox of controls, the profession has developed subtler mechanisms of enforced compliance that do not appear to involve domination. Academia is a "relatively autonomous field" with "rigorous mechanisms" that impose "necessity" on agents. Rites of passage like master's exams, orals, field exams, dissertations, and defenses systematically harass graduate students to expect, and even demand, this normalizing, self-regulating process. The graduate student, so primed to direct his or her politicized gaze outside of the academic setting—decrying classism, imperialism, colonialism, sexism, logo- and phallogocentricism—is never given even the vaguest permission to criticize the totally dominating system that controls his or her personal destiny in graduate school. Here submission to authority—the type of false collegiality sometimes thought necessary to obtain needed recommendations and patronage—is learned and practiced with a subaltern's strategic cunning. When graduate students are then processed, largely through the combined good offices of the Modern Language Association and the Sheraton or Hilton corporations, and then through the bureaucracy of college and university departments and administrations, they are ready to face the totalizing environment of domination and observation involved in the process of contract renewal, tenure, and promotion.[1]

But I have only described the lot of the lucky few. Many others will be even more systematically observed and controlled in precarious one-year and adjunct positions where the slightest deviation from collegial behavior and intellectual or personal propriety will result in ejection into the "free market." And the academic market is particularly unfree since the renewal/tenure system negatively marks anyone who fails to be renewed or is denied tenure. In the business world changing positions, budget cuts, or termination of contract are norms rather than marks of dismissal, as they are in the academic world, where the expectation is of continuous, untroubled unfurling of career from the cradle of graduate school till the grave of endowed chair. Could a more effective process to control, disempower, marginalize, and subject beings without the use of overt violence or force have been created with deliberate forethought?[2]

It is to the credit of many in the profession that they have not only survived such a process but remained politically committed as well as devoted to teaching and learning. And let us recall that the dismal picture of social engineering that I have drawn has on occasion been lightened by the warm touch of individual compassion, benevolent departments, and even some sense of solidarity. While not everyone experiences total humiliation and domination, most have felt some rough abrasion of the milling process in the formation of the procrustean subject position I have described.

While it may seem strange to see a conference like the annual Modern Language Association convention as part of a hegemonic process that dominates the individual rather than a kind of confraternity that encourages collegiality and cordiality, we must recall the functions of such professional organizations. These institutions are first and foremost compulsory bureaucracies. Few who join do so in an act of free will. And this compulsion begins early with that most exquisite moment of domination—the job interview. Not only are candidates for academic positions required to subject themselves to a kind of gaze of power (which is made all the more explicit by its taking place in a hotel room—with popular associations of assignations and prostitution), but they must pay a hefty fee for the privilege of wearing an identifying badge. Without this badge they are without official identity; neither can they enter certain restricted locations, such as the book exhibits or even panel presentations. The overt policing of the organization by hired security guards (only begun within the past 10 years) simply makes more explicit the regulatory nature of this organization.[3]

The banning of the public is also worth considering. With the advent of security guards, members of "the public" are prohibited from attending most of the sessions of Modern Language Association. That no hue and cry has been raised by the public-at-large in the face of this overt act of censorship only confirms the fact that the goings-on at this convention are not intended to be anything other than self-regulating mechanisms of an internal economy. Ironically, the only events open to the public at the 1995 convention in San Diego were screenings of films or readings by "authors" rather than talks by scholars. The assumption is that anything that goes on in the convention of a professional nature would not interest the public. If that is the case, why ban public access? Perhaps the reason is that there really is nothing public about a board meeting, a religious convocation, or a tenure review committee—or a professional organization.

For those who have tenure, the strategic set of rewards and punishments associated with attending professional conferences is perhaps less obvious but no less effective. Speaking at the convention is a visible sign of one's intellectual capital. Keynote or invited speakers are assigned a special position in the profession, and they can command more money, power, and prestige in their own institutions as well as negotiate for more lucrative positions. Speaking at all in the conference guarantees that the member is still "active" in the profession and reassures his or her department and employer that he or she is worthy of promotion, tenure, and increases in salary. Being chosen as a member of a particular division or committee also serves a self-regulating function of elevating those who have "fame" to an inner circle of selection.[4]

As such, professional organizations have served a normalizing role in the dispersal and distribution of information, the creation of hierarchies within disciplines, the maintenance of formal and informal networks, and the lubrication of gate-keeping functions in the peer-review processes—whether in reviewing articles for journals, assessing grant applications, acting as a reader for university presses, vetting tenure reviews, promotions, and so on. This gate-keeping function is not to be underestimated since promotions and tenure depend heavily on evaluations, recommendations, and assessments by those already credentialed.

Professional organizations also promote "star" academics. The notion of a "star" academic whose work is a must-read corresponds nicely with the "star" system and must-see movies developed in Hollywood, a system now seen as an essential part of the commodification of film. Stars—not directors—sell movies; likewise, "name" scholars sell books, advance a university's prestige, and determine a profession's direction. When professional organizations showcase stars, they are participating in the commodification of knowledge that is part of a corporate, capitalist agenda. As with the circulation of women pinpointed by Gayle Rubin, and the relations of desire created through women between men noted by Eve Sedgwick, the circulation of star academics through professional conferences creates value and meaning in an virtual economy.

The paucity of interdisciplinarity, often bemoaned by professional organizations who then try artificially to enforce interdisciplinarity, is not accidental. Likewise, the organization of associations around particular centuries or areas is no aberration. As Gerald Graff has pointed out, the division of departments into dynastic pigeonholes serves to limit debate and discussion about methods and—really—political issues (28–30). If a Miltonist can never really talk to a modernist, then neither will have to defend the rationale for either of their assumptions. There need be no discussion between leftists and liberals, feminists and chauvinists, or historians and literary critics because the business of departments is rigorously bureaucratized. Professional organizations neatly mirror these divisions and incorporate them into larger umbrella groups like the Modern Language Association.

Even the format of professional conferences—the unyielding three papers, one moderator, no time for discussion, or the plenary speaker elevated to "star" status and then respectfully questioned from afar, contributes to a colonization of the recipients of knowledge, the conference-goers (primarily graduate students, junior faculty, and those from less elite positions). This standardized format disperses antagonism and opposition through ritualized, self-policed, legitimized encounters. When was the last time one witnessed a genuine debate or extended clash of opinions or political outlooks in these orchestrated forms of information management? Or, in another ritualized encounter, observe the ritual of badge-checking, the furtive glance to the lapel, serving to self-enforce hierarchies of rank and class, signifying status by prestigious location (and not indicating, for example, areas of knowledge or interest—which would facilitate conversation and informal encounters).

What I am pointing to, if quickly, are some of the systems of overt and covert social control, the microtendrils of power that create and justify professional organizations. More bluntly, the spirit of reform of the sixties and the insights of cultural critique, postmodernism, feminism, and genealogical and discursive criticism have all failed to penetrate to the level of practice in professional organizations. While some teachers have worked at translating their theory to praxis in the classroom and in reforming the curriculum, few have done so in this institutional venue.

The problem arises in the way one rationalizes the function of a professional organization. One has to ask, why do we bodies[5] gather together in strange cities in megahotels? Face-to-face interaction seems to be part of a sense of community that cyberspace has not yet succeeded in creating. Perhaps the immanence of touch, of the possibility of moving from one place to another, of eating together, of real-time spontaneous repartee, of interaction on a number of intellectual and physical planes, of a nonlinear form of language interaction draws us together in groups. Our human sense of coming together in meeting—from family gatherings, collective worship, political demonstration, or colloquy, the Greeks assembling by the glow of rosy-fingered dawn, the Jewish imperative to gather ten worshipers—has been travestied by these faux gatherings of the tribes announced by mail and completed by payment of check. What intellectual, social, political functions can be accomplished in such gatherings?

Most professional organizations fall into two types: either societies or bureaucracies. Societies model themselves after exclusive clubs. They imagine themselves as emulating other self-selected gatherings like salons or literary clubs, and they usually devote themselves to the admiration of a single author or type of writing. Societies emulate an upper-class model of behavior or fantasies of upper-class behavior—encouraging the refined adulation of a particular author or a particular fantasy of the style of a historical period. Sometimes they may simply be more tendentious versions of fan clubs replacing Madonna with Dr. Johnson. However, societies can easily become bureaucracies as their numbers increase and their exclusivity diminishes.

Bureaucracies are formations whose aim is to maximize order, create continuity, and above all to create a structure that guarantees the smooth running of some activity by limiting disruption and transgressive behavior. The bureaucrat typically places smooth functioning of operations above any other priority. This aim is achieved by creating a hierarchy that at its center is controlled by a self-selected elite. Elections can be held, but the candidates are carefully filtered through nomination committees or some such other process. Change, in any real sense, cannot be accomplished, although relatively minor alterations can take place by means of a carefully controlled process that ensures fellow players' interests are not put into danger.

One enters a bureaucracy as a single, isolate unit. One can proceed and succeed in a bureaucracy only by operating according to the rules of the system. In this sense, a bureaucracy provides a place of belonging—but only to interchangeable units. Another way of putting this is that a bureaucracy is like a home, but only for those who have lost, through the exigencies of alienation and reification, the possibility of home. A bureaucracy solves the problems of where to belong and how to function without addressing the problem of being a subject. It is a haven in an heartless world, but only to heartless and alienated subjects.

To Marx, "life (i.e. production and consumption) begins where its [the bureaucracy's] power ends" (Bottomore 57). As Marx specifies, "the bureaucracy is the imaginary state alongside the real state" (qtd. in Bottomore 57). The bureaucracy considers the state as its private property. In this sense, the bureaucracy convinces us that it is the system, that it owns the system, but in fact it constitutes an imaginary of the system. The bureaucracy of the professional organization, in effect, attempts to displace other possible locations of knowledge, colloquy, intellectual life. In a bureaucracy, knowledge as such becomes commodified, controlled, and profoundly cut off from a dialectic of theory and praxis—in effect depoliticized. Politics appears as treason against the bureaucracy. It is perhaps not inappropriate to realize how much of our sense of knowledge, of the right way to do scholarship, about how the profession is macro- and micromanaged is profoundly imbricated with the bureaucracy and the bureaucratic process—from the giving of papers, the publication of articles, the business of departments, promotion, tenure, hiring, and so on. In fact, the idea of a life-tenure is, as Max Weber notes, one of the prime characteristics that distinguishes the bureaucrat from the employee (202).

Georg Lukács continues this discussion by placing the bureaucracy in the center of a capitalist transformation of the state: "Bureaucracy implies the adjustment of one's way of life, mode of work and hence of consciousness, to the general socio-economic premises of the capitalist economy" (98). In this way of knowing, knowledge becomes rigidified, and methods for presenting such knowledge shape that rigidity. As Lukács notes, "all issues are subjected to an increasingly *formal* and standardized treatment and in which there is an ever-increasing remoteness from the qualitative and material essence of the 'things' to which bureaucratic activity pertains" (99). Linked to this is what Lukács calls "an even more monstrous intensification of the one-sided specialization which represents such a violation of man's humanity" (99). From this perspective, the quality of our lives as intellectuals, once molded in the crucible of the professional organizations, among other institutions, begins to resemble the kind of alienated labor described as the problem of the working classes. While I am not equating academic life with life in the iron mills, I do think it serves no benefit to pretend that intellectual life is somehow exempt from larger trends.

As opposed to the bureaucratic or a societal form of a professional organization, one might consider the idea of a cooperative. A cooperative association (or "associated mode of production") was seen by Marx as an ameliorative but incomplete solution to the problem of capitalism. As Marx wrote, "these [cooperative] factories represent within the old form the first sprouts of the new, although they naturally reproduce, and must reproduce, everywhere in their actual organization all the shortcomings of the prevailing system" (III, 521). Marx saw the cooperative mode as one that would negate wage labor, but felt that the danger of cooperatives were that they would remain local, particular, and not address larger issues of production.[6]

For the purposes of this essay, I want to propose this model of a cooperative over that of current bureaucratic institutions. Cooperative links the idea of community to work. Obviously, no organization can actually be a community, but it is possible to resist being a bureaucracy. As a cooperative is only a partial solution to a larger problem, nevertheless it represents the way "a new mode of production naturally grows out of an old." Can a professional organization offer this alternative, and can we think of a transformational kind of politics within that ideological sphere?

An essential step in transforming professional organizations into cooperatives is to define in advance the commonality of experience, purpose, and work. The problem with professional organizations for the most part is that they take no activist position, they articulate no politics, they merely assume that there is a field of study (or adulation).[7] Umbrella organizations like the Modern Language Association simply require the participants to be in "literature." They never achieve communitarian cooperation because there is no common political agenda, no sense of solidarity, no political reason to be together, and no defined sense of work. When 1 or 2 or 10 thousand gather in the name of literature, they are coming together under a concept too broad, ambiguous, and uncentered to provide for a collective creation of agency. While in the past some political stances were taken on a piecemeal basis—the Modern Language Association came out officially against the war in Vietnam, refused to hold its conference in a state with sodomy laws or one that did not observe Martin Luther King, Jr. Day, it apparently will no longer take such positions. A recent *MLA Newsletter* (Fall 1994) contains a letter from Barbara Foley protesting an amendment to the MLA constitution that prohibits the Delegate Assembly from taking political stands on issues not directly relevant to the teaching of the humanities.[8] In this sense, the MLA furthers its role as an advanced bureaucracy. While future conventions may argue over this new stance, the discussions that go on in individual sessions, when and if there is time for discussion, will necessarily be of a distinctly apolitical nature. And if politics are discussed, there will only be time or occasion for the most superficial and strident oppositions. This attempt to make the organization objective is specified by Lukács as a characteristic "specific type of bureaucratic 'conscientiousness' and impartiality . . ." (99).

What professional gatherings lack, for the most part, is any sense of "working through." I am deliberately using Freud's term [*Durcharbeiten*] here because the process of psychoanalysis implies a determined, exhaustive, and long-term attempt to make sense of conflicts. Conflicts are not minimized or ignored, but are exploited in the process of the working through to achieve a dialectical understanding. An engaged intellectual analysis demands the play of conflicting ideas, the give and take of opinion backed by evidence leading to some kind of political activity. Professional organizations generally operate by discouraging conflict, by structurally fragmenting thought into 75-minute segments, each then subdivided into 20-minute papers that essentially leave little or no room for discussion and "working through." The bureaucratizing of thought involved in panel-formation fragments any kind of discussion that could possibly ensue. Each panel-goer is a unit, disconnected from other panel-goers. And each panelist is, for the most part, acutely aware of the isolate nature of his or her observation and the lack of engagement between his or her paper and the other papers. The feeling of letdown following this kind of anti-intellectual engagement is not unfamiliar to anyone who has been part of the process.[9]

One feels this sense of disappointment because one is in effect coerced into a process of alienated thought. Like commodified labor, being is divided up into units that appear to have an exchange value (a job, promotion, tenure) as well as a use-value (furthering knowledge, making change, developing teaching skills). But the use-value of intellectual work is denigrated in this process to pure exchange value. The contents of the intellectual sensorium are put into the service of the economy of competition rather than of symbolic production leading to the reformation of social structures. This academic competition, like the touted beneficial competition in the so-called free market, serves a powerfully regulating function in creating the personally cut-throat (and therefore paradoxically institutionally docile) bodies and minds fighting each other rather than the forces of oppression and power. There may be working, in the sense of symbolic production, in academic life—but there is little working through.

In general professional organizations seem designed to prevent a working through of ideas that would necessarily imply a notion of agency, a political goal, a necessary sense of conflict, a group activity. New ideas generally suggest, demand, or even provoke a change in social structure. Even Carlyle once said, "Speech that leads not to action still more than hinders it, is a nuisance on the Earth" (qtd. in Steiner 28). Although professional organizations appear to be groups that encourage speech, they are in fact mechanisms for managing individualism, braking mechanisms to halt in its tracks any connection between the analysis of ideas and the inhering notion of change that abides with new ideas. Unregulated groups are in fact dangerous things, especially if they have agendas. Hence the regulatory function of professional organizations.

What would a new type of professional organization look like? I ask this question with a certain sense of self-concern since I have been part of a collection of people who are in the process of shaping such an organization. We have called our collectivity Group for Early Modern Cultural Studies [GEMCS].[10] Having attended our first three annual meetings, I can relate a bit what the future might look like, but I can also see that such an organization must resist the demand for the bureaucratization of the group.

Such a new type of organization needs to consider all the aspects of power inherent in contemporary disciplines. GEMCS attempts to create a space that is relatively safe from disciplining, the gaze, and hierarchies of power and control. To do this, there really has to be a minimum of organizational structure. We seem to have done fairly well with a precarious sense of near anarchy. If the organizing branch of the group is kept completely porous then anyone who wants to start something, do something, or undo something can simply join a committee or start their own. This Shirley Temple–Mickey Rooney sense of "let's put on a play" could be easily disparaged as unprofessional—and it is. That is precisely the point. Forms of organization alternate to bureaucracy appear chaotic and act to disquiet people.[11]

Further, we have eliminated the issue of "star" speakers by refusing to have plenary lectures.[12] The idea behind this move is to emphasize that anyone who comes to the meeting does so on a level playing field. No one is paid to come; no one is invited. We are all in this sense equally interested in doing the work—in working through. When the idea was first suggested, a noted historian wrote me a letter pointing out that if no plenary speakers were announced, no graduate students or junior faculty would come. Presumably "low-status" scholars would only be drawn to a conference if they could bask in the intellectual brilliance of a "high-status" scholar. As it turned out, our conferences are more than well represented by younger scholars, and there were plenty of senior people as well. The issue of stardom, it turns out, seems to be part of a process of bureaucratic self-selection more than it is about genuine intellectual ability.

Related to this issue of power, graduate students and junior faculty need to be completely integrated into any such organization so that there is not even a question of including them as part of any decision-making process. Many organizations have a kind of tokenism in which younger scholars are included but always alone as sole representative of their constituency. GEMCS has made an effort to keep prices down and reduce fees for graduate students and the unemployed since the cost of attending a professional conference has a powerful class-bias built into it. It is in bad taste to mention high fees, expensive hotels, and so on (the assumption in academia, as in the rest of America, is that we are all one class), but these financial issues need to be kept in the foreground in planning.

The group has taken a position that we should have an advocacy role. The aim is to recognize the politics inherent in education and to discuss and deal with this sphere as part of our goals. Indeed, one of the issues that came up very strongly in discussion was that we should devote a block of time solely to issues of pedagogy. The dichotomy between research and teaching is one that troubled many people, and there was a sense that a role for a conference of college and university teachers should relate to how we teach what we know. Linked to this issue, of course, was how our institutions contribute or interfere with that process. We also want to maintain an awareness of the differences between the roles of graduate students and junior faculty who teach introductory, remedial, and writing courses and senior faculty who get to teach their subject more openly.

In addition to these issues, questions about the relationship between the conference and the locale of the conference came up. There was discussion in the most recent meeting of trying to forge links with local organizing groups so that GEMCS did not float, like imperial Laputa in *Gulliver's Travels*, above a particular city without some connections to grass-roots organizations.

The rubric of "Early Modern," which is admittedly limiting, allows us to span the period 1450–1850, thus loosening the stranglehold that particular organizations have on certain centuries.[13] This choice of breadth represents a central political decision. It is possible to say that disciplinarity as enforced by periodization is not an accident but a distinct product of bureaucratic knowledge. Periodization prevents a sense of communal endeavor. An enlightenment project of dividing up time into discernible grids controlled by a series of professional organizations serves as a de facto turfing of the intellectual life. So, in trying to reduce the power of bureaucracies to control spheres or periods of thought and being, we have adopted a notion of the long (some might say *very long*) Early Modern period.

Cultural studies stresses interdisciplinarity, questioning the roles of the various intellectual disciplines. Historians cannot smugly assume that what they do is "real" history, while postmodern literary critics must question whether they can address anyone who thinks that texts can signify. One of the best by-products of this amalgamation was the rather surprising and pleasant set of impressions that arose when one sat down at particular sessions and took note of the breadth of knowledge that usually is excluded by the straitjacket of periodism. The bureaucratized notion of specialist must constantly be challenged by questions across areas of expertise.

Beyond that, the rubric of cultural studies creates an umbrella that can cover a variety of left-leaning methodologies. Strategically, "cultural studies" works as a rubric in the same way that "Early Modern" does; it aims at a kind of guerrilla action, a war of position, against an established army, so it can disperse as frontally organized traditional disciplines approach. For our purpose cultural studies identifies an intellectual space that permits a gathering in its name in a very different sense than "literature" permits. The concept of literature, in recent history, is one that obscures its normalizing and regularizing politics, whereas the politics of cultural studies are more or less worn on its sleeve. In other words, cultural studies is a banner that identifies us (most of us) as in, if not near, the camp of a set of assumptions about race, class, gender, sexual preference, and disability. Of course, this is not an iron-clad, PC-approved list of things we agree on, but it is not a value-free, objective set either. We can then begin our discussions without having to justify these somewhat common assumptions—again another relief from many other professional organizations whose politics are not only *not* on their sleeve—they are not even on the soles of their shoes.

Cultural studies, however, does not assume a consensus on all issues. "Working through" allows—indeed demands—a notion of conflict. Bureaucratic organization manages conflict so that agreement appears to exist, particularly through an emphasis on impartial voting. *Robert's Rules of Order*[14] and carefully controlled elections create the illusion of democracy and debate. Agreement, however, only means a tally of half plus one of votes in the room. There can be sniper activity, but dissension is managed. As opposed to this managed vision of electoral politics, GEMCS aims for a dialectical sense of conflict and consensus. Perhaps borrowing from the Quaker prejudice against voting, based on a fear that majority rule infringes on the rights of what can be a sizable minority, a consensus model based on argumentation and persuasion is more appealing and less bureaucratic.

GEMCS aims to foster working through by encouraging panel proposals that would be more workshop-oriented. However, institutional constraints and force of habit have caused many people to propose traditional papers. The trained academic knows the way to the stable very well. In spite of the dead hand of tradition, the conferences still have managed to wrest free and generate intense discussion. Sessions that have worked best were ones on general topics like cultural studies, or the possibilities for interdisciplinarity, as well as ones that "read" particular texts collectively. Our aim for future conferences is to figure out ways to organize the program and publicize its aims so that members are more comfortable with alternate forms of presenting and discussing information.

Strange as it may seem, academics are starved for conversation with each other that goes beyond shop talk. As one advances in the profession, the opportunity to be in a class of one's peers diminishes. We generally praise the dynamic of the classroom, but we are most often the teacher there. Many of us went into teaching because we liked the dynamic of the classroom, and so we need to re-create classrooms filled with people of varying degrees of accomplishment but with high levels of interest. And here it is important to mention that we should encourage community-based people living in the conference venues to attend, but we can only do this if our work and our language are relevant to their issues. And this can only be accomplished through a genuine sense of political engagement in our academic work. A true challenge is to break down the wall between town and gown, even if the gown is from another town.

It may seem irrelevant to add that one strong sense of commonality came from having a dance. Bruce Clark, editor of *The Eighteenth-Century: Theory and Interpretation* and former member of the rock group of Sha-Na-Na, has brought his band up from Lubbock, Texas, for two of our conferences. The conference-goers danced to some incredible rock music until late in the night. One almost feels apologetic for mentioning what seems to be a "social occasion" in a serious discussion of professional organizations, but that embarrassment has to be noted and discussed. Pleasure, physical pleasure, movement, touch, energy—these are only some aspects of the body that are banished in the general postlapsarian view of academic work. The sweat of the brow is a permissible signifier for academic work but not the sweat of the body. The inclusion of the body and of its play in a professional organization is not only to be admitted but encouraged. I am not advocating that professional organizations start to look like a Norman O. Brown utopia or like the Essalen Institute, but the fact that professional organizations resemble these not at all is a bad sign.[15] In addition to active resistance to institutions, then, there is always the possibility of dancing in the dark.

To this awareness of the body, I would add another point. We need to rethink venues. Why do professional organizations all too often hold their conferences in large, garish, corporate hotels? Does it make sense to discuss Shakespeare or even *Fanny Hill* in a windowless conference room still bearing the traces of the previous days meeting of petroleum products sales representatives (or, as at one conference I attended, sharing the hallways with Pentagon officials)?[16] Do we want to donate our monies to multinational corporate hotel and entertainment chains that spawn these monuments to sterility and garish taste? The willful suspension of awareness of surroundings is an ideological adjunct to alienation. Although there are practical reasons why one might use hotels, there are also many other kinds of retreats available to groups who wish to be less alienating venues. These might also be more conscious of environmental issues, alternative lifestyles, physical comforts, and financial ability.

It might actually make sense for some groups to limit their size to avoid the gigantism of the Modern Language Association. This elephantiasis of the professional body can only be advantageous for pecuniary or hegemonic reasons. In fact, some groups may want to be small enough to have dinner together or go to the movies. Professional organizations might be made less necessary if academics would create small, working groups of like-minded, politically concerned people with similar aims and goals. Many such groups exist—in which people present ongoing work, read texts together, and perhaps engage in some common pro-active goal. These may even have a political agenda, such as developing a curriculum, fighting for minority studies programs, or publishing a magazine. However, there is a delicate balance between fragmentation and unification that one has to consider. To return to Marx's doubtful attitude toward cooperative associations, we must recall that the disadvantage of small groups or localized ones is that they inevitably have a lower vantage point from which to view the horizon. But, as Marx also pointed out, cooperative organizations are one stage in a greater transformation.

There is a level of violence in the inherent assumptions and operations of business as usual in the institution of Literature. Some might think I am being churlish, unrealistic, or idealistic in proposing any sense of an alternative. And some will wait for GEMCS to fail or simply to become another in the many of allied organizations in this country. I cannot guarantee that either of these outcomes will not happen. But the success or failure of GEMCS is an irrelevant issue. What is more to the point is that those of us in the postsixties generation have suffered from a huge failure of the imagination. We have successfully mounted an enormous critique of racism, sexism, capitalism, imperialism, colonialism, logocentricism, ableism, and so on. As a generation of scholars, we have probably produced the largest consistent body of knowledge devoted to reforming institutions and understanding social mechanisms since the beginning of print; yet, we have simply adopted the structures and functions of our predecessors. The effect is to change the furniture and carpeting in the university without changing the buildings.

What I have been saying is not merely that something is rotten in the state of academia, but that the very structure and function of knowledge is bound tightly into the institutions of the profession. Further, the ills of this set of practices are not simply uncomfortable or irritating but metastatic, proliferating a practice of knowledge that is based on a systematic inequality of power and position, a reproduction at the level of ideas and practices that parallels the abuses of race, class, gender, and ability in the larger postmodern, multinational world, or that in fact are linked to that world. While it is true that academia is still one of the only places where left discourse occurs, it happens as a kind of epiphenomenon to the routine exercises of power and discipline that blandly proliferate daily. We need a revolution in the quasi-medieval, quasi-enlightenment structures of thought and production called academia. Cooperatives, communities, communitarian formations point the way, as they did in the nineteenth century when they signaled alternatives to the factory system.

A challenge for the millennium is to rethink the institutions of knowledge. This means not simply the way we teach but the circumstances of our teaching and learning, the way we gather together, the purpose of those gatherings, what needs are met and what needs are not. Marx wrote that "the abolition of bureaucracy is only possible by the general interest *actually*—and not, as with Hegel, merely in thought, in *abstraction*—becoming the particular interest, which in turn is only possible as a result of the particular actually becoming the *general* interest" (III, 25). So too with the institutions of knowledge, the attempt must be made to reshape the bureaucratic notions that have governed the general categories of knowledge and the general modes for achieving these. But to do so is not so easy. As Weber points out, "once it is fully established, bureaucracy is among those social structures which are the hardest to destroy . . . and where the bureaucratization of administration has been completely carried though, a form of power relation is established that is practically unshatterable" (228). Of course, while we may be ultimately be seeking a change in the state, here we are speaking of an Ideological State Apparatus. To do so we need to understand the way that commodification, Taylorism, ideology, alienation of labor fit into the profession and professional organizations. The sacred cows of tenure and promotion need to be rethought in this analysis. Only then may we be able to achieve a dialectic of theory and practice; what is at stake is a kind of revolution that involves a profound reexamination and reorganization of the institutions of our profession. Such a change obviously can only happen from the bottom up, and creating new professional organizations may be an effective way to begin such a process. We owe this reexamination to ourselves and our students; till then we are still dancing in the dark.

Notes

1. Let us not even mention the linkage of this institutional gaze to the marketplace of publishing—another set of conjunctions that observes with vigilant eyes whether the scholarship one pursues is of interest to the handful of readers for academic presses or journals who are culled from the same bureaucratic upper echelon that constitutes the academic slice of the professional-managerial class. The market conditions the academic workplace, adding another layer of ideological compulsion and compliance.

2. Another functional result of this system is that academic freedom is putatively maintained while being denied in practice. Tenure may guarantee academic freedom; but the system of surveillance of graduate students and junior faculty insures that no untenured member of a department can truly express her or his politics, particularly if at variance with the common ideology, without fear of reprisal. Through a process of virtual operant conditioning, younger members of the faculty learn to selectively express, covertly believe, and act with a calculation bordering on hypocrisy in the name of expediency to the end that any impulse toward radical politics is crushed in the womb. By the time such faculty members get tenure, they have unlearned academic freedom.

3. It is perhaps a postmodern irony that now security guards are hired by New York City high schools to make sure that students do not arrive with guns, and by the Modern Language Association to make sure that unauthorized professors do not enter the book exhibit or listen to other professors' lectures. Such patrolling methods do not work very well at schools, where students learn how to pass through metal detectors undetected and at MLA where deviant graduate students and professors have learned how to use the duplicate tags of friends.

4. Since I wrote this essay, I have been nominated and elected a regional delegate to the MLA from New York State, become a member of the Standing Committee on Disability, and been elected to a position on the Executive Committee of the Division on Restoration and Eighteenth Century Literature. My position as an "outsider" has clearly been seriously compromised. However, I think the points I make in this essay still stand as valid. I might justify my involvement in several ways. First, I can say that the whole policy of the MLA toward people with disabilities and toward disability studies has been radically altered by some long, tough discussions. Second, I hope that my presence in the Delegate Assembly, along with that of other radicals, can help change some policies of the MLA—including ending the policing of members and dehierarchizing the organization. In fact, I am happy to have been part of a vote that condemned Yale University for taking punitive actions against graduate students organizing a union. But finally, one has to acknowledge that with the MLA as with capitalism, one can never truly be in the system and outside of it. Long live the Fifth Column!

5. Of course, the virtual reality of the e-mail bulletin board forces us to reconceptualize the whole idea of a gathering of any sort, as print forced us to think about the nature of the idea of the public. No longer do we need bodies to constitute a gathering. Print made it possible to speak of a reading public whose presence was not physically immanent, although that presence might be more powerful by virtue of the absence of bodies. Cyberspace changes the relationship of author, text, and public without requiring immanence.

6. One might want to reconsider the idea of cooperatives today. In the current moment, there seems less of a possibility of complete worker control of industry than there did in Marx's time. While communism exists in China and Cuba at the moment, it is not characterized by worker control but rather by bureaucratic control by party members. It is true, nonetheless, that such societies give greater guarantees of workers' rights, including housing, education, medical care, and so on. But given a transnational model of capitalism, one might do well to consider worker cooperatives as more than simply a failed step between capitalism and communism. Worker cooperatives, still few and far between, do provide, in Europe (particularly Spain) and in some factories in the United States, alternative forms of production that certainly hold a great deal of advantage over the model of the traditional corporation. Universities, we must recall, still follow the corporate model much more than the cooperative model. While departments within universities have a certain amount of cooperative autonomy (as long as the members are tenured), the university still determines salaries, budget allocations, working conditions, and so forth.

7. James Thompson has focused on this false sense of purpose in period studies like the eighteenth century in which the researcher/scholar receives the imperative to adulate the material he or she studies. One must revere Dr. Johnson, even imitate him, appreciate Richardson, revel with Fielding. And not to do so is in some sense not to be "in" the eighteenth century.

8. At the December 1995 meeting of the MLA, Barbara Foley attempted to rescind this ruling, but a lawyer's report citing a putative threat to the tax-exempt status of the MLA if its engagement in political activity in the form of passing resolutions was largely persuasive in convincing delegates to defeat the Foley amendment. Bureaucracy triumphant!

9. One of the strange compensatory mechanisms people have developed to try to overcome this sense of isolation is the comment, usually made at such sessions, about "how well the papers came together." What this usually means is that similar topics were covered, rarely that the participants actually addressed each other's theoretical or political assumptions. This confluence is like the symmetry (or asymmetry) museum curators try to achieve when they hang paintings next to each other.

10. A rather funny situation has arisen because we have tried to keep controlling forces to a minimum. GEMCS has no official way of pronouncing its acronym. Initially some people began with the rather elegant "Gems." I jokingly put forward the yiddish-sounding variant for East Coasters: "gemkiss"

with a hard *g* sound. I began hearing another variation "G-max." I am quite happy with this state of indeterminacy. But the more telling lesson is that there is no official practice here—and no one to assign a correct pronunciation.

11. An organization like GEMCS has to deal with the sociojuridical status of institutions. If one wishes to have a continuing structure, legal requirements begin. Does one seek nonprofit status? Create bylaws. Have elections for a board of directors that is required by law for nonprofit organizations? In recent meetings we have been wrestling with these issues, with some members wanting to institute more defined structures. In the 1995 meeting in Dallas, membership decided to table possible bylaws and allow creative anarchy to reign. The aim was to work toward consensus without the compulsion of majority rule politics. However, as some members have objected, then an inner core of activists may end up taking over the organization, not by intent to hijack but simply by filling a void that others choose not to occupy. It remains for us to work out these problems.

12. A practice apparently followed by the Marxist Literary Group as well.

13. Even this rather commodious time span breaks down at the edges as we creep toward the medieval and modern periods.

14. Some may find it worth noting that the eponymous parliamentarian was actually Brigadier General Henry Martyn Robert (1837–1923) of the United States Army. How appropriate that this putatively democratic guide to controlled group governance was in fact the product of a military mind.

15. The Society for the Study of Narrative Literature conference and the Shakespeare Society also have dances.

16. The Marxist Literary Group, for one, solves this problem with a meeting in which all participants stay in the dormitories of a university.

Works Cited

Bottomore, Tom, et al., eds. *A Dictionary of Marxist Thought.* Oxford: Blackwell, 1983.

Bourdieu, Pierre. *Outline of a Theory of Practice.* Trans. Richard Nice. Cambridge: Cambridge UP, 1977.

Graff, Gerald. "Why Theory?" *Left Politics and the Literary Profession.* Ed. Lennard J. Davis and M. Bella Mirabella. New York: Columbia UP, 1990. 19–35.

Lukács, Georg. *History and Class Consciousness: Studies in Marxist Dialectics.* Trans. Rodney Livingstone. Cambridge, MA: MIT P, 1971.

Marx, Karl. *Capital.* 3 vols. Trans. Ernest Untermann. Chicago: Charles H. Kerr, 1909.

Rubin, Gayle. "The Traffic in Women: Notes Toward a Political Economy of Sex." *Toward an Anthropology of Women*. Ed. Rayna Reiter. New York: Monthly Review, 1975. 157–210.

Sedgwick, Eve Kosofsky. *Between Men: English Literature and Male Homosocial Desire*. New York: Columbia UP, 1985.

Steiner, George. *Language and Silence: Essays on Language, Literature, and the Inhuman*. New York: Atheneum, 1967.

Thompson, James. "Introduction: What Is Left of the Left?" *The Eighteenth Century: Theory and Interpretation* 32.3 (1991): 195–203.

Weber, Max. *From Max Weber: Essays in Sociology*. Ed. H. H. Gerth and C. Wright Mills. New York: Oxford UP, 1971.

Chapter Nine

The Star System in Literary Studies

David R. Shumway

> Flying down to Charlottesville is just an ordinary piece of business in the life of many academics. By "Charlottesville," I don't mean that all conferences are in Charlottesville, but I mean that people regularly go to conferences. It's really a phenomenon, and it has changed the structure of the way in which we do business.
>
> —Stanley Fish

In 1913, the critic Stuart Sherman published an essay in the *Nation* on George Lyman Kittredge, arguably the leading literary scholar of the day. The occasion was the publication of a Festschrift celebrating Kittredge's twenty-fifth anniversary at Harvard. Part of Sherman's task in the essay—which laments philology's evil influence on the teaching of English—is to demonstrate that Kittredge is a significant figure in spite of his obscurity to the public. As Sherman explains, Kittredge "has not dulled his palm by the entertainment of newspaper reporters, nor popularized his science for the magazines. . . . He has kept his name austerely within professional circles. Yet he has had his way in his profession. . . . He has exercised, indeed, a kind of overlordship upon English instruction in this country" (228). Sherman's article has something in common with more recent laments in the press about literary studies. For example, Sherman cites the subjects of the articles in the Festschrift to demonstrate just how arcane the knowledge was that Kittredge and his followers produced—a tactic that contemporary journalists have made a cliché in their coverage of the MLA convention. But unlike these journalists, Sherman cannot accuse his subject of being a slave to fashion or of seeking the limelight.

Kittredge, who virtually founded Chaucer studies in the United States, stood at the head of a professional genealogy that controlled the field for many years after his death, but he was not a star. Nor were any of his illustrious contemporaries or near contemporaries, such as John Manly, John Livingston Lowes, and so on. Why they were not stars and Judith Butler, Jacques Derrida, Stanley Fish, Henry Louis Gates, Jr., Fredric Jameson, Gayatri Chakravorty Spivak, and other figures in the academy are is the subject of this essay. In examining the academic star system, whose existence has been widely perceived but not explained,[1] I begin with the development of the theatrical and cinematic star system as a distinctive form of celebrity, then discuss the broader culture of celebrity that has developed in the United States. Media images reveal the star character of today's leading literature scholars, but to explain why these scholars have become stars, I examine changes in academic practice such as the growth of the conference circuit and the rise of literary theory. I also consider the effects of academic stardom, most important, the way it functions in authorizing knowledge. I conclude that the star system inhibits the production of collectively held knowledge and has weakened public confidence in the profession.

❦ ❦ ❦

Since the rise of theory in the 1970s, a star system, a new form of intellectual authority and professional status, has become significant and perhaps dominant in literary studies. There have been scholars like Kittredge, who were more powerful, more famous, and more influential than their colleagues, since the discipline was established in the late nineteenth century. As Robert Merton observes of eminent scientists, these literature scholars probably received disproportionate recognition for their contributions compared with that accorded less-well-known scholars for comparable work (443–47). But to use Sherman's term, influential literature scholars offered only an "austere face" to the profession and to the public. Just as they couched their scholarship in the dispassionate rhetoric of science, they presented themselves as impersonal and disinterested. One indication of the lack of personality presented by these scholars is the pictures we have of them: institutional photographs—head-only, black-and-white shots that hardly distinguish one scholar from the next (Figs. 1 and 2). Even formal portraits in oils are austere. Their undifferentiated photographic images were not widely disseminated, and because their travel was limited, relatively few members of the profession saw and heard them in person. In a response to an earlier version of this essay, however, Douglas Bruster pointed out that scholars like Kittredge and Lowes had a comparatively wide audience beyond the profession: "Paradoxically, some early-twentieth-century academics possessed a public voice that none of the more recent stars has commanded" (439), giving well-attended public lectures, and their books were widely reviewed in newspapers and magazines. As I will show, the star system itself partly explains this paradox.

In the nineteenth century, writers, politicians, scientists, and generals obviously achieved fame, but the concept of the star first emerged in the theater, which had had a star system since the early nineteenth century (deCordova). What distinguished theatrical stardom was the visual presentation of personality. Actors were always present when their personalities were experienced or consumed. Writers lived through their words, scientists through their discoveries, politicians through their campaigns, and generals through their victories. Portraits or images of these figures may have been available, but they could not compare with the compelling presence of the actor onstage. The theatrical star developed in relation to a particular kind of consumer, the fan, who sought not to imitate the star's achievements or to gain from his or her power but to have an imaginary personal relationship with the star.

The advent of the cinematic star system around 1910 expanded the experience of stars to virtually every outpost and backwater. Many more people could become fans, and movie stars had much greater celebrity than early stage stars did. In fact, movie stardom changed the character of celebrity: politicians, writers, generals, and other famous figures were increasingly personalized as the public increasingly responded to them as fans. This process was aided by the tremendous proliferation of visual representations of the famous during the twentieth century. First in newspapers, then in glossy magazines, and finally on television, the images of celebrities became ubiquitous. As a result, celebrity pervaded the culture, and since about 1960 its form has mutated again. Joshua Gamson observes that contemporary celebrities are developed and marketed not only on the basis of their abilities or qualities but also on the separable "capacity to command attention" or on sheer "knownness" (58). As John Ellis asserts, television tends to produce not stars but figures who

Fig. 1. Austere image: George Lyman Kittredge. Courtesy of Harvard University Archives.

Fig. 2. Austere image: F. O. Matthiessen Courtesy of Harvard University Archives.

are "famous for being famous" (107). Inevitably, other groups in society deploy such strategies. A recent book by several professors of communication argues that "visibility is . . . what every professional seeks. It is the crucial ingredient that can make lawyer X the most sought after in town, talk show host Y the most popular in her market, and surgeon Z the most highly paid in his city" (qtd. in Gamson 57).

The pervasiveness of celebrity may help account for the star system in literary studies, but it is important to distinguish the star from the mere celebrity. The appeal of studio-era stars (as opposed to that of later TV celebrities) is the illusion of depth, of a rich, complicated personality that exists beyond film roles. Where stage stars achieved fame through their seeming ability to become the characters they portrayed, movie stars were consistent personalities re-created in each new movie in spite of the roles they played.[2] Greta Garbo is always playing Greta Garbo whether she is portraying Queen Christina, Marguerite Gautier, or Ninotchka. Moreover, as Gamson notes, fans took the Hollywood star as a model, someone to identify with and to imitate (145–47). Jackie Stacey has shown that identification is central to how women responded to stars of the 1940s and 1950s both while watching movies and at other times. The narratives of Hollywood films positioned their audiences to identify with the characters the stars played, so it was easy for the viewer to carry that identification over to the star.

Stars are often said to be different from the rest of us because of their "star quality," which Budd Schulberg defines as a "mysterious amalgam of self-love, vivacity, style, and sexual promise" (qtd. in Brown 241). But as Denise Scott Brown notes in an article on the star system in architecture, "Stardom is something done to a star by others. Stars cannot create themselves" (241). The invention of stars' public images needs to be understood as a collaborative project,[3] but the success of that invention clearly depends on audience response. The studios built a publicity apparatus to ensure that the personality portrayed in the movies would be further developed in other media and that images of the star's offscreen life would continue the fans' relationship with the star between film releases.

It is onscreen, however, that Schulberg's star quality is realized. The components of star quality correspond to two components of audience response: identification and desire. Self-love is important because an individual lacking self-love tends not to be regarded as worthy of imitation or identification. Sexual promise, conveyed through the portrayal of romantic relationships, is at the heart of what the dream factory makes and sells. This promise can be realized in identification, as Woody

Allen illustrates in *Play It Again, Sam*. But movie stars themselves were objects of desire. The roles the stars played usually involved romantic relationships, so that movie stars came to be the very embodiment of romance for much of the public. The fans were meant to dream about having a sexual relationship with the star. The star's attractiveness thus works both directly and vicariously in the minds of the fans, who want either to have the star or to be the star.

These desires, to use Brown's term, "create" the star. Stardom is an effect of a relation between the celebrity and the fans. The movie star is, after all, defined by performance at the box office. If the fans do not buy tickets to see a performer, the performer is not a star. But stardom is not just a matter of economics. Adoring fans make the star adorable; thus studios staged premieres and other events for the display of public worship, made sure that fan mail received responses so that fans would send more mail, and helped build quasi-religious shrines such as the Walk of Fame. But if adoration could be encouraged and given opportunities for display, it could not be produced at will. Players often failed to become stars in spite of the studios' best efforts.

Whether stardom is a result of achievement or a product of a "machine" designed to turn ordinary folks into celebrities has been debated since P. T. Barnum, but as Gamson shows, during the twentieth century cultural weight has shifted from merit to production (15–16). Whereas the great stars of the studio era were rendered authentic by offscreen publicity, the new celebrities are presented as produced images that are endlessly discussed and manipulated in public. Fans no longer expect the authenticity that the studios worked so hard to produce. The studios once did their best to spread only the right kind of gossip about their stars, but in the current environment of hypercelebrity, such control is next to impossible and largely irrelevant. Where stars were once made to appear like gods, contemporary celebrities are often distinguished by their pathologies or deviances. The new skepticism about celebrity should inform an analysis of the public's response to the academic star system.

Although I have discussed stardom as a specific form of celebrity that found its characteristic expression in the movie stars of the studio era, stardom obviously exists in other fields of entertainment—rock and roll, for example—as well as in professions such as architecture. And although the spread of stardom was doubtless influenced by the movies, it should be more generally considered an effect of the development of the mass media. If writers like Fitzgerald and Hemingway enjoyed something like star status as early as the 1920s, this status cannot be attributed solely to the cinematic model. The media defined these writers as personalities in news articles about their extraliterary experiences. Previously, leading writers in the United States had been defined primarily by their work and their ideas; their personalities were a function of their writing. Now the situation was reversed, and the writing was only one expression of the personality (see my *American Civilization* 224–26). I am not, then, arguing that movie stardom is a direct historical cause of the star system in literary studies. I am suggesting that the importance in contemporary America of celebrity in its many forms, including stardom, helps account for the rise of the academic star system. Moreover, the workings of the cinematic star system can help us understand those of the academic one.

It took longer for a star system to develop in the academy than in the larger literary culture. Before World War II, the dominant literary historians continued in the austere mode, keeping their personalities on the sidelines. The first significant generation of academic critics, which included F. O. Matthiessen and John Crowe Ransom, displayed more personality than literary historical scholars had but did not achieve the fame and influence of critics outside the academy such as H. L. Mencken. Matthiessen's suicide ironically may have made him something like a cult star during the 1950s, but this phenomenon does not account for the authority of his work. After World War II, Lionel Trilling gained fame beyond the academy, and his personality became discursively available in ways that Kittredge's was not, but Trilling was not constructed in the visual terms that define stardom. Moreover, while his extra-academic activities increased his prestige and authority within the academy, they defined him as an intellectual rather than as an academic star. The intellectual is a public figure but not necessarily a public personality. The academic star may or may not be a public figure—a "universal intellectual"—but is always a public personality in the academy.[4]

This history of early manifestations of personality in literary studies needs to be supplemented with an understanding of changing theoretical assumptions in the discipline. As a form of authority, the star system is closely linked to criticism outside the academy, which has long depended on the authoritative personalities of individual critics such as Mencken. The philologists and literary historians who founded the modern language disciplines saw themselves as scientists, and they sought to ground their work in disinterested, impersonal judgment. However, they continued to value what was personal, unique, or original in literary works. After World War II, when the dominant practice of literary studies became criticism, the personal became important in academic writing as well.

Academic critics began to think of themselves as having distinctive voices or perspectives. But because literary studies remained a discipline, the values associated with science were not completely rejected.

The emergence of academic stars, which has occurred only within the past 20 years, marks a fundamental shift in the profession of literary studies. During that time, academic literary study has produced stars whose brilliance shines within the profession, though that brilliance is produced both directly by academic activities and indirectly by reflection in nonacademic media. Literary theory stars have been featured in articles in the *New York Times Magazine*, in newsweeklies, and even on the *McNeil-Lehrer News Hour*. These public media may reveal star construction better than academic publications do, but public exposure reflects literary theorists' professional roles.[5]

Rather than give literary-theory stars fame among the general public, popular images of such stars enhance their star quality in the academy. Professors are suddenly suffused with a glamour usually reserved for public celebrities.[6] Colin Campbell's "The Tyranny of the Yale Critics," which appeared in the *New York Times Magazine* in 1986, was perhaps the first major exposure of academic stars in the national media. The article's words are far less significant than its pictures—large color portraits, three of which hardly seem likely to convince anyone of their subjects' "sexual promise." These pictures of Harold Bloom, Geoffrey Hartman, and J. Hillis Miller contextualize their subjects: Bloom appears in a messy but well-appointed study (Fig. 3), Miller reads a book in a pizza parlor, and Hartman stands against a stained-glass window whose six-pointed stars allude to his interest in Judaica. Bloom's expression suggests worry so deep as to verge on despair, while Hartman looks merely serious, and Miller seems as though he might have smiled the second after the shutter closed. In spite of the severe looks, these pictures personalize and individualize their subjects in ways that earlier photographic and painted portraits do not. Moreover, there is an additional image—the most starlike of the four—of Jacques Derrida (Fig. 4). While the other photos contextualize their subjects, Derrida dominates this scene, the background being dark and serving to frame the figure. The chiaroscuro lighting dramatically features one side of his face as he leans forward and offers an indistinct expression, one similar to Miller's but made more dramatic by the lighting. Even Derrida's clothing is dramatic—a black corduroy jacket rather than the usual tweed sport coat—and it also serves to set off the star's face. The other three images are interesting pictures of professors; Derrida is presented like a movie star.

Fig. 3. Harold Bloom in context. Courtesy of the photographer, Benno Friedman.

Fig. 4. Star image: Jacques Derrida. Photo: Julio Donoso/Sygma.

Since the "Yale Critics" article, the *Times Magazine* has presented other star images of literary academics on a number of occasions. The most famous is surely the photograph of Frank Lentricchia—taken from a book jacket—in which he is dressed in an open-collared shirt and blue jeans and posed against a graffiti-covered wall, arms folded and a scowl on his face (Atlas; Gilbert and Gubar; Lentricchia, "Andiamo!"). A comparison of this image with that of James Dean on the poster for *Rebel without a Cause* makes clear the role in which Lentricchia is casting himself. Photographs accompanying Adam Begley's "Black Studies' New Star" portray Henry Louis Gates, Jr., in dramatic lighting like that used for Derrida's portrait and include images that give the reader a sense of Gates's personal life. Such images provide a glimpse of the construction of personality crucial to the star system.

Perhaps the most striking visual expression of the academic star system, however, is Mark Tansey's painting *Derrida Queries de Man* (1990; Fig. 5). According to Arthur Danto, "The painting of two figures wrestling with one another on a rock shelf, which makes one dizzy simply to look at it, is based on Sidney Paget's famous illustration of Sherlock Holmes and Doctor Moriarity in combat at Reichenback Falls" (29).[7] By casting Derrida and de Man as two of the best-known figures of popular narratives in virtually every conceivable medium, Tansey raises them to mythic status. It matters little whether this gesture is meant to be ironic—though of course it is—because once the association is made, it cannot be erased. Tansey's painting places Derrida and de Man (it is not immediately obvious who is who) in a company of stars ranging from Basil Rathbone to Jeremy Brett. These external representations of academic stars reflect the way academic stars function within the discipline of literary studies, just as photo spreads of movie stars reflect those stars' status in the industry.

The most important catalyst for the emergence of academic stars is the conference and lecture circuit. As Stanley Fish has observed, literary academics now "regularly go to conferences. . . . [A]nd it has changed the structure of the way in which we do business" (Interview). Although there have been professional conferences in literary studies since the first meeting of the MLA in 1883, the listings in MLA publications reveal that these conferences proliferated in the 1970s. This growth resulted both from an exponential increase in the number of learned societies—spurred by the MLA's provisions for convention sessions sponsored by allied organizations—and from the rapid emergence of the thematic conference as a regular feature of professional life. Thematic conferences and

Fig. 5. The theorist as pop-culture hero: Mark Tansey's *Derrida Queries de Man*, 1990, oil on canvas, 83 ¾" x 55" (212.7 x 139.7 cm), collection of Michael and Judy Ovitz, Los Angeles, CA. Courtesy of Curt Marcus Gallery, New York; © Mark Tansey 1990.

conferences organized by learned societies differed from meetings of traditional professional organizations—the MLA, NCTE, CCCC, the regional MLAs—in that they did not have a ready-made audience of members for whom participation was a form of professional recognition. The new types of conferences needed famous scholars to attract participants and attendees.

These new conferences exhibited a hierarchy that had previously been understood but that had not been reflected in the structure of professional meetings, which aimed to allow the exchange of new information and ideas among a community of contributors. By using the famous as drawing cards and by giving them a privileged role, the new conferences positioned the famous and their audiences in a new relationship. In repeated appearances at invited lectures the famous do not merely present arguments but also make available a personality exhibited in the performance of the lecture or paper, in responses to questions and comments, and perhaps most significant, in informal conversations before and after the performance. For example, those of us who have witnessed Gayatri Spivak's public performances cannot fail to remember them when reading her prose. There is not only the distinctive voice but also the striking face, the sari, and the characteristic tics or patterns of delivery. Whatever Spivak has to say is different merely by virtue of her having spoken the words. Some stars seem to be particularly adept at exploiting the opportunities public performances provide. Stanley Fish reads clearly and with unusual attention to effective emphasis, but the most distinctive feature of his performance is the way he responds to questions and comments. A master of the humorous put-down, which he is as likely to use on a friendly questioner as on a hostile one, Fish often follows his one-liners with a rapid rhetorical destruction of an opponent. Despite his aggressiveness, Fish wins the audience, not only by making his position seem unassailable but also by coming across as honest, open, and approachable—a regular guy, neither ethereal nor exotic. Where Spivak conveys the gravity of the issues she addresses and Fish the presumed self-evidence of his claims, Jane Gallop's self-presentation corresponds to the wordplay characteristic of her work, which is also highly self-referential. Her most distinctive style of performance is a burlesque of conventional notions of femininity, which might include heavy makeup, seamed stockings, and a form-fitting dress. Gallop may choose to sit on the speaker's table rather than behind it. Ideas uttered by this very much embodied Gallop are distinguished by the conditions of the performance.

In calling attention to performance style, I do not mean to diminish the content of these stars' work. The view that this approach is belittling may derive from the antirhetorical assumption that ideas should speak for themselves. It may also be related to the ranking of publication over teaching, since good teaching often depends on dramatic performance. Fish, Gallop, and Spivak have reputations as master teachers. Even scholars who present themselves more conventionally are perceived differently as a result of frequent appearances in the flesh. Public appearances give many conference-goers or lecture attendees the feeling that they know the famous one. It is the feeling of personal connection that transforms the merely famous scholar into a star.

Of course, the growth of the lecture and conference circuit could occur only recently, with the advent of rapid and relatively inexpensive jet travel. As literary scholars' correspondence from the 1930s and 1940s confirms, the journey to the MLA convention was a hardship for many. Prominent scholars did visit other campuses to lecture, but their trips were limited in number and distance by travel time. Jet travel makes it possible for stars to appear all over the nation and even on other continents without missing—or perhaps without appearing to miss—an irresponsible number of classes. The effects of stardom are self-generating. The stars' reputations allow them to demand special travel budgets, support for research assistance, and more frequent leaves, all of which enable even greater mobility and thus the opportunity to appear at more conferences and to accept more lecture invitations.

The conditions for the development of the conference circuit and of the star system were not just technological. They have their roots in the disciplinary form that the research university imposed on literary studies in the late nineteenth century (see my *American Civilization*). This form entails collective, interinstitutional evaluation of contributions to peer-reviewed journals. The development of the Ph.D. as a professional credential for the professoriat produced individuals trained not only in the methods, theories, and facts of a particular discipline but in practices and behavior required in all disciplines. Scholarly publication was built into the system that required an original contribution in the doctoral dissertation. According to Christopher Jencks and David Reisman, by World War II most college students attended institutions staffed by academic professionals, and only a shortage of Ph.D.s prevented even more colleges from hiring such faculty members (21). The expansion of universities after the war allowed a higher percentage of literature faculty members to pursue vigorous, productive careers in research, careers for which they had been trained but which had been precluded by heavy teaching loads.[8] However, it is true that an increasing percentage of institutions—including liberal arts colleges and teachers' colleges—came to require research for tenure and promotion. As institutions that had previously required only teaching of their faculty began to require research as well, more and more faculty members had to write academic papers. Moreover, at many of these institutions, giving a paper at a conference came to be regarded as earning credit for promotion or tenure.

These factors, along with the exponential growth in the number of practitioners, meant that a tremendous amount of critical writing was produced after the war. But contrary to Jonathan Culler's claims, since literary studies had long been a discipline, the "horizontal system of evaluation" (30) characteristic of this form of knowledge production could not be a significant factor in accounting for the star system. However, two more recent conditions mentioned by Culler are probably relevant. The job crisis of the 1970s and 1980s was yet another stimulus to publication: "As current wisdom has it, more publications are needed to get a job interview today than were required 20 years ago for tenure" (27). Such an intensely competitive professional environment among scholars and institutions contributed to making stars of those who produced the most or the best publications. As Culler observes, "[F]or deans in the American system, 'visibility' may have become more important than what is called 'soundness'" (31). Soundness was the preeminent value of Kittredge's era, while visibility, as I have shown, is precisely what star systems demand and promise. Accordingly, institutions that were not considered the most prestigious tried to lure stars with light teaching loads and high salaries—a practice that has resulted in bidding wars among institutions and frequent job changes for many stars. Institutions that could not afford to hire stars offered them lucrative deals to visit and teach—or perhaps merely consult—for periods as short as a week.

The star system in literary studies, like that of the studio era, involves identification with a person who represents an ideal. Most academics, however, cannot hope to follow the stars' career paths; in fact, the current trend toward reduced funding for higher education suggests that opportunities for even an ordinary career in research are increasingly limited. James Sosnoski has aptly named those who occupy the extreme range of careers in literary studies "token professionals" and "master critics."[9] The care and feeding of stars has exacerbated these disparities. The symbolic capital a university acquires by having stars in its literature department has meant that stars command an ever larger share of shrinking resources.[10] During the current period of academic retrenchment, the average faculty member's real wages have been falling. The star system may have contributed to this trend and may have encouraged the hiring of more part-time and temporary faculty members.

Changes in the mode of academic performance, however, are not sufficient to account for the rise of the star system. A change in the disciplinary object was also a necessary prerequisite. Since the early 1920s, literary studies has been more a collection of subdisciplines than a unified field. Before then, scholars like Kittredge could dominate the entire discipline because it was so narrowly focused. As the discipline developed, however, its practice was increasingly conducted by scholars who specialized in a period or other division of the field and whose fame and influence were largely confined to a particular community of specialists. Specialties with larger followings obviously produced more-famous scholars than those with smaller ones did. However, the advent of academic criticism in the late 1930s meant that theories and methods could be applied to all literary specialities and thus that scholars could acquire broader reputations.

The advent of literary theory coincided with the expansion of the conference and lecture circuit, and the two phenomena doubtless fed each other. Theorists, like the New Critics before them, had the entire discipline as a potential audience. Since theorists challenged the premises underlying all literary study and offered or seemed to offer new, more valid or useful approaches to the study of literature, the practitioner of any specialty could be—and it was said, should be—engaged in theory. Although most literature scholars did not attend to theory, enough did—or said they did—to make theory, which first emerged as a marginal activity and was to become just another specialization, the broadest discourse in the discipline. Leading theorists won recognition from practitioners of virtually all specialties. Journals devoted to theory, such as *Critical Inquiry* (first published in 1974) and *New Literary History* (first published in 1969), became among the most influential in the discipline.

Theory not only gave its most influential practitioners a broad professional audience but also cast them as a new sort of author. Theorists asserted an authority more personal than that of literary historians or even critics. As we have seen, the rhetoric of literary history denied personal authority; in principle, even Kittredge was just another contributor to the edifice of knowledge. Criticism was able to enter the academy only by claiming objectivity for itself, so academic critics could not revel in personal idiosyncrasy. They developed their own critical perspectives, to be sure, but all the while they continued to appeal to the text as the highest authority. In the past 20 years theory has undermined the authority of the text and of the author and replaced it with the authority of systems, as in the structuralist and poststructuralist privileging of *langue* over *parole* or in the demystifying readings of Marxism or psychoanalysis. Sometimes the theory seems to eschew all authority, as in some renderings of deconstruction. And yet these claims are belied by the actual functioning of the name of the theorist. It is that name, rather than anonymous systems or the anarchic play of signifiers, to which most theoretical practice appeals. Thus one finds article after article in which Derrida or Foucault or Barthes or Lacan or Zizek or Althusser or Spivak or Fish or Jameson or several of the above are cited as markers of truth. It is common now to hear practitioners speak of "using" Derrida or Foucault or some other theorist to read this or that object; such phrasing may suggest that the theorist provides tools of analysis, but the tools are not sufficient without the name that authorizes the procedure.[11]

Foucault observed this phenomenon when he noted that Freud and Marx serve as founders of special formations of knowledge called "discursive practices," to which their names are indispensable:

> The initiation of a discursive practice, unlike the founding of a science, overshadows . . . its later developments and transformations. As a consequence, we define the theoretical validity of a statement with respect to the work of the initiator, whereas in the case of Galileo or Newton, it is based on the structural and intrinsic norms established in cosmology or physics. (134)

Because authority in the natural sciences is rooted in a consensus about such norms, the hierarchies in these fields have not developed into star systems of the sort I have described here.[12] Nobel laureates in the sciences may get more credit than they deserve, in part because their status can make a discipline listen to what it might otherwise discount, but such new knowledge does not continue to be authorized by the laureates' names, much less by their personalities. By contrast, the field of literary studies is made up of conflicting discursive practices, each of which depends on at least one theory star of greater or lesser magnitude. And knowledge in literary studies is defined not by virtuosity of critical performance or by the accumulation of facts but by the enlisted names of the fathers (and increasingly the mothers, though the stars remain predominantly male). This form of authority both produces the star system and is reproduced by it.

In some respects, Derrida may be the best example of this phenomenon, the most starlike of the stars. To be sure, his magnitude owes something to his being the only major poststructuralist still alive, but he represents a quintessential combination of star qualities. Derrida is the jet-set academic, a professor who seems to spend more time in the air between gigs than on the ground at any particular job. He has held recurring or regular visiting appointments at Yale, Johns Hopkins, and the University of California, Irvine, while holding permanent positions first at the École Normale Supérieure and then at the École des Hautes Etudes en Sciences Sociales. His appearances on the lecture and conference circuit keep him before his fans, but they are infrequent enough to be major events. These events are performances of deconstruction in action and of Derrida's personality in construction. Derrida's work depends on performance for its authority: one reads each new Derrida not to find out where deconstruction is going but to see what Derrida will do with a new object. And yet these performances do not merely contribute to our appreciation of the master's virtuosity. Each performance—to the extent that it is successful—extends Derrida's personality further into the terrain of intellectual life. To some extent—and sometimes to a very great extent—Derrida is always constructing a personality in his work. The public performances with their identifying features—the length of the lectures and their disregard for the usual limitations of aural comprehension—correspond to the bits and fragments of autobiography that are part of his written texts. Derrida's fans know him not mainly as the initiator of deconstruction but as a character he plays onstage.[13]

Among American stars, Fish is doubtless the most adept at exploiting the star system.[14] Since he took up reader-response theory, he has used the first-person pronoun more often than is typical of theorists, and he has also seemed to be writing about himself as much as about anything else. This self, however, is not sexual or even private but, rather, professional. In his recent collections of essays, the most important framing device is Fish's own intellectual autobiography. He begins *Is There a Text in This Class?* with an introduction titled "How I Stopped Worrying and Learned to Love Interpretation," which itself begins, "What interests me about many of the essays collected here is the fact that I could not write them today" (1). In the era of Kittredge, the response to both these statements would surely have been, "Who cares?" It was the collective mind of the discipline, not the individual mind, that mattered. In the heyday of New Criticism, the same stricture would have applied, albeit less strictly. In the current environment, however, Fish can make theoretical arguments—arguments about the conditions of interpretation and knowledge production—more persuasive by writing about himself than he could by leaving himself out. Because Fish's personality—carefully developed in the essays themselves and in his public appearances—authorizes his work, his changes of mind are significant.

Current theoretical assumptions and recent trends in scholarly practice have expanded the role of gossip, which has become as significant to academic stardom as it is to film stardom. It is the feeling of personal connection that transforms the merely famous scholar into a star, and the circulation of gossip about academic stars confirms this element of their construction. Indeed, one might argue that what distinguishes the stars from the rest of us is the velocity and breadth of the gossip that circulates around them. While gossip may deal with any aspect of the star's life—that Stanley Fish drives a Jaguar, that Jane Tompkins works in a cafeteria two days a week—as with gossip everywhere, sexual predilections and relationships are the most discussed issues. Conferences are not merely the scene of professional performance; they are also, as David Lodge has perhaps most effectively illustrated, rife with sexual opportunities—or at least the appearance of the same. The behavior of stars at conferences thus may become a central element of their personae: Will X get drunk again this year and take a graduate student back to her room? Does Y's wife know he's here with Z? Of course, gossip often refers to nonconference doings, to the star's life at home or in the department, but it is at conferences where the gossip is most quickly disseminated—except, of course, when it appears in print.

Gossip—or matters that were once thought to be gossip—are increasingly appearing in scholarly publications. Because of the widely held notion that one can speak only from one's own gendered, racial, class, sexual, or professional position, increasing numbers of literary scholars are engaged in describing their positions. Personal matters, once regarded as extraneous to disciplinary discourse, have become central to it. Queer theory has made the sexual life of the theorist one of its principal preoccupations. It has been argued that "[i]f you can follow the permutations of [Eve] Sedgwick's identity, an understanding of queer theory is within your grasp" (Begley, "I's" 57). The discipline has more knowledge about the sexual tastes of Eve Sedgwick than the *National Enquirer* provides about those of most celebrities. Another queer theory star, Judith Butler, is the subject of what is to my knowledge the only fanzine about an academic star: *Judy*. Written in the hyperbolic style of movie and fan magazines, *Judy* is of course a parody of the academic star system, but what better confirmation can one have of the system's widespread recognition?

The importance of gossip and of other types of public discussion of the private lives of the stars is manifested in the current rash of autobiographies written by literary academics.[15] A recent article by Adam Begley in *Lingua Franca*—a periodical whose very existence attests to the star system and to the importance of gossip—discusses autobiographies by Cathy Davidson, Alice Kaplan, Frank Lentricchia, Jane Tompkins, and Marianna Torgovnick, in addition to the autobiographical revelations in Sedgwick's theory and criticism. Begley offers a number of possible explanations for this turn to autobiography: individualism run rampant, the exhaustion of the dominant critical idiom, an expression of midlife crises ("I's"). My own view is that autobiography is a means by which some of these critics attempt to establish their own authority under the conditions of the star system. The current discourse of literary studies has made the construction of personality a means of acquiring cultural and academic capital.[16] Tompkins employs this tactic explicitly in "Me and My Shadow," where autobiography is used to make an academic argument, and it is implicit in Lentricchia's and Torgovnick's narratives. This autobiographical movement should be distinguished from some appeals to personal and shared experience in women's studies, African-American studies, gay studies, and other such knowledge formations. In these fields, autobiography has been used in an attempt to establish communal identity, while the current crop of autobiographies seeks to distinguish the author from everyone else.[17]

As theory has called into question the traditional means by which knowledge has been authorized, it may be that the construction of the individual personality has become an epistemological necessity. Such a turn of events would be ironic since poststructuralism has aimed to undermine the subject along with other epistemological foundations. And yet reliance on the autobiographical self does not contradict the more general poststructuralist attack on the sovereign subject as the source of objective knowledge. The authorization of knowledge by personality is in fact consistent with poststructuralist questioning of the shared, public authority of knowledge.

In "No Bias, No Merit," Fish addresses the issue of author-anonymous review, which can be seen as one of the discipline's responses to the star system. In the late 1970s, the MLA Executive Council voted to institute a policy of blind submission for *PMLA*. Previously the authors of papers submitted to the journal had not been anonymous to the reviewers. Why after nearly 100 years of publication did *PMLA* institute anonymous review? I suspect that there are several reasons. One of them, surely, was the increasingly heterogeneous discourse within the discipline; such heterogeneity made people more likely to believe that their work was judged unfairly. And it was not just discourse that was becoming more heterogeneous. The new policy was initially suggested by the MLA's Commission on the Status of Women, which wanted to ensure that questions of gender, race, institutional affiliation, and rank would not enter into the evaluation of manuscripts. But I believe that the incipient star system was also a factor, especially when understood in the context of increased heterogeneity. As I have noted, there has always been a hierarchy of authority in the discipline, and the work of the most authorized scholars had a greater likelihood of publication. Fish makes this circumstance an ethical point in "No Bias, No Merit," where he identifies merit with professional hierarchy: "There will always be those whose words are meritorious (that is, important, worth listening to, authoritative, illuminating) simply by virtue of the position they occupy in the institutions . . . merit is inseparable from the structure of the profession" (167).

At one time, most members of the profession believed that its hierarchy did embody correct judgments of scholarly merit, and they agreed on the criteria for good scholarship. The disintegration of relative consensus in the 1970s made practitioners view judgments of professional status and merit as arbitrary and capricious and seek to remove signs of authorial identity, including personality, from the review process. It is ironic—but also significant—that this change occurred precisely as the personality of the contributor was becoming more important to the contribution. As a result, author-anonymous review diminished *PMLA's* influence. Once the dominant forum for publication in the discipline, *PMLA* lost its standing to new theory journals, such as *Critical Inquiry*, that could use the star system to their advantage.[18]

Fish's argument against blind submissions depends on his assumption of an identity between professional status and professional merit. But no one really accepts such an identity. We all agree that some people are not as interesting or important or as much worth listening to as their positions suggest they should be, and we all know of others who we believe are unfairly neglected. Fish correctly points out, however, that a speaker's or writer's authority is never a matter of the content of his or her words alone. Indeed, in my view, the star system is not to be condemned because it authorizes judgments on the basis of extraneous considerations of personality and status. All systems that authorize knowledge entail such considerations. It follows that the quality or value of an individual's work should not be impugned because it has been authorized by the star system. All those who become academic stars have achieved professional success and recognition through accepted disciplinary procedures, such as peer review. In this essay I have specifically refrained from mentioning any star whose work I do not find valuable. Although under any system of authority some individuals will seem not to have earned their positions, I do not believe that the star system has produced a disproportionate number of such individuals.

The problem is not that the star system mistakes celebrity for value but that it confuses the two. Many fear that their idols are merely well known but cannot easily dismiss the value and authority that reside in them. When combined with the disparity of rewards, this confusion breeds resentment not just of the stars but also of the profession that makes them. Moreover, the star system reflects a shift in symbolic capital from the collective judgment of the discipline to individuals, a shift that further diminishes the discipline as a source of identification, breaking it down into incommensurable camps. There are not many Judith Butlerites, for example, who are devoted to Stanley Fish, nor are there many Foucauldians who follow Derrida. Ironically, the individualism of the star system is at odds with the theories many stars propound, theories promoting a knowledge grounded in communal interests. Marxism, feminism, queer theory, and the various ethnic-studies projects have all attempted to build knowledge collectively. The star system has been and will continue to be an obstacle to such collectivity. The star system depends on fans, an impoverished community focused on individuals who are not part of the community. It would be better for literary scholars, teachers, and students to stop being fans and to recognize that they can authorize knowledge without the name of a father or mother.

Such a change might make the discipline of literary studies more effective as a professional enterprise. Professions are not self-enclosed systems but, rather, groups that contend for control of work within society (Abbott 2). Thus professionals must be concerned with demonstrating to the public their competence to perform the work they control. Disciplinary consensus is a source of internal confidence and external legitimacy for the science disciplines that define knowledge in the culture at large. Literary academics have not been terribly effective of late in demonstrating such competence. Indeed, literary academics have lost whatever partial control they had over literary journalism during the 1950s and 1960s, perhaps because disciplinarity requires that practitioners write for one another rather than for the public at large. But by locating authority in disciplinary stars, the star system has reduced the legitimacy of the discipline's discourse in the culture at large. The star system has given literary academics greater public visibility, but this celebrity has not made the knowledge that the stars produce any more widely known or given that knowledge greater public authority. On the contrary, to the public academic stars are curiosities rather than intellectual leaders.[19] We in literary studies can only begin to regain public confidence in the knowledge we produce if we are willing to claim an authority for our work wider than that vested in the stars.

Coda

The unstated difficulty with the suggestion that professional authority be conceived differently is that it would require not merely a shift in professional practice, but a theoretical shift as well. If I am right that the star system arose out of a particular constellation of sociological and intellectual forces, it is likely to remain in place until different conditions develop. But even if members of the profession can make successful efforts to change practices, there remains a genuine theoretical conundrum that cannot simply be wished away. The problem has to do with epistemology, but it is unlikely to be solved in that discourse. The profession has vested so much authority in stars because other sources of authority have been eroded. Critics of poststructuralism and other contemporary theory often write as if the relativism that seems to follow from these positions was an easily correctable mistake. I am not convinced that relativism does follow logically from such theory, but I think it is fair to say that literary studies today often betrays a sort of commonsense relativism. This state of affairs came about less as a result of any theory's claims than of experience of several decades of academic literary interpretation. That experience showed that a consensus about the meaning of a literary work could not be produced. Theory arose first as a means of producing consensuses, but triumphed not only by producing an even a broader range of disparate readings but also by explaining and justifying the failure to achieve consensus. Theory, however, has not done a very successful job of explaining the value of multiple interpretations to those outside of the field. Moreover, when such explanations are attempted, they often end up making it seem as if that consensus were equally impossible to reach on other intellectual questions as well. In other words, literary theorists sound exactly like the relativists they are alleged to be.

When literary scholars practice in their specialties, however, they do not behave like relativists. They argue that their interpretations or theories are better or truer than rivals. They usually do not claim to be presenting the only valid reading of a text, but they present their own as having a compelling claim to which the profession ought to attend. This does not make these scholars hypocrites, but it does reveal the weakness of epistemologies that establish narrow and inflexible standards for what counts as knowledge. The solution to the problem is to recognize that knowledge comes in a variety of forms, some of which involve the possibility of a high degree of consensus and some which function without it. Literary studies needs to be able to show that a range of interpretations of texts are valuable, while at the same time acknowledging that a range of positions about the truth of, say, evolution is unjustifiable. Literary studies cannot abandon the insight about texts that its history has produced, but neither can it proceed as if everything were merely a text. To delegitimate the star system, literary studies must be willing to locate the value of knowledge to some extent in its adequacy of representation or truth. Such a move would not eliminate personal authority, but it would provide an alternative, a means by which the powerful personality could be called to account.

Notes

I want to thank Brian McHale for inviting me to give the first version of this essay as a lecture at West Virginia University, Morgantown. I am grateful to the faculty members and graduate students in the English department at that institution and to Michael Bérubé, Peter Brunette, David Damrosch, Joel Foreman, Linda Kauffman, David Kaufmann, Dana Polan, and Jeffrey Williams for their important questions, suggestions, and comments.

1. Print references, such as Jeffrey Williams's mention of "academostars" (1281), remain scarce.

2. See Dyer for complex readings of these personalities in their historical and filmic contexts.

3. I develop this point with respect to rock stars in "Rock and Roll as a Cultural Practice."

4. There have always been a few scholars who also function as intellectuals and achieve fame as a result. At the moment Edward Said and Cornel West seem

to fit that mold; they therefore differ from the properly academic stars with which this essay is concerned.

5. Academics like Camille Paglia who have become talk-show celebrities are exceptions. But in my view Paglia is not an academic star, partly because her TV appearances reduce her capital within the academy but mainly because her work is not highly regarded.

6. Of course literary theorists are at best very minor celebrities compared with movie, television, sports, or rock stars.

7. Tansey has done other paintings that comment on the star status of artists and critics. In *The Triumph of the New York School*, André Breton, of the school of Paris, is depicted in a military surrender to Clement Greenberg, while various artists of both camps look on. The painting's allusion to Velázquez's *The Surrender of Breda* would likely be familiar only to art critics and art historians.

8. Thus Jonathan Culler's argument that after World War II teachers came to think of themselves as researchers is somewhat misleading (28).

9. James Sosnoski attributes this problem to a "Magister Implicatus," a personification of critical orthodoxy (73). This may be an accurate representation of some earlier state of the field, but at the moment we have stars who demand notice rather than masters who require obedience.

10. On symbolic capital, see Bourdieu.

11. For evidence that this practice represents a change in literary studies, see Conarroe's January 1980 Editor's Column.

12. What is in play in Merton's discussion of the reward structure of science is only recognition for contributions. The contributions themselves are not defined or authorized by the status or personality of the scientist.

13. For a powerful illustration, see Derrida and Bennington, which contains snapshots from Derrida's family album. It is unclear whether Bennington's role is that of fan, disciple, or both.

14. Fish gets star treatment in Begley, "Souped-Up Scholar."

15. One might also cite biographies that dwell on material that would previously have been dismissed as gossip (see, for instance, Miller's *The Passion of Michel Foucault*).

16. Not all stars overtly construct a personality in their theoretical writings. Fredric Jameson, for example, who works in a Marxist tradition that views individualism with suspicion, offers not a hint of personal revelation in a body of criticism that nevertheless has an unmistakable voice.

17. Whether autobiography functions as intended in Women's Studies and other fields is questionable. For a critique, see Kauffman.

18. The institution of author-anonymous review followed a change in editorial policy (adopted in 1973) that required articles to be "of significant interest to the entire membership" (Schaefer, Editor's Column [1975] 3). By the late 1970s William Schaefer recognized that this policy had not produced the desired results; in a 1978 Editor's Column he more or less admitted that PMLA had not generated great interest in the profession. The next editor, Joel Conarroe,

announced in a 1979 Editor's Column that the editorial policy was in need of revision, but it was not formally changed at that time. The author-anonymous review policy was adopted in 1978, and a revised statement of editorial policy was first published in October 1979 (Statement).

19. The anti-intellectualism of American culture contributes to this problem.

Works Cited

Abbott, Andrew. *The System of Professions: An Essay on the Division of Expert Labor*. Chicago: U of Chicago P, 1989.

Allen, Woody. *Play It Again, Sam*. Dir. Herbert Ross. Paramount, 1972.

Atlas, James. "On Campus: The Battle of the Books." *New York Times Magazine* 5 June 1988: 24+.

Begley, Adam. "Black Studies' New Star." *New York Times Magazine* 1 Apr. 1990: 24+.

———. "The I's Have It: Duke's 'Moi' Critics Expose Themselves." *Lingua Franca* Mar.-Apr. 1994: 54–59.

———. "Souped-Up Scholar." *New York Times Magazine* 3 May 1992: 38+.

Bourdieu, Pierre. *Outline of a Theory of Practice*. Trans. Richard Nice. Cambridge: Cambridge UP, 1977.

Brown, Denise Scott. "Room at the Top? Sexism and the Star System in Architecture." *Architecture: A Place for Women*. Ed. Ellen Perry Berkeley. Washington: Smithsonian Inst. P, 1989. 237–45.

Bruster, Douglas. Letter. *PMLA* 112 (1997): 438–39.

Campbell, Colin. "The Tyranny of the Yale Critics." *New York Times Magazine* 9 Feb. 1986: 20+.

Conarroe, Joel. Editor's Column. *PMLA* 94 (1979): 3–4.

———. Editor's Column. *PMLA* 95 (1980): 3–4.

Culler, Jonathan. *Framing the Sign: Criticism and Its Institutions*. Norman: U of Oklahoma P, 1988.

Danto, Arthur. *Mark Tansey: Visions and Revisions*. New York: Abrams, 1992.

deCordova, Richard. *Picture Personalities: The Emergence of the Star System in America*. Urbana: U of Illinois P, 1990.

Derrida, Jacques, and Geoffrey Bennington. *Jacques Derrida*. Trans. Bennington. Chicago: U of Chicago P, 1993.

Dyer, Richard. *Heavenly Bodies*. London: British Film Institute, 1987.

———. *Stars*. London: British Film Institute, 1979.

Ellis, John. *Visible Fictions*. London: Routledge, 1982.

Fish, Stanley. Interview. *Thinking in the Twentieth Century*. Prod. Joel Foreman. Maryland Public Television, 1985.

———. *Is There a Text in This Class ? The Authority of Interpretive Communities*. Cambridge: Harvard UP, 1980.

———. "No Bias, No Merit: The Case against Blind Submission." *Doing What Comes Naturally: Change, Rhetoric, and the Practice of Theory in Literary and Legal Studies*. Durham: Duke UP, 1989. 163–79.

Foucault, Michel. "What Is an Author?" *Language, Counter-Memory, Practice: Selected Essays and Interviews*. Trans. Donald F. Bouchard and Sherry Simon. Ed. Donald F. Bouchard. Ithaca: Cornell UP, 1977. 113–38.

Gamson, Joshua. *Claims to Fame: Celebrity in Contemporary America*. Berkeley: U of California P, 1994.

Gilbert, Sandra, and Susan Gubar. "The Man on the Dump versus United Dames of America; or, What Does Frank Lentricchia Want?" *Critical Inquiry* 14 (1988): 386–406.

Jencks, Christopher, and David Reisman. *The Academic Revolution*. Garden City: Doubleday, 1968.

Kauffman, Linda. "The Long Goodbye: Against Personal Testimony; or, An Infant Grifter Grows Up." *Changing Subjects: The Making of Feminist Literary Criticism*. Ed. Gayle Greene and Coppélia Kahn. London: Routledge, 1993. 129–45.

Lentricchia, Frank. "Andiamo!" *Critical Inquiry* 14 (1988): 407–13.

———. *The Edge of Night: A Confession.* New York: Random House, 1994.

Lodge, David. *Small World.* New York: Macmillan, 1984.

Merton, Robert K. *The Sociology of Science: Theoretical and Empirical Investigations.* Chicago: U of Chicago P, 1973.

Miller, James. *The Passion of Michel Foucault.* New York: Simon & Schuster, 1993.

Schaefer, William D. Editor's Column. *PMLA* 90 (1975): 3–4.

———. Editor's Column. *PMLA* 93 (1978): 859–60.

Sherman, Stuart. "Professor Kittredge and the Teaching of English." *Nation* 11 Sept. 1913: 227–31.

Shumway, David. *Creating American Civilization: A Genealogy of American Literature as an Academic Discipline.* Minneapolis: U of Minnesota P, 1994.

———. "Rock and Roll as a Cultural Practice." *Present Tense: Rock and Roll and Culture.* Ed. Anthony DeCurtis. Durham: Duke UP, 1992. 117–33.

Sosnoski, James J. *Token Professionals and Master Critics: A Critique of Orthodoxy in Literary Studies.* Albany: State U of New York P, 1994.

Stacey, Jackie. *Star Gazing: Hollywood Cinema and Female Spectatorship.* London: Routledge, 1994.

Statement of Editorial Policy. *PMLA* 94 (1979): 875.

Tompkins, Jane. "Me and My Shadow." *Gender and Theory: Dialogues on Feminist Criticism.* Ed. Linda Kauffman. Oxford: Blackwell, 1989. 121–39.

Torgovnick, Marianna De Marco. *Crossing Ocean Parkway: Readings by an Italian American Daughter.* Chicago: U of Chicago P, 1994.

Williams, Jeffrey. Letter. *PMLA* 107 (1992): 1280–81.

Chapter Ten

The Life of the Mind and the Academic Situation

Jeffrey J. Williams

I

To be called an "academic" isn't usually a compliment. Ranging somewhere between an attribution of pedantry and an outright insult, it frequently takes a pejorative connotation. This is not entirely without warrant, for there is a way in which the academic location of many contemporary intellectuals—and the conditions and protocols of that location, such as tenure, committee work, field strictures, research requirements, and grant procedures, as well as and probably more deeply, the affects and ideological purview intertwined with those conditions—function effectively to absorb them into the circulation of academiana. This prospect for academic-intellectual life accords with the model of the traditional scholar, for the most part self-contained in his or her scholarly pursuits, and has migrated into everyday mythology, represented by stereotypes of the ivory tower variety (the patched-tweed-wearing, pipe-smoking, absentminded professor), and underwritten by the assumption that academics worry about things that no one in the real world would, like metaphysics or comma splices, and transact their business in a sheltered zone without much connection to normal events of the world.

While this image has a long history, presumably originating in the clerical model of the medieval university, there is now extant a revamped image of the academic-intellectual, as one who consults for business, develops profitable new products, jockeys fat grants, runs rich centers, or shows up on TV to lend expert commentary. This ties into what is sometimes called "the cult of expertise," whereby academic-intellectuals assume a kind of entrepeneurial or technocratic consultant position, facilitating the activities that they comment on, whether in business, agriculture, bomb-making, law, or policy.[1] This projects a new stereotype of professorial life, of the well-coiffed and expensive-suited academic who appears on *Geraldo* or *CNN*, or who jetsets from conference to capital cities, lunching with staffers from congressional committees or multinationals, periodically touching down at the university to check mail or give a lecture, buffered by a phalanx of graduate assistants and secretaries.[2]

Both of these characterizations illustrate distinct versions of professionalism: the first I would call an *insular* or *parochial professionalism*, whereby academic-intellectuals seek to propagate work within the confines of their particular "fields," tending the gardens of their "specializations." Their work is circumscribed by the social sphere of the university not only in terms of the audience for whom they publish but in terms of protecting and lobbying for their interests, to maintain their particular divots of turf within their respective departments and schools as well as disciplines. Thus a significant part of their work might also encompass sitting on committees that decide course offerings or personnel decisions, writing memos within their departments, voting in faculty meetings, chatting at the departmental coffeepot, and the like. The second I would cast as a *consultant* or *corporate professionalism*, whereby academic-intellectuals serve in the corridors of industry, finance, media, and government, not as independent scholars but as accredited experts, advising on policies, strategies, and product development. Their work might include, for sociologists, taking surveys for an upcoming election and counseling which districts to target, or for those in economics, advising on the effects of long-term fiscal policies, or for those in chemistry, running an experiment for a pharmaceutical company, or for those in biology, testing out the effects on mice of a product from a cosmetic company, and so on.[3]

On the one hand, this latter version of professionalism supposes a more obviously worldly component and would probably set itself, pragmatically if not glamorously, in opposition to the cloisteredness of an insular academicism. On the other hand, the first version of professionalism frequently carries with it a nascent snobbism, that one is concerned with more purely intellectual matters, the state of knowledge, and the vitality of one's discipline, without dirtying oneself with unsavory things like business or government. Thus, against a consultant professionalism, it claims more intellectual integrity. While this is not a hard-and-fast dichotomy, the first version of professionalism largely typifies activity in humanities departments, which do not usually have direct uses in business or government and rarely garner significant sums of external grant money (but are not beholdened to it), and the second applies more to hard social science and practical science departments. The growing number of "practical" courses, such as business and technical writing in many English departments, particularly at less elite universities, complicates this scheme, and part of the problem with the current reconfiguration of the university is that there is more pressure for the humanities to pay its own bills, bristling against its traditional self-conception.

These distinctions are obviously in very broad strokes, and there is frequently a wide disparity between the image of professionalism that we project to validate our work and the actual work that most of us do in universities. Many people at less than elite universities—the remaining 90 percent of us—rarely see a grant or do much jetsetting, and time is taken up with teaching four, five, or even six courses a term, grading piles of papers, holding office hours, doing "service" work, and so on—regardless of discipline.[4] This construction of professionalism is decidedly insular, although one might more caustically call it a *dickensian professionalism*, befitting the age of "speed-up" and downsizing. One can see this particularly in the distinction between professors and adjuncts or lecturers, who are in a nether zone, doing poorly paid piecework as professors-in-waiting, sustained by the chimerical promise of an eventual professional franchise. However, this marks an *effacement* of professionalism, constituting professorial work as a job rather than a vocation, more in keeping with what secondary school teachers are required to do. This is not to slight school teachers; rather, they are precisely *not* treated with the privilege, monetary and otherwise, accorded to the "higher professions," that are certified with advanced degrees and other markers of professional entry. The distinction is similar to that between doctors and nurses or nurse-practitioners, who work according to a time clock.[5]

I have sketched these two prevalent versions of professionalism not to take part in yet another jeremiad, casting the university location of intellectuals as irredeemably fallen, as Russell Jacoby does in *The Last Intellectuals*.[6] Nor do I say this to tap into a typical self-abasement of academic-intellectuals, the tendency toward self-loathing that Stanley Fish provocatively if not perversely depicts in "The Unbearable Ugliness of Volvos." Rather, I want to use them as a frame to investigate some of the specific factors that constitute academic-intellectual life, particularly for those of us in the humanities, and how we are made by our institutional location. We frequently declare our "positions"—as a Marxist, feminist, traditionalist, and so on—but there is an implacable way in which our institutional positions make us. As a test case, I will examine a recent autobiographical account of the days in the life of a humanities professor, James Phelan's *Beyond the Tenure Track*, which offers an inside look at life in the academic-intellectual world and its attendant model of professionalism. Lastly, I will try to stake out an alternative prospect of professionalism—what I call a *secular professionalism*—countervailing both the tropism toward insularity and the pull of accommodation. Insofar as the university offers a relatively autonomous zone, there can still be advantages to working in an ivory tower.

II

James Phelan's *Beyond the Tenure Track* is a telling document, most immediately because it presents a series of diary or journal entries exposing the day-to-day details of the life of an English professor. Less immediately but more significantly, it is also telling in its depiction of the rationale for doing intellectual work—for which Phelan invokes the traditional notion, "the life of the mind"—and its disciplinary determinants—what I will group under the rubric of tenure. Phelan records his activities, his interests and concerns, and his worries and goals for roughly 15 months, from January 1987 to March 1988, recounting the not-so-gritty and mostly pedestrian goings-on of his professorial life. His brief dated passages alternate, for the most part, among: telling about how his teaching is going and his dealings with graduate students; family matters like picking up his children at day care; how his research is progressing (a conference paper, finishing a book chapter); his relationship with mentors like Sheldon Sacks and Wayne Booth; how he and his wife manage to negotiate—successfully—a double academic career and a family; his residual jock impulses (as a runner and basketball player); and finally, his professional fix and ambitions (Will he get a book contract? Will he get a job offer for an endowed chair?).

On first sight, *Beyond the Tenure Track* seems to fit the recent, widespread trend of academic-intellectual autobiography or "personal criticism," as Nancy Miller labels it in *Getting Personal*. However, Phelan's book strikes me as more properly a diary or daybook rather than a formed or stylistically mannered autobiography, and in this regard it is something of a curiosity. It is evidently intended for a general audience to describe what exactly professors do—as one might to friends and family who do not know, as well as to others in the business. As Phelan puts it, it serves to "explain [. . .] my version of academic life to a hypothetical audience of the curious ('What's it like being an English professor?') and the noncomprehending ('So you only teach eight hours a week? Must be nice')," as well as to explain it to himself (ix). Although this gestures to the worthwhile goal of "public access" and to dispel myths about academic work, still the actual audience of *Beyond the Tenure Track* is hardly a mass market but a fairly esoteric one. Published by Ohio State University Press, it almost seems to fit the genre of a kind of local history, speaking to those within the professional circle, who would understand and be interested in what Phelan talks about. I take its value, then, as a quasi-ethnographic report of the days in the life of a professor, exposing the work habits and habitus, as well as the self-representation of and rationale for that habitus.[7]

In general, Phelan conceptually organizes what he does under the rubric of "the life of the mind." As he puts it, he is teaching his students "about the pleasures of a commitment to the life of the mind," which is predicated on "the process of mutual exchange, agreement, and disagreement," that is "great fun . . . when it goes well" (11). Specifically, the process revolves nearly exclusively around discussions of issues such as the "first principles" of critical articles on *Wuthering Heights* (10), character in Calvino, or voice in Hemingway. To locate him among critical camps, Phelan's definition of intellectual activity largely subscribes to latter-day Chicago school practices, drawn from Phelan's graduate training there, promoting the value of induction and uncovering first principles (the neo-Aristotelian angle, via Richard McKeon, R. S. Crane, Elder Olson), pluralism (from Crane and Phelan's mentors, Sacks and Booth), and dialogue (the more recent theoretical spin, via Booth and contemporaries like Don Bialostosky).[8] In other words, his version of the life of the mind carries out the line of humanistic pluralism, with a dialogic upgrade.

Phelan goes on later to elaborate: "The heart of this life is being an intellectual who is able to contribute something substantial to the work of other intellectuals and able to communicate to students that knowledge and some enthusiasm for the life of the mind" (168). There are a few things to note here. Phelan's succinct definition of professionalism is decidedly circular, closed off from any external public or from any political concerns, other than those of the professional circle. The life of the mind is a *spiritual* rationale, for individual edification, rather than a public one, basically following the Aristotelian justification of philosophical activity, which is valuable for its own self-contained good and pleasure. The dialogue Phelan talks about—contributing to the "critical conversation," as it is frequently put—is strictly intra-academic, occurring in the pages of *PMLA* (the journal he uses as a test-case for his students to decipher "first principles") or like journals, and passed on in a classroom. In that one passes on stories—"knowledge"—of literary texts in specific, generally formalist (plot, character, etc.) ways to others in the academic circle, this presents insularity by definition as a condition of appropriate and gratifying ("fun") professional engagement.

Astonishingly but consistent with his definition of the life of the mind, there is little mention of any larger politics outside the realm of Ohio State and its policies, despite the book's being a record of 15 months in late twentieth-century America. Other than one brief mention of graduate students writing letters to Congress for tax exempt status for stipends (181), Phelan does not consider, not to mention engage, any social concerns or political events of the day (for instance, how the question of taxing stipends ties to the regressive tax "reform" of the eighties, targeting low-income people and social programs, redistributing income upward). His work and life are narrowly circumscribed between home and university. Phelan appears to be a conscientious and thoughtful teacher and citizen of Ohio State, but his professional self-definition, however well-intentioned, is predicated on the omission of any consideration of larger social or political issues.

Further, in Phelan's view, one participates in intellectual work not only to contibute to the work of other like professionals, presumably in "the field," but to propagate apprentice scholars. How students function in this is as recruits or novitiates, to be brought into the intra-intellectual pool of the "conversation," with the promise or telos of self-generating pleasure ("great fun"). However, in a way that Phelan's model—and most models of liberal education—mask, students also bluntly form a labor pool. As Evan Watkins argues in *Work Time*, academic activity in "English" is about circulating students within the university (nearly every student takes comp) as well as "intellectual work," about evaluating and sorting them for the advanced labor pool. And within the profession, grad student "apprentices" constitute the labor pool that fairly directly enables higher faculty to have the leisure to do research. This division of labor has become ever more apparent in the current job crisis in the humanities. In other words, English education is not neutrally taken up in mindful topics, but those mindful pursuits serve to reproduce the very structure—ideologically as well as in material terms of employment—of the university and of white collar, techno-managerial culture that universities feed. Phelan's and the standard humanistic justification of innate pleasure ("fun") effaces this other function, and thus is bluntly ideological in its construction of and reliance on an imaginary projection of the actual ends of university work.[9]

This is not just a quibble, but has real consequences. Part of the reason why the current job crisis has been met with such mystification ("it was supposed to be better by 1990 . . . 1992 . . . 1995 . . . 1998") and inaction is this ideological gap, between the imaginary projection of motivation and goals in the humanities (fun, spiritual improvement) and the actual conditions of employment in universities. These conditions parallel the post-Fordist reconfiguration of life, that is, ruthless job retrenchment, downsizing, de-unionization, and so on, that affect all areas of work, from formerly secure corporations (that were once considered tenured sinecures, in their own ways), such as IBM or Sears, to what Douglas Coupland in *Generation X* calls McJobs. In their job ads, McDonalds also declares the "fun" of working there.

Strikingly, Phelan's definition of the life of the mind occurs after he tells a disturbing story of an old friend he met at a conference who was denied tenure at an Ivy. She lands another job, but "feels burned by the whole experience" (168). Academic tenure stories like this ring all too true, and Phelan expresses what seems appropriate outrage: "Stories like that make me sick" (168). For him, such dealings do not live up to the ethos of the life of the mind. However, this gets at precisely the problem: that life occludes issues like the job structure in universities and whom they serve, as belonging to an external zone, outside the closed circuit of stimulating class discussion and academic articles. It is not that the values Phelan talks about—discussion, uncovering first principles—are unimportant, but their practice is inseparable from and circulated within an institutional economy. The idealized category of the "life of the mind" delimits an insulated zone without recourse to dealing with the material problems that embed it.

Phelan's observation of the problems of tenure and other academic predicaments—most obviously, those of his graduate students—does not push an opening in this sealed zone, so that he can extend his trenchant first reaction ("sick") and his ethical discomfort to the place where it most immediately bears and might effect change: the labor politics of the university. Phelan's only recourse, instead of social critique or political action, is *pathos* (his feelings of outrage and sympathy). The resort to pathos is not unique, especially in response to the job prospects of the present generation of humanities scholars. For instance, past-MLA president Patricia Meyer Spacks, in a column in the *MLA Newsletter*, calls attention to the horrific job market for most fledgling professors in English and modern languages. However, this observation prompts worry (Spacks repeatedly remarks how worried she is), rather than concrete proposals for change or new policies. While such feelings may spur effectual change, the mere expression of "support" frequently substitutes for it, as a well-intentioned placebo.

There are a few other uncomfortable moments in *Beyond the Tenure Track* about jobs, one in which Phelan tells about a friend from graduate school who has committed suicide after not getting tenure (70–72), and one when he tells about visiting a small college in Texas to give a paper. In the latter he mentions, after finding out about the severe conditions under which the people there work (five courses a term, etc.), that he feels as if his job is a sinecure (69).[10] Phelan brings these instances up out of conscience, but again his response never leaves the realm of discomfort or translates into an extended diagnosis of the institutional factors that generate such conditions, nor proposals to remedy them, not to mention any larger consideration of the material relations of the postindustrial world that might cause them. Not only does his version of an insular professionalism not lend any effectual resistance to unfair job practices, but it finally amounts to a quietism that sustains those practices.[11]

III

I want to stress that my reading of Phelan here is not to single him out for reproach. He is not exceptional in subscribing to this version of professionalism; the "life of the mind" is, after all, a commonplace rationale for what we presumably do in universities, especially in the humanities. Phelan himself points to some of the ways in which the life of the mind goes wrong for his students and for his friends and colleagues; the problem lies not with him but with prevalent modes of institutional formation that embed all of us.

Alongside the ideal vista that the life of the mind presents, there is another significant layer in the process of professional formation that Phelan recounts: the pragmatic career imperatives, institutional rules, and social relations that I would summarize under the rubric of tenure. By this

I do not mean the simple contractual mechanism of job security—one that really is not as unique as it seems, which civil servants like police officers, state accountants, and so on, are granted after a short probationary period—but the social psychology of relations engendered by the processes of hiring, tenure, promotion, and academic "membership." The life of the mind projects an abstract professional purview, akin to the hippocratic oath in medicine, whereas this dimension projects more concrete consequences and might be more aptly characterized as disciplinary. It is enacted through disciplinary structures of evaluation of the academy, akin to board qualifiers, certification, and licensing in medicine. These structures, however, are not external and temporary, but generate a certain mind-set or what Pierre Bourdieu calls a "system of dispositions." While the life of the mind holds out the ideological carrot at the end of the proverbial stick, hiring, tenure, and promotion take the part of blinders and harness.

Although Phelan titles his book to indicate a kind of transcendence of the tenure issue ("beyond"), his account is permeated with talk about tenure and career, whether it be stories of his graduate school friend who committed suicide after being rejected for tenure and or the woman denied Ivy tenure; a description of a faculty meeting at Ohio State in which three junior faculty members are denied rehiring (their work was not good enough, according to Phelan [85–90], though one then wonders why they were hired); another of people in his department voting on promotions to full professor (three people are voted to full professor, two not [157–160]); and, for him, a reminiscence of his own tenuring (89), the question of the stepladder up to full professor (167–170, 204), and most prominently, his being courted for an endowed chair at Trinity College in Hartford, Connecticut (170 passim). In fact, this job prospect causes Phelan to extend his record beyond the discrete unit of a year that he had initially planned, to include his visit to Trinity and the unfolding of that job search. In narrative terms, this effects a generic shift in the book: rather than a simple chronicle of the incidents of "a year in the life," it becomes very visibly a *narrative of career*, the Trinity job providing a telos toward which the action inevitably moves ("some events *demanded* to be followed" is Phelan's coy way of putting it in the preface [my italics; x]).

Phelan himself neatly summarizes the markers of career—the processes of tenure and promotion—as "the academic ladder." As he puts it:

> The [severe] reactions of both friends [denied promotion to full professor] reveal a lot about the whole academic ladder that they—

> and I—are trying to climb. The ladder has only a few rungs—grad student, assistant professor, associate professor, full professor, and (sometimes) chaired professor—and it gets narrower as it goes up. Once you've reached the third rung, you can stop climbing and just stay on the ladder. *But by then you're used to the climb and you think about your life at least partly in terms of it.* So making that fourth rung typically takes on a significance comparable to the first three. (my italics; 159)

Phelan is disarmingly self-conscious about this, saying "I think that there's something not quite right here," but still he goes on to confess, "And yes, I want to be promoted." This seems a perfectly understandable aim and ambition, but the point I want to underscore here is that the "tenure track" is not a simple apprentice hurdle, an initiatory step that then grants an independent purchase of academic freedom, as one might expect and as it is usually advertised. Rather, it is an ongoing process in which Phelan and his colleagues are absorbed and which structures their aspirations, habits, activities, hopes, desires, disappointments, and social relations. As Phelan frankly observes, it determines his life. And it is inculcated by institutional channels, protocols, and codes.

Tenure is not an external signpost peripheral to the life of the mind, but fully internalized, governing the behavior of those engaged in the academic field and permeating that life. Even after crossing its presumably momentous threshold, it overwrites Phelan's thinking about his junior colleagues (whether they deserve tenure or not), his senior colleagues' and his own ambitions (to be promoted), and his work relations. In this way, the concatenation of practices gathered under the rubric of tenure function as the habitus of the academic-intellectual, as Pierre Bourdieu defines it—that is, the "system of dispositions common to all products of the same conditionings" ("Structure" 59). For my purposes here, "habitus" offers a way to characterize the institutional practices and conditions that actualize ideology. Ideology is not simply an ideal prospect or set of beliefs, but realized through institutions, which inculcate certain behaviors. As Bourdieu argues, the habitus sustains institutions by incorporating individuals into their set of practices ("the *habitus* is what enables the institution to attain full realization . . . through the capacity for incorporation" [57]), by regulating those practices, but also by permitting a certain degree of improvisation (what Bourdieu calls the "generative principle of regulated improvisations" [57]), thus making the institution durable.[12]

How this translates to academia, particularly in the humanities, is that qualifiers, examinations, obviously the dissertation, and the more vague but nonetheless tangible construction of professional decorum (in social gatherings as well as in courses and seminars) incorporate graduate students into the practices of the academic institution, normalizing and disciplining their behavior. In this sense, "professional discourse" and "the current conversation" serve a disciplinary function as well as being for the sake of pleasure or knowledge, providing the path through which students are incorporated into the languages and conceptual mannerisms of established behavior. For faculty, the ritualistic thresholds of hiring, tenure, and promotion, less momentous but still crucial formal measures such as yearly reviews and teaching evaluations, informal job conditions such as who gets a good teaching schedule or a window office, and various kinds of everyday interchange, from seating at faculty meetings to comments at the mailbox, all contribute to this process of regulation, reinforcing the trappings of rank and disciplinary order.

I would emphasize the cluster of affects circulating around tenure—fear and anxiety as well as desire and hope for the untenured, often envy and resentment for those in the middle of the tenure track, and sometimes high-handedness and snobbism for those on top. Tenure is effective because of the affects it inculcates, which discipline presumably independent intellectual wills, desires, and ideas. (Even if senior colleagues are generous and solicitous, that recognizes the assumed coercive effects of tenure.) In short, despite the salutary aim of protecting freedom or simply granting job security, tenure in this sense enforces a regimen of complicity and conformism.[13] You can see how its incorporation works on Phelan: rather than being beyond the tenure track, he is fully enmeshed in it, concerned with his job, the possibility of promotion, committee meetings, the Faculty Senate, and not much else.

The coercive "disposition" of tenure feeds off, for the most part, the distinctively middle-class anxiety of professionals, the kind that Barbara Ehrenreich details in *Fear of Falling: The Inner Life of the Middle Class*. As Ehrenreich argues, the professional middle class attains its class position via education rather than capital—or, in terms closer to Bourdieu, its cultural capital distinguishes it from and enables it to rise above the working class. Professors, particularly in the era of increased access to university education post-World War II and given the contemporary advent and growth of state universities, are archetypical members of this newly arrived professional middle class. And, as Ehrenreich argues, the middle class has historically been motivated by fear and dread of losing its tenuous and newly gained class position. The tenure process banks on precisely this fear, holding out the image of falling as a constitutive condition of employment.

Further, the habitus designated by tenure is not a static and rigid structure, but a flexible mode of regulation that changes over time and from institution to institution, making it all the more durable. For instance, it is a commonplace that it now takes more publications to get hired than it did 20 years ago to get tenured, creating strange disparities between older and younger faculty members and their levels of professional accomplishment and savviness.[14] And while tenure seems to be transinstitutional and thus predicated on a universal principle of fairness and unbiased value, its actual operation is variable if not arbitrary, pragmatically determined within its specific institutional locale, case by case. For instance, the rule of thumb in the regional state university where I used to teach was five or six articles, whereas the flagship state university where I now teach is one book, and rumor has it that it takes not one but two books to get tenure at Ohio State and God's intercession to get tenure at Harvard or Yale. (This, of course, is the formal research requirement, and does not include other less concrete criteria, such as "quality," not to mention "collegiality.") In Bourdieu's terms, the regulating mechanism of tenure ensures the reproduction of extant socio-institutional arrangements and hierarchies by its continual adjustment and revision.[15]

At some points, Phelan recognizes these institutional dimensions, and at one point he rebukes career concerns—salary and prestige—that take away from ("infect" is his term) purer "intellectual activities," the pleasures of teaching and writing (214–15). However, this resorts to a kind of clerical model, eschewing the dirt of worldly concerns essentially as vanity, at the same time that Phelan's narrative posits the necessity and inevitability of those concerns.[16] This parallels the ideological swerve of the life of the mind: precisely when the question of the larger world ("the larger context of our capitalist culture," as he puts it) presses on Phelan's construction of intellectuality, he withdraws to the insularity of "pure" "intellectual activities." The problem of tenure and career becomes one of personal attitude and individual performance, inciting soul-searching ("I need to look at the way I've been infected" [215]), instead of pointing to any social or political frame, not to mention course of action. Soul-searching might be a start toward change, but here turns inwards, toward spiritual well-being and self-performance.

Self-cultivation is of course a traditional justification of the humanities and in general of the university. It might represent a human good, but the problem with it is that it usually implies an individualistic rather than a collective notion of intellectual life. In general, the overriding ideological force of "the life of the mind" and of tenure is individualistic, the life of the mind cultivating one individual for his or her own benefit and edification, and tenure a process that one goes through alone, literally a contractual relation of an individual rather than a group. It need not be this way: for civil service workers, as for most unionists, it is after all a collective contract. In individualistic terms, what to do about careerism becomes a moral problem—an "infection"—instead of a social problem. The institution, in this line of thinking, becomes an amoral mechanical structure, rather than a mode of organization that people make and use.

IV

Again, this is not to reproach Phelan, but to decipher the operation and effects of insular professionalism which disempowers him from staking out a better intellectual life for himself and those around him. That's the power of ideology: not that we have imaginary beliefs and are mystified (who among us can claim an entirely demystified purchase on the world?), but that those beliefs, tacit or explicit, work precisely against our common concerns and interests in actual practice.

One possible conclusion from my somewhat bleak analysis is that the academic-intellectual situation is irremediable and an inevitable result of professionalization. It is not hard to see why professionalism often carries a negative charge and seems at best a necessary evil, that interferes with and constrains intellectual activity (the red-tape, bureaucratic sense of institution), or warps intellectuals into a narrow academicism, or serves as a kind of careerist devil's bargain, prompting intellectuals to sell out—for prestige, power, money, or simply a secure middle-class life. Edward Said takes it this way in his succinct overview, *Representations of the Intellectual*, where he finds professionalism to be the cardinal sin of contemporary intellectuals: "The particular threat to the intellectual today, whether in the West or the non-Western world, is not the academy [the institutional structure per se], nor the suburbs [as Jacoby claims], nor the appalling commercialism of journalism and publishing houses, but rather an attitude I will call professionalism" (73–74).

While I do not think the choices are quite so simple—current pressures on intellectual life are part of the gamut of relations of the "knowledge industry" and its function in the social, cultural, and economic spheres, as well as a specific ideology of professionalism—Said articulates four ways in which professionalism debilitates intellectuals: (1) specialization, which shuts out any historical or political sense and fosters narrowly following the dictates of those in your "field" (77); (2) the cult of the certified expert, which rules out dissent by disallowing those not authorized by the professional field, or those not speaking the correct professional language, from intervening critically in debate, say, on policy (77, 80); (3) a drift toward governmental power and perogatives, shunting free inquiry (80); and (4) "research . . . programs that further commercial as well as political agendas" (81)—in other words, selling out to corporations as well as government.

To recall the general distinctions with which I started, Said's first caveat—specialization—roughly adheres to the parameters of an insular professionalism, and the remaining three—serving government or corporate interests, underpinned by the ascription of expertise—comprise what might be considered a consultant professionalism.[17] In contrast to Said, I would maintain a twofold dichotomy, because I think that it represents opposite poles of the same continuum, basically the closing in of a clerical model and the selling out of an anticlerical model. While Said here places most weight on the dangers of consultant professionalism, I would argue that the insular is actually the majority mode of the university, both in its traditional ideological bearing—the pursuit of knowledge in one's discipline, leading the life of the mind, the monkish model of attending to higher concerns set against the trappings of the world—and in the prospects that are available to most academics, particularly those 90 percent of us at less elite universities. The consultant model that Said indicts applies for the most part to those at elite institutions like Harvard, Columbia, Yale, MIT, Stanford, as well as some flagship state universities, which draw huge external funds, and from which leading professors might shuttle between teaching and jobs, say, in the State Department or the Federal Reserve. Bluntly, you do not usually hear of someone from Southwest Missouri State College being called to serve as assistant secretary of education or as a consultant for NBC News.[18] Thus the distinction between an insular and consultant professionalism might be further inflected by one's place in the academic hierarchy, consultant professionalism an elite model unavailable to many of us, and insular professionalism a more common model, especially in the humanities.

Said's solution is to reassert the category of amateurism to counter the corruptions of professionalism and to stake out a domain exempt from career pressures and the lure of power and money. Amateurism allows for an autonomous and disinterested position from which an intellectual can speak against injustice and the abuses of power—in Said's famous motto, "speaking truth to power." However, though this counterrepresentation promises what appears an attractive solution, I would argue that it presupposes a troubled and unrealistic set of relations. While projecting a position of disinterest beyond financial pressure—which is what tenure ideally does—the notion of the amateur taps into a suspect representational network, recasting the intellectual as a gentleman hobbyist if not dilettante. Whatever the flaws of the university, this model evacuates the worth of scholarly academic work and any belief in the authority attained through such work, which presumably grounds one in speaking out. Further, it assumes a system of patronage or the luxury of inherited wealth that grants the leisure to pursue intellectual activities. One would have thought this is more rather than less disinterested than the flawed but relatively democratic system of support of the university.

Perhaps most tellingly, the attribution of amateur status is patently inaccurate when applied to engaged intellectuals like Noam Chomsky or Said himself, who can make public statements and have access to large-scale media partly because of their prominent professional positions, and who draw a certain public authority from their estimable professional reputations. Indeed, it is precisely Said's professional position (as the author of widely influential critical books, and as an eminent, endowed professor at Columbia, in some ways the heir to Lionel Trilling as New York's great, urbane man of letters) that grants him access to speak out (on *Nightline* or in the *New York Times*) about Palestine and other political issues, that otherwise would not be available to him as an unaffiliated "amateur" at large—particularly not as a Palestinian. My point is not that professionalism therefore represents a salvational role, but that neither amateurism nor professionalism present a position outside the extant systems of power and authority; the choice, rather, is which presents a more viable position for disinterested intellectual work. And contrary to Said's argument for amateurism, I believe—partly on the evidence of Said's own career—that there is a lot more to be lost than gained in evacuating the prospect of professionalism for amateurism.

I would reconstitute the concept of professionalism more neutrally as a description of where we are situated, akin to other words like *institutionalization*, which might have debilitating effects but also grant certain pragmatic possibilities. As Bruce Robbins puts it in a slightly different context, "What we make of this possibility will depend on the extent to which, learning to pronounce the word institutionalization [or, for my purposes, professionalism] without the usual sinister innuendo, we distinguish particular institutional alternatives from each other rather than condemning (or praising) them all together" ("History" 768). The choice, then, is not between professionalism and antiprofessionalism, but between different versions of professionalism, and different ways to act within institutions.[19]

Against the tropisms toward insularity or selling out, I would stake out an alternative model of professionalism. From the former, I would take the notion of disinterested scholarship, but disavow its tendency toward narrowness, extending it to encompass research beyond field boundaries and bringing into the conversation considerations of the role of the university and labor there, as well as other relations to society. From the latter, I would take the prospect of engagement with "real world" concerns, but maintain a certain vigilance toward and autonomy from the influence of authoritarian, corporate, or other motives in research. Borrowing from Said's impassioned argument for an engaged, historically conscious and politically responsible criticism in "Secular Criticism," I would call this version a *secular* or *worldly professionalism.*[20] Thus I would reclaim the current professional position of academic-intellectuals—within the university—as one that enables our taking up precisely the kind of secular criticism that Said advocates. For whatever the dangers, problems, and irritations, there are still considerable advantages, as Noam Chomsky points out in his classic "The Responsibility of Intellectuals":

> In the Western world at least, they [intellectuals] have the power that comes from political liberty, from access to information and freedom of expression. For a privileged minority, Western democracy provides the leisure, the facilities, and the training to seek the truth lying hidden behind the veil of distortion and misrepresentation, ideology, and class interest through which the events of current history are represented to us. The responsibilities of intellectuals, then, are much deeper than what [Dwight] Macdonald calls the 'responsibility of peoples,' given the unique privileges that intellectuals enjoy. (60)

That site of leisure and training occurs largely within the university—moreso than, say, the estate of journalism and public media—and under the auspices of its professional purview. As Chomsky underscores, there are distinct advantages to its essentially cloistered position, permitting a degree of freedom of inquiry and criticism, access to information beyond propaganda or press releases, training to cull through that information, and stable economic support. In other words, the university, in its best prospect, fosters precisely the precondition of relative disinterest that Said finds in amateurism—and that can enable rather than cut off an engagement with social and political concerns. Professionalism, in this light, represents a term of negotiation with the public sphere, not its effacement.

I would stress this liminal opening that the university and professionalism present; the university is frequently deprecated as an ivory tower, but in reality comprises a significant contemporary public sphere, that is open to relatively large numbers of people, where one can address and debate issues that inform social and political policy and actions. As Henry Giroux points out, we are already in a public sphere by virtue of being in a classroom. Beyond the classroom, the university presents a significant public forum, as Edward Said reflects in an interview: "But there's no question that, in some ways, neither Chomsky nor myself would have had the audiences we've had without the university. A lot of the people who listen to us when we speak . . . are university students. The university provides one with a forum to do certain things" (145). Further, the professional base of the university garners a certain social legitimacy and position from which academic-intellectuals can cross over to larger media channels and other public venues, as oppositional intellectuals like Said, Chomsky, Cornel West, Patricia Williams, and many others have. This crossover, however, should not only be to make our professional discourse more publicly accessible, as Michael Bérubé advises, but also to open that discourse to public and worldly concerns.

Finally, I do not mean to recuperate the current professional situation and academic location of intellectuals, under the banner of secular professionalism, as flawless and unequivocally salutary. No doubt there is a deep ambivalence or tension in that location and purview, as Phelan's account attests and as the predominance of insular and consultant versions of professionalism make clear. However, a secular or worldly professionalism offers a channel of negotiation between the more narrowly defined activities of a university work location and larger world concerns. Rather than seeing professionalism as a danger, as Said does, or as a quarantine, as Phelan does, this alternative vista offers a kind of press pass to the public sphere and public policy—which in my view constitutes not only a choice but an obligation of intellectual life.

Notes

1. For instance, think of economists and current econometric exercises, which chart and validate present arrangements of wealth and labor and the way in which wealth and surplus value is circulated, rather than questioning or criticizing the blatantly inequitable material conditions and social relations that result from that circulation. Not to mention those who work on nuclear, chemical, and biological weapons.

2. For a relevant representation of such an image, see Jane Smiley's portrait of Dr. Lionel Gift in her satire of contemporary academic life, *Moo*, which is exceptional in its depiction not only of the vicissitudes of English professors—the standard plot fodder of academic novels—but the interrelation of student life, professors, research grants, administration, and state budget mandates.

3. The "corporatization" of the university is familiar by now; see, for some daunting examples, Lawrence Soley's exposé *Leasing the Ivory Tower*.

4. James Sosnoski illustrates how this disparity sorts out in literary studies in *Token Professionals and Master Critics*.

5. For the standard discussion of professionalism and the way in which professions such as medicine distinguish and sustain themselves, see M. S. Larson's *The Rise of Professionalism*. See also Brint's *In an Age of Experts* for the shifting role of professions from public service to expert rationales.

6. Jacoby sets up an elegaic narrative in which the New York Intellectuals represent the last of the truly public intellectuals, and he bemoans the contemporary relocation of intellectuals to the academy, finding current intellectual work to be overly specialized, without relevance to larger public concerns, and overly jargonized, without address to a more general audience. For Jacoby, the move to the universities parallels the death of the cities and the flight to the suburbs. While there might be some truth to Jacoby's characterization—I too question the insularity of academia—it is dubious in its representation of a fall from grace (the New York Intellectuals were not by any means a broadly popular movement, and in some ways they represent an earlier, albeit more urbane, academicism—think of Lionel Trilling), and in its representation of the present moment (many current academic intellectuals, such as Edward Said or Noam Chomsky, have decided public force, probably moreso than any of the New York Intellectuals). Ironically, neoconservative critics of the academy and of academic intellectuals, such as Roger Kimball in *Tenured Radicals*, see it precisely the opposite way: modern-day academic-intellectuals are *too* political and too much concerned with public issues, and should go back to the more quiet times of the fifties, presumably taking up appreciative analyses of literary masterpieces (in some ways, as Trilling did). For a relevant analysis, see Sarchett.

7. This admittedly takes some liberty with *Beyond the Tenure Track*. I appreciate James Phelan's thoughtful response, "The Life of the Mind, Politics, and Critical Argument: A Reply to Jeffrey Williams," as well as his tolerance of what must seem my rough handling of his personal exposure.

8. For a firsthand account of the Chicago School, see Wayne Booth's "Between Two Generations"; Booth inducts Phelan, among others, into its third generation (23). The Chicago School held a significant position in the rise of American formalism, which is now usually elided under the misapplied label, the New Criticism. For a useful history of the Chicago School and its views, see Leitch 60–80. On the question of dialogue, recall that Booth provided a pivotal letter of introduction for Bakhtin to the American scene; see his introduction to Bakhtin's *Problems of Dostoevsky's Poetics*. The concept of the dialogic in Bakhtin provided an apt fit with for Booth's version of pluralism, and it is no accident that Booth's students—like Don Bialostosky—have gone on to do significant work with Bakhtin. My specific point here, though, is that Phelan's concepts of dialogue, intellectual exchange, and the life of the mind derive from his Chicago school training.

9. The reference is obviously to Louis Althusser's definition of ideology as "represent[ing] the imaginary relationship of individuals to their real conditions of existence" (162). As Richard Ohmann notes in his still unsurpassed *English in America*, classes in composition, for instance, teach not just the humanistic virtues of "good writing," but proper comportment, how to do assignments on time, functional communication skills, and so on. The university thus functions as a weeding and preparatory device for entry into the (professional) middle class, a prospect that is usually swept aside in the traditional rationale of literature as inculcating aesthetic appreciation, or in the updated rationale of "critical thinking" or "expression."

10. In a relevant review, Terry Caesar comments on these uncomfortable moments when the academic hierarchy begs exposure. Caesar—not surprisingly from the author of "On Teaching at a Second-Rate University"—points out the unquestioned, elite professional expectations that Phelan has.

11. In his response, Phelan finds my argument unpersuasive because of my unexamined political assumptions, but does admit at one point: "For him, the 'uncomfortable moments,' and especially the problems in academic life they point to, ought to be more than noticed: they ought to be addressed through action. If the woods are burning, I ought to do something more than say 'what's that funny smell?' and then go back to my next conference paper. Williams's case here seems to me much stronger, and, at a general level, I accept it—as well as the point that I and others like me should devote more time to reforming the institution" (156). My point precisely!

12. As Bourdieu elsewhere defines it, "The habitus, the durably installed generative principle of regulated improvisations, produces practices which tend to reproduce the regularities . . . while adjusting to the demands inscribed as objective potentialities in the situation . . ." (*Outline* 78). Bourdieu's concept explains how institutions—concrete structural arrangements—operate in practice and sustain themselves over time.

13. C. Wright Mills does not pull any punches about this: "Insitutional factors naturally select men for these universities and influence how, when, and

upon what they will work and write. Yet the deepest problem of freedom for teachers is not the occasional ousting of a professor, but a vague general fear—sometimes politely known as 'discretion,' 'good taste,' or 'balanced judgement.' It is a fear which leads to self-intimidation and finally becomes so habitual that the scholar is unaware of it. The real constraints are not so much external prohibitions as control of the insurgent by the agreements of academic gentlemen" (297). On the gamut of affects indicated by tenure, see my companion essay, "The Other Politics of Tenure."

14. See my "Posttheory Generation," esp. 59–61; see also Michael Bérubé's chapter in this volume.

15. To quote Bourdieu again: "Produced by the work of inculcation and appropriation that is needed in order for objective structures, the products of collective history, to be reproduced in the form of the durable, adjusted dispositions that are the condition of their functioning, the *habitus* . . . is what makes it possible to inhabit institutions, to appropriate them practically, and so to keep them in activity, continuously pulling them from the state of dead letters, reviving the sense deposited in them, but at the same time imposing the revisions and transformations that reactivation entails" ("Structure" 57).

16. In the aptly titled *Secular Vocations*, Bruce Robbins underscores this paradoxical crux of professionalism, straddling between worldliness and eschewing worldliness.

17. In "Secular Criticism," Said also pointedly targets "the ethic of professionalism" (4–5); in this earlier expression of antiprofessionalism, his focus is more strictly the specialized development of literary theory that he castigates as being based on "a philosophy of pure textuality" (a.k.a. deconstruction), cut off from society and history, whereas he expands the range of his criticism in *Representations of the Intellectual.*

18. As a case in point, compare Said's model of the career ladder to Phelan's: "Your hope is to be asked back, to consult, to be on a board or prestigious committee, and so to remain within the responsible mainstream; someday you hope to get an honorary degree, a big prize, perhaps even an ambassadorship" (100–01). The question of an ambassadorship might apply to someone at Harvard School of Government, but I would hazard to guess it does not present itself to most of the rest us in academe.

19. Stanley Fish argues trenchantly against what seems a pervasive antiprofessionalism, noting that "power not only constrains and excludes, but also enables," and that we never act purely but are embedded in institutions and their categories ("Anti-Professionalism" 239; 242–43). However, he characteristically collapses any distinction among professionalisms to a monolithic professionalism.

20. In a parallel revision, Bruce Robbins proposes the term "oppositional professionals." While I myself would advocate our being oppositional intellectuals, I believe that "secular professionalism" is more germane, as not all of us will claim an oppositional politics.

Works Cited

Althusser, Louis. "Ideology and Ideological State Apparatuses." *Lenin and Philosophy and Other Essays*. Trans. Ben Brewster. New York: Monthly Review, 1971. 127–86.

Bérubé, Michael. *Public Access: Literary Theory and American Cultural Politics*. New York: Verso, 1994.

Booth, Wayne. "Between Two Generations: The Heritage of the Chicago School." *Profession 82* (1982): 19–26.

———. Introduction. *Problems of Dostoevsky's Poetics*. By Mikhail Bakhtin. Trans. and ed. Caryl Emerson. Minneapolis: U of Minnesota P, 1984. xiii–xxvii.

Bourdieu, Pierre. *Outline of a Theory of Practice*. Trans. Richard Nice. Cambridge: Cambridge UP, 1977.

———. "Structure, *Habitus*, Practices." *The Logic of Practice*. Trans. Richard Nice. Stanford: Stanford UP, 1990. 52–65.

Brint, Steven. *In an Age of Experts: The Changing Role of Professionals in Politics and Public Life*. Princeton: Princeton UP, 1994.

Caesar, Terry. "Frameworks and Free Agents." [Rev. of James Phelan, *Beyond the Tenure Track*.] *the minnesota review* n.s. 45–6 (1996): 275–83.

———. "On Teaching at a Second-Rate University." *Conspiring with Forms: Life in Academic Texts*. Athens, GA: U of Georgia P, 1992. 145–65.

Chomsky, Noam. "The Responsibility of Intellectuals." *The Chomsky Reader*. Ed. James Peck. New York: Pantheon, 1987. 59–82.

Coupland, Douglas. *Generation X: Tales for an Accelerated Culture*. New York: St. Martin's, 1991.

Ehrenreich, Barbara. *Fear of Falling: The Inner Life of the Middle Class*. New York: HarperCollins, 1989.

Fish, Stanley. "Anti-Professionalism." *Doing What Comes Naturally: Change, Rhetoric, and the Practice of Theory in Literary and Legal Studies*. Durham, NC: Duke UP, 1989. 215–46.

———. "The Unbearable Ugliness of Volvos." *English Inside and Out*. Ed. Susan Gubar and Jonathan Kamholtz. New York: Routledge, 1993. 102–08.

Giroux, Henry. "Academics as Public Intellectuals: Rethinking Classroom Politics." *PC Wars: Politics and Theory in the Academy*. Ed. Jeffrey Williams. New York: Routledge, 1995. 294–307.

Jacoby, Russell. *The Last Intellectuals: American Culture in the Age of Academe*. New York: Basic Books, 1987.

Kimball, Roger. *Tenured Radicals: How Politics Has Corrupted Our Higher Education*. New York: Harper & Row, 1990.

Larson, Magali Sarfatti. *The Rise of Professionalism: A Sociological Analysis*. Berkeley: U of California P, 1977.

Leitch, Vincent B. *American Literary Criticism from the Thirties to the Eighties*. New York: Columbia UP, 1987.

Miller, Nancy. "Getting Personal: Autobiography as Cultural Criticism." *Getting Personal: Feminist Occasions and Other Autobiographical Acts*. New York: Routledge, 1991. 1–30.

Mills, C. Wright. "The Social Role of the Intellectual." *Power, Politics and People: The Collected Essays of C. Wright Mills*. Ed. Irving Louis Horowitz. New York: Oxford UP, 1963. 292–304.

Ohmann, Richard. *English in America: A Radical View of the Profession*. New York: Oxford UP, 1976.

Phelan, James. *Beyond the Tenure Track: Fifteen Months in the Life of an English Professor*. Columbus: Ohio State UP, 1991.

———. "The Life of the Mind, Politics, and Critical Argument: A Reply to Jeffrey Williams." *College Literature* 23.3 (1996): 143–61.

Robbins, Bruce. "The History of Literary Theory: Starting Over." *Poetics Today* 9.4 (1988): 767-82.

———. "Oppositional Professionals: Theory and the Narratives of Professionalization." *Consequences of Theory*. Ed. Jonathan Arac and Barbara Johnson. Baltimore: Johns Hopkins UP, 1991. 1–21.

———. *Secular Vocations: Intellectuals, Professionalism, Culture*. New York: Verso, 1993.

Said, Edward. Interview. Imre Salusinszky. *Criticism in Society: Interviews with Jacques Derrida, Northrop Frye, Harold Bloom, Geoffrey Hartman, Frank Kermode, Edward Said, Barbara Johnson, Frank Lentricchia, and J. Hillis Miller*. New York: Methuen, 1987.

———. *Representations of the Intellectual: The 1993 Reith Lectures*. New York: Pantheon, 1994.

———. "Secular Criticism." *The World, the Text, and the Critic*. Cambridge: Harvard UP, 1983. 1–30.

Sarchett, Barry. "Russell Jacoby, Anti-Professionalism, and the Politics of Cultural Nostalgia." *the minnesota review* n.s. 39 (1992–1993): 122–42.

Smiley, Jane. *Moo*. New York: Knopf, 1995.

Soley, Lawrence C. *Leasing the Ivory Tower: The Corporate Take-over of Academia*. Boston: South End, 1995.

Sosnoski, James J. *Token Professionals and Master Critics: A Critique of Orthodoxy in Literary Studies*. Albany: SUNY P, 1994.

Spacks, Patricia Meyer. "The Academic Marketplace: Who Pays Its Costs?" President's Column. *MLA Newsletter* Summer 1994: 3.

Watkins, Evan. *Work Time: English Departments and the Ciculation of Cultural Value*. Stanford: Stanford UP, 1989.

Williams, Jeffrey. "The Other Politics of Tenure." *College Literature* 26.3 (1999): 226–41.

———. "The Posttheory Generation." *Day Late, Dollar Short: The Next Generation and the New Academy*. Ed. Peter C. Herman. Albany: SUNY P, 2000. 25–43.

Part IV

The Job of Literature

Chapter Eleven

Time Out of Mind: Graduate Students in the Institution of English

Louise Mowder

It is a commonplace that graduate students, particularly in the arts and humanities, are subject to a crushing wheel of pressures.[1] The tensions of the late 1980s and 1990s were particularly acute; university funding squeezes, the contentious disputes over the state of the curriculum, and the almost suicidally depressed job market appear to have left graduate students in the field of English with barely enough energy to complete their doctorates. Remaining invisible is the construction of the concept of the "graduate student." Each graduate student in the field of English is a text as well as a body, theorized and defined by academia, by the student's field and its professionals, and by the students themselves. The tremendous power, tacit and explicit, of an entire institution is brought to bear on the individuals who occupy the position of "graduate student." This system of discourse demands that they shape and reorder not only their interests and intellects, but their very lives and definitions of self in order to be considered as full participants within their fields. Even the students' own counterdefinitions, meant to resist larger institutions, can be equally hegemonic.

At the same time the expectations associated with the definition of "graduate student" can differ from campus to campus, even from adviser to adviser. The mystery of what it means to be a truly successful graduate student in English is demonstrated by the numbers of students who crowd whatever publication workshops or job-strategy clinics a department may offer. The mystery of just what one is supposed to be is matched by the enigma surrounding just what sort of future one will have if one stays in a doctoral program. If the profession seems to acquire an aura of empyrean incalculability, it can also radiate a sense of godlike power and omnipotence. Graduate students seem to view the institution of English itself as vast, monolithic, and seemingly uncontrollable, a perception that can lead the individual student into a state of extreme passivity toward the institution. How much commitment to transforming the field can any one student muster when that student has no faith that he or she will ever be permitted employment in the institution, even on completion of the doctorate? With so many crucial demands on time or energy, how can a student even begin to see the institution whole, much less envision how to shape and remodel the field?

Today's graduate students are the ostensible members of and heirs to the profession. Yet rather than attempting to influence the world which they will inherit, most are busy trying simply to survive and to anticipate the demands of tomorrow's marketplace. The graduate student culture that has resulted is often highly individualistic and professionally reactive.

There has been a good deal of debate over the "crisis" in graduate studies over the past decade, epitomized by William Bowen and Neil Rudenstine's influential *In Pursuit of the Ph.D.* Using a model derived from the somewhat rarefied statistical base of ten major research universities (Berkeley, Chicago, Columbia, Cornell, Harvard, Michigan, UNC, Princeton, Stanford, and Yale), their findings are by now the clichés on which departmental policies are built. Completion rates for the doctorate—as opposed to the baccalaureate—degree were found to be quite low, and the "time to degree" (TTD), that is, the amount of time spent pursuing the degree before completion, was lengthening with each passing year. According to federal statistics, graduate students in the arts and humanities are evidently taking longer to complete their degrees. The 1992 *Federal Report on Educational Statistics* shows that there has been an increase from median time lapse of 9.6 years in 1975 to 12.0 years in 1987 (269). This last statistic has been the most worrisome, and Bowen and Rudenstine devote a good deal of analysis to the problem of "lengthening TTD." They lay the primary blame for it on financial considerations; the chief culprit is the increasing reliance on assistantships to provide graduate student funding, as opposed to the previous practice of fellowship awards. They emphasize quite strongly that funding, especially in the course-work years, should consist of fellowships rather than TAs. Ronald G. Ehrenberg, a labor economist, has also adduced definitive evidence that graduate students in the arts and sciences are more likely to complete their doctorates—and in less time—if they receive fellowships, especially in the first year of Ph.D. work, rather than teaching or research assistantships.

University and program administrators across the country paid close attention to Bowen and Rudenstine's articulation of a "coming crisis" in faculty staffing and developed new graduate programs in direct response to their findings. Revamped programs in graduate English are specifically designed to trim the time spent in graduate school. These programs, however, often attribute "lengthening TTDs" to student intransigence. The 1990 Kagan-Pollitt plan at Yale, developed in direct response to Bowen's earlier report, *Prospects for Faculty in the Arts and Sciences*, provided a euphemistic "incentive to finish" by cutting the number of teaching fellowships awarded each year up to 25 percent. In addition, most students were barred from teaching in their fifth and sixth years. Instead, a one-time "dissertation fellowship" was to be awarded in the fifth or sixth year; after that, there would be no more funding for graduate students ("Yale Plan"). This plan was designed to light a fire under the feet of sluggardly graduate students, who were apparently so contented with their lot that they were loath to leave the ivied halls.

Bowen and Rudenstine noted that funding limits by themselves will not work to spur completion, but many universities, already in troubled fiscal states, have used Bowen and Rudenstine's highly regarded conclusions to provide an inarguable rationale for adopting aid restrictions. In addition, programs have attempted to deal with lengthening TTD by placing shorter deadlines for the various segments of the degree process—less time to complete course work, a limited amount of time to read for and pass orals and comprehensives, and fixed deadlines for all stages of the dissertation. Typically these deadlines are directly connected to limits on the number of years of funding that a graduate student can receive.

I contend that the institutional emphasis on shortening TTDs is at best shortsighted and inaccurate, and at worst cynical and self-serving. This model of the problems that impede graduate students from degree completion and its proposed solutions are divorced from the reality of current graduate student life. While funding problems can effectively torpedo an aspiring academic career, there are also other unexamined problems for graduate students that are just as terminal.

The model of graduate education that Bowen and Rudenstine assume, implemented at Yale and elsewhere, is a vestige of past expectations, even though graduate students themselves have changed markedly over the past 30 years. These changes are not simply philosophical or intellectual, but deeply demographic in nature. Bowen and Rudenstine's study is flawed, I believe, by its limited statistical basis and elite bias, as all their evidence is drawn from Ivies or noted research universities. When we examine the statistics of the entire population of graduate students in literature across the country, a very different picture of the "graduate student" emerges, and that difference has profound effect on prospective solutions to the "crisis" in the field. For example, one culprit strongly implicated in the projected shortage is the attrition rate. From their sampling, Bowen and Rudenstine are sanguine about retention and completion rates, estimating completion rates for those entering in the early 1970s to be about 55 percent, with a better than 80 percent completion rate for those achieving ABD status (112). While no overarching examination of completion statistics for all 340 graduate programs in literature has yet been undertaken, we can get some idea of what appears to be a truly astounding rate of attrition from the federal statistics on all U.S. graduate programs. In 1984–85, 1,239 Ph.D.s were granted in the field of "letters," about 4 percent of the total 32,943 Ph.D.s granted (*Digest* 238). The median age at receipt of the doctorate was 35; 55 percent were married; the median time lapse from the bachelor's to the doctoral degree was 12.1 years; the average total amount of time registered in their programs of study was 8.2 years.

But these statistics are about those hearty, diligent souls who have completed the degree. What were the numbers like for the entire entering cohort of their classmates? If we go back eight years, to fall 1976, we find that these 1,239 Ph.D.s were part of a class of 23,618 first-year students enrolled in programs leading to advanced degrees in letters.[2] Eight years later, only 5 percent of them had completed their Ph.D.s. Even if we allow for terminal master's candidates, the 1976 class of "second-year and beyond students" numbers 20,364; we are still left with a retention and completion rate of 6 percent. Those who fought in the Battle of the Somme had a better chance of survival.

Was the lack of fellowship awards, as Bowen and Rudenstine hypothesize, the major factor for this stunning rate of attrition? Evidence suggests otherwise. In the same year that they were researching their volume, the Council of Graduate Schools asserted that one of the most significant barriers to completing a humanities doctorate was the dissertation itself. In its 1991 report, the Council inculpated the varying forms that the dissertation can assume:

> In the humanities, the dissertation often takes the form of a manuscript that could be later published as a book. On the other hand, a few engineering and science departments surveyed allow students to simply bind together their previously published articles and submit them as a dissertation. ("Dissertation")

Even on campuses where such practices are not acceptable, exceptions are made in the interest of speedy completion. "Hard science" dissertations, for example, are often comprised of previously published experiments (sometimes undertaken in conjunction with a faculty member), accompanied by a new logical discussion. Arts degrees, in stark contrast, require a book-length piece of original research and writing. In history the dissertation increasingly demands time-consuming archival research, and similar patterns of archival research are developing in English.

For all of their omissions, the federal statistics still tell another story. During the past 30 years, the graduate student body in "letters" has been definitively reshaped, becoming primarily female, markedly older, and noticeably less white. Perhaps the major demographic change has been the increase in women. Women Ph.D. recipients in letters remained fairly constant in the decade between 1950 and 1960—about 21 percent of the degrees granted each year. By 1970 the number had crept up to 31 percent. The percentages grew through the 1970s, and by 1980 women received 47 percent of Ph.D.s in English. Throughout the 1980s women received more than half of Ph.D.s granted in English, holding steady at 57 percent during 1985–86 and 1986–87. The age of the average Ph.D. recipient steadily increased as well, moving from a median age of 30.1 in 1970 to 35.4 in 1987. White candidates, who made up 85 percent of the Ph.D. recipients in 1975, were 77 percent of the total pool by 1987. In contrast, the percentage of Asian, Hispanic, and African-American scholars all increased.

By examining these changing demographic patterns and by scrutinizing Bowen and Rudenstine's assumptions, one can interpret the "problems" that might beset graduate students in English much differently. On the much-bemoaned issue of "increasing TTD," for example, an increase in the median age of doctoral graduates from 30 to 36 suggests that students are taking longer to finish their degrees. However, a closer look at the number of years that these students are actually registered in their degree programs indicates that something else is going on. Actual registered time has increased only slightly from 7.3 years in 1977–78 to 8.5 years in 87–88. What accounts for the difference is that most graduate programs reported an increase in their "returning" population—many after pursuing other careers or beginning families, and usually women—but their "TTD" is not adjusted.

An older female graduate student will probably face different obstacles to completion than those encountered by the typical doctoral candidate of 30 years ago, who was a 24-year-old male. A student graduating from a Ph.D. program in 1976, when the median age on completion was 30, could still anticipate devoting him- or herself to the academic world for several years before beginning a family. The present-day new female Ph.D., with a median age of nearly 36, may very well have begun her family while in graduate school. For such a student, obtaining affordable day care may present a greater difficulty than writing a dissertation while teaching two and one. Contemporary studies provide no insight into the ways in which family and child-care responsibilities might lengthen the degree.

Graduate programs, like the rest of the academy, have been slow to recognize the extent to which reliable family care opportunities increase productivity. A University of Montreal study of 1,123 Canadian career women stated that almost anything that employers do to help employees balance the demands of work and family can have positive impact. Among the helpful items were: flexible work schedules; time off for family responsibilities; supervisors who understand employees' family needs; employer-sponsored child care at or near work; and financial or logistical help from the employer in finding childcare.[3] Annette Kolodny broke a path at the University of Arizona for providing similar life- and family-support systems to both faculty and students, but the vast majority of departments deal with such concerns informally, if at all.

The impact of family stress on completing the graduate degree has not been studied, but we can get an idea of the variety and force of such problems by looking at the different forms of specialized psychological assistance near campuses. "Specialty counseling," such as married student counseling, is itself indicative of an even more familiar, and even less analyzed, graduate school phenomena: the close relation between graduate study and therapy. Psychoanalysis and the intellectual have always been closely aligned, and in graduate school the intellectual can often find both the time and the insurance coverage to pay for it. The soul-searching and the quest for the intellectual self involved in graduate study frequently seem to lead to the therapist's office as well as to the library. But while graduate study and therapy may often go together, production of written work and therapy are often incompatible. How much Prozac aids dissertation completion remains anecdotal.

Graduate student depression is not, however, purely the product of too much isolated meditation. It can also be seen as a predictable response to an extremely difficult institutional lifestyle. It is ironic that the academy, which casts itself as more humane and thoughtful than the brute utilitarian corporate world, is in many ways an antiquated sweatshop when it comes to family and work issues. In January 1993 professors at Rutgers University, where I was a graduate student, found their labor negotiations at a standstill after 18 months; one of the major issues of division between the faculty and the administration was the issue of family care. Faculty asked for 3 months of unpaid leave following the birth or adoption of a child or to care for an ill family member. Administration rejected the request, proposing instead a contract that officially recognizes that professors cover for each others' classes when one is absent. "Formal time off is not needed," according to University spokespersons ("RU Talks"). This is the sort of response that we heard from corporate C.E.O.s 25 years ago.

Yet, even if university administrators are 30 years behind the times in their approaches to family and childcare, they are taking their employment practices directly from today's business pages. One of the most prominent importations, all too familiar by now, is "outsourcing," the process through which businesses reduce their benefits costs by replacing permanent employees with temporary workers, euphemistically called "consultants." On campus, we have seen this "outsourcing" in the increasing reliance on part-time lecturers and adjunct faculty to teach courses previously assigned to full-time faculty. Part-time professors made up 38 percent of the nations' professoriate in 1987, although that figure has surely grown since. Fifty percent or more of the classes at some institutions, such as community colleges, are taught by part-timers, adjuncts ineligible for tenure. Many institutions defend the use of adjuncts, claiming it gives them needed "flexibility." However, as a 1992 AAUP study of the growing trend toward hiring temporary faculty argues, this hurts the quality of higher education as well as weakens the tenure system (see "The Use and Abuse of Part-time Faculty"). From these statistics, it is now apparent that the predicted "shortage" of faculty members of such concern to Bowen and Rudenstine, and upon which so many graduate students banked their hopes, has vanished in the face of corporate tactics.

We graduate students are intimately familiar with these employment positions, because "temporary" lines, which can be renewed for decades, may be the sole source of funding that we can find after being cut off from other forms of assistance as doctoral programs push to shorten our stays. In English departments across the country graduate students are becoming the new sharecroppers of the academy. The purported concern over "lengthened TTDs" has led to a self-serving administrative position whereby graduate support is axed, so graduate students are forced into working as adjuncts, creating a pool that the administration can use to avoid hiring tenure lines. Cut off from fellowships and teaching assistantships but desperate to stay working in our chosen field as we complete our degree, we take an ill-paid part-time lecturer position, thereby freeing the university from the necessity of hiring a recent Ph.D. on a permanent basis. Graduate students, ever more isolated, overworked, and wretched, lack the solidarity that would prevent their unwitting participation in a system of academic cannibalism.

This dismal state has frequently led to the argument that part of the problem is simply that there are too many of us. In a characteristic response in the *Chronicle of Higher Education* in December 1992, an endowed professor of English at Wellesley described his receipt of over 1500 letters of application for one position, from which he concluded that "It's obvious that there are too many Ph.D. programs, and too many graduate students in them. But this bad state of affairs continues because professors want those graduate students in seminars and because universities need yet another source of cheap labor" (Cain).

What can we do, when we have already invested years in such a program, besides quitting immediately? We look at the hiring figures, and we try to figure out how we as individuals can beat the odds, in a more intellectually advanced form of the specialization planning that our undergraduates engage in. Maybe those other students won't get the job, but I can, if only I am professional enough, write enough articles for the right journals, write the best dissertation that is optioned by the best press, and give enough papers at enough prestigious conferences like the MLA. This is the conventional wisdom, bruited in cafés, libraries, and lounges across the country.

But in order to truly empower ourselves, individual effort will not be enough. The institution is undergoing systemic change, which we must comprehend and address as a group. We must learn to critique the ideology of individualism that dominates our own field, just as we have mastered it in the texts we are writing about. We must expand our social horizons, fight against the wisdom of professionalization that tells us that we succeed best by remaining enmeshed in the small community of our department, our field, our profession. We must start to draw more vigorous social and political connections with those both inside and outside of the university. What might some of these necessary moves be?

1. We should develop innovative new support mechanisms, within our departments or schools and local community. Programs involving family care, family leave, graduate student therapy groups, and dissertation groups are certainly best utilized if created and supported by our departments or university administration. But an official unwillingness to provide on-site day care does not prevent us from forming our own babysitting cooperative.

2. We should take a labor perspective. What implications does the university-as-corporation model hold for us as its employees? We must support unionization efforts and join our own campus chapter. Like faculty, graduate students have traditionally been dissuaded from union participation by the argument that such labor activity is "uncollegial." Donald Kagan, then dean of Yale College, explained that Yale students attempting to organize mistake seeing themselves as "workers and potential laborers" rather than as students and potential faculty. Kagan intoned, "You didn't hear these complaints when there were only 400 graduate students. And if we're right, you won't hear them in five years, because students will be thinking about themselves right" ("Putting a Limit"). Yet the university system itself is run as a business which strategically uses us as workers and laborers. And as union members, we must strongly promote the AAUP call for a limit on the use of adjuncts to 15 percent of classroom teaching.

3. We should broaden the perception of our place within the profession and begin to utilize its resources and opportunities as a class rather than as individuals. For example, we should lobby the MLA to conduct a more thorough study of graduate students registered in literature and languages, one that asks questions about the types of problems beyond those of funding. We need a more accurate statistical portrait of the graduate student population, one that can be used to obtain more specified support services for both graduate students and untenured faculty.

4. We should enlarge our awareness of the impact that national issues have on us. We must be aware of and work for political action that affects our future. We must lobby for such things as national health coverage;

many universities wish to avoid hiring permanent faculty for the same reason that other businesses are loath to—benefits costs. Lobbying does not mean that we have to camp out on our representatives' office doors. We are, after all, teachers and writers; we can write letters, opinion pieces, and articles. Some universities and colleges even have specialized programs that assist faculty in getting opinion and comment pieces in local, state, or national publications; inquire at your institution's public relations office.

5. Finally, we should develop a sophistication about our economic position in the institution of English and about that institution's place in the greater economic community. We should look at the demand within the university for our services, and at the demands placed on the university in general. Administrators will hire us if they believe that we can provide a product that their clients, the students and their parents, will want to buy. Our products in the past have been the traditional skills of good writing—grammar, syntax, rhetoric, and so on—and literature. The presumable benefit of the literary canon was that it formed the basis for an educated man's system of knowledge and value. But a combination of factors, of which canon busting itself may be one, seems to have convinced students that what we can teach them is not necessary in today's world. This can be seen directly in the declining enrollment figures of English majors over the past 15 years.

What we now have to persuade our students and their parents is that our training has given us a skill that they also want to obtain, and is in fact necessary to their success in all forms of life after college. While our language and texts may differ, we all learn in graduate school how to read, how to write, and how to think critically—all the skills that Robert Reich, in *The Work of Nations*, has attributed to "symbolic analysts." We learn the skills of abstraction, system thinking, experimentation, and collaboration. Reich states that these skills are of paramount necessity for success in twenty-first century capitalism—where we all will probably be living—but that less than 15 percent of our students receive this education (229).

That I have followed up a condemnation of corporate capitalist practices in the academy with an injunction to make oneself more desirable to capital may seem contradictory. However, I envision the ways in which we are able to change society's response to capitalism itself. If we are able to help our students achieve the skills and insights required to think more rigorously, to manipulate abstractions, to move beyond naive narratives, then the current system of manufactured consent will itself be more frequently critiqued and altered. Critical thinking is a prerequisite tool to democracy and intellectual freedom.

To follow through on the types of actions that I have outlined here will mean a new narrative of the academic institution of English, of its place in the world, and of our place in it. It has come time to revise our notion of the "professionalist" student, to move beyond the image of the lone individual in the carrel or at the conference, and see both our own and our institution's intimate connections to the larger field of American life, even those areas that we eschew.

Notes

1. For typical and generally bleak views, see Ohmann; Rudd; Von Blum; and Ziolkowski.

2. *The Digest of Educational Statistics* reproduces the same figures for fall 1976 enrollments throughout all of its enrollment charts in the annual volumes produced between 1977 and 1989, so I have had to work with this figure.

3. This study disputes the popular image of the "stressed-out supermom." See "For the Professional Mother."

Works Cited

Bowen, William G. *Prospects for Faculty in the Arts and Sciences: A Study of Factors Affecting Demand and Supply, 1987–2012.* Princeton: Princeton UP, 1989.

———, and Neil Rudenstine. *In Pursuit of the Ph.D.* Princeton: Princeton UP, 1992.

Cain, William. "Different Perspectives on Part-time Faculty." *Chronicle of Higher Education* 16 Dec. 1992: B26.

Digest of Educational Statistics. 1992.

"Dissertation Still 'Alive and Well,' but Not Advising." *Chronicle of Higher Education* 16 Jan. 1991: A22.

Federal Report on Educational Statistics. 1992.

"Fellowships, Not Assistantships, Said to Be Key to Completion of Doctorates." *Chronicle of Higher Education* 23 Mar. 1990: A1.

"For the Professional Mother, Rewards May Outweigh Stress." *New York Times* 9 Dec. 1992.

Ohmann, Richard. "Graduate Students, Professionals, Intellectuals." *College English* 52 (1990): 247–57.

"Putting a Limit on How Long Graduates Teach." *New York Times* 21 July 1990.

Reich, Robert. *The Work of Nations: Preparing Ourselves for 21st Century Capitalism*. New York: Knopf, 1991.

"RU Talks Resume Tomorrow." *New Brunswick Home News* 20 Dec. 1992: B1.

Rudd, Ernest. *A New Look at Postgraduate Failure*. New York: Guilford, 1985.

"The Use and Abuse of Part-Time Faculty." Special issue. *Academe* Nov.–Dec. 1992.

Von Blum, Paul Stillborn. *Education: A Critique of the American Research University*. Lanham: UP of America, 1986.

"Yale Plan to Shorten Duration of Doctoral Studies Angers Faculty Members and Graduate Students." *Chronicle of Higher Education* 13 July 1990: A13.

Ziolowski, Theodore. "The Ph.D. Squid." *American Scholar* 59 (1990): 177–95.

Chapter Twelve

Getting Hired

Terry Caesar

In order to have a job, you've got to be hired. If you've got a recent academic position, however, the process by which you were hired is likely to have been one of the most interiorized, prolonged, politically fraught, and severely rationalized it is possible to undergo in any field. Getting hired for an academic position is not like business where the interview is at the decisive center of the process. Indeed, one of the curiosities of academic hiring is that it is consequent on a decision whose center is everywhere and whose circumference is nowhere. You are never sure precisely what will prove decisive even if you get as far as the on-campus visit, meet with the graduate students in order to ask them if they have to share office space with the faculty, luxuriate throughout in some sort of minority status, and get a jolly chuckle from everybody during the interview when you express relief at not having been asked to pee into a bottle. How has the hiring process changed, and how has it changed, in turn, the very idea of an academic career?

I am not sure it would be possible to determine exactly how getting hired has changed during the last 40 years. Take simply the matter of expectations. A hiring, like a marriage, redefines a larger institutional structure each time. Henry Wilbur begins his entry in *The Academic's Handbook*, "On Getting a Job," with the following statement: "The first task of the new Ph.D. is to obtain an academic position." Then he refers to his own experience. His first paragraph concludes as follows: "On the basis of that experience, I immediately qualify my opening sentence: before you set out to obtain a job in a college or university, you should do some frank and honest soul-searching" (63). Forty years ago, would Wilbur have felt the need to make his qualification? Thirty years ago? Twenty? When did academics begin to align themselves with businessmen as wage-earners? When did it become imperative to caution "entry-level" candidates about the rigors of committee work? When, for that matter, did it become necessary for a book to appear with a chapter such as Wilbur's? One feels that if he turned any more of his skepticism on the very process he aims to elucidate, he simply could not provide his wise counsel to leave hobbies off your c.v. or to be sure to appear in business clothes if the department has asked about your marital status. When did getting hired, one could ask, become so thoroughly routinized that some attempt at detachment from it now only appears to be idle or fatuous?

It is very difficult not to posit some point in time during which hiring was easier, more humane, and on a more casual scale. Therefore historical perspective unavoidably becomes an exercise in idealization. Let me consider in this regard B. L. Reid's charming memoir, *First Acts*, which concludes with his working as a milkman in 1946, before an employment agency in Chicago notifies him of a position at Iowa State College. He and his wife are both offered jobs without interviews. Although Reid mentions "an exchange of letters," presumably none of them were letters of recommendation. I think we can further presume that Reid did not submit either a cover letter or a c.v., and it probably would have been as inconceivable for his new employers to have asked him to deliver a formal lecture as it would have been to check their offer against affirmative action guidelines. We do not, in short, understand Reid's situation today according to the one characterized by Kafka in *The Trial*: "The verdict doesn't come all at once, the proceedings gradually merge into the verdict."

Nonetheless, idealization can be resisted insofar as proceedings did obtain, which enable Reid's initial good fortune to be understood as merely part of a more comprehensive sentence. Four years later, while teaching at Mount Holyoke, the intelligence was discreetly given to Reid that he would be fired because he lacked a Ph.D. It took Reid until 1956 to get one—at age 39, from the University of Virginia, while teaching as an instructor at Sweet Briar College. The age at which Reid got his doctorate was perhaps more unusual then than now, but I believe it is typical of how tempting it is to emphasize discontinuities when one could just as justly stress continuities in the professional narrative of getting hired. Rather like an astutely career-minded grad student today, Reid sent off his course papers to the *Sewanee Review* and the *Kenyon Review*. Furthermore, whether he intended it or not (Reid does not say), Sweet Briar could not hold him, for he was in a better bargaining position with a Ph.D. Mount Holyoke duly offered not only more money but tenure. Back at Holyoke, Reid was secure. Eventually he published a few books, got nominated for a Pulitzer for his biography of John Quinn, and was named to an endowed chair some years before he retired in 1983. He enjoyed a career, in other words, very much in line with contemporary notions of success.

It is not at all clear that Reid would ever have benefited from advice such as Wilbur's. It is not even very clear what Reid took the profession to be, beyond one in which he was able to follow the scholarly logic of his own interests, generously conceived. Could he have realized he was all along more specialized than he imagined if he had had to subject himself to the elaborately credentialized and sequentialized process of getting hired as it exists today? Once again, hard to say. What can someone about to undergo this process today make of a Reid, who mentions that his academic career only came about in the first place because of the need for teachers created by the G.I. Bill? There is no comparable need for teachers anymore in higher education. For decades there have even been too many institutions. S. S. Hanna mentions (the time is "the early seventies") that he got a letter from "a small college in Nebraska," which gave his letter of inquiry the following response: "Sorry, we have been forced to close down the college. If we reopen and need you, we'll call you" (11).

How does a profession change when one seeks entry into it with the knowledge that one is competing against hundreds? (And often competing for positions at colleges one has barely heard of?) Reid simply indicates no historical awareness—not even by 1956—about being one among many. The real clarity his experience provides us with has to do with the one past phenomenon on whose basis a clear difference is usually declared from the present: the fabled "old-boy network." This network is not a myth. Yet it can easily be enlisted to make a myth. What gets lost is a career such as Reid's. He was not a product of an old-boy network. He appears to have made his way upward through a succession of jobs pretty much on his own.

We may contrast Reid's career with that of the pseudonymous Simon O'Toole, who at one point, after publishing an edition of McPherson's letters while teaching at "Baraboo University," is invited to take over the courses of a famous old editor of letters at "his famous old university."

O'Toole declines until things are spelled out: if he likes it, he can stay—and thereby have a teaching load of four hours a week, a handsome salary, an assistant to help correct papers, and a sure Guggenheim. "Did I yield?" writes O'Toole. "I yielded" (67). It is a measure of how shadowy and self-serving O'Toole feels the whole careerist enterprise to be—*Confessions of an American Scholar* is possibly the strangest book ever written about academic life—that he gives no specifics about when the great moment of his career took place. (It seems to have been roughly about the time Reid got his Ph. D.) He would probably want to emphasize how problematic was his own lifelong relation to any "network" rather than how certain it proved to be in one crucial instance.

Nevertheless, O'Toole discloses enough about his own career to reveal how profoundly implicated it was in the very rhythms of elite affiliation, privilege, and mutual interest. It is apt that his account is so muffled and painfully inward, as if the better to emphasize a professional level where the significant moves are closed to outside influences. I take this to be fundamentally the same state of affairs that continues to this day when top professors change jobs or even when top institutions try to get senior faculty. Dolores Burke's research study about faculty recruitment in the eighties quotes one senior person who relates the following procedure: "I gave a seminar in the department and they called me a couple of weeks later and asked me if I wanted the job. I didn't even know there was a job" (72). Such agreeable astonishment could not be further from the earnest attentiveness Wilbur entrusts to his young professor-to-be, who has first to be told to look where positions are advertised. "The 'old boy network' is more alive in some fields than others," states Wilbur (65). He can say no more. He does not say that this network does not advertise. Perhaps he does not have to. You do not get hired within this field, not even starting out. You get chosen.

A senior professor is quoted in Burke as follows about then and now: "Back in the fifties it looked like an old boy network but it really wasn't. There were just fewer of us. The American Astronomical Society had 800 members when I was treasurer; now there are 3600. When I became treasurer, I knew every graduate student in the country personally. It was a totally different world back then" (58). So all that has changed is numbers? But this ignores how elites perpetuate themselves. A general truth about professions is repeatedly demonstrated in Magali Sarfatti Larson's fine study of professionalism: "*A profession is always defined by its elites*," as she puts it at one point (227; her italics). The best way to enforce definition is not only to maintain inner solidarity but to avoid visibility, especially concerning mundane procedures (old boys just pick up the phone to get something done) and perhaps most especially of all concerning hiring. One looks in vain for clear, detailed accounts of how old boys make good on the promise of *jobs*. Perhaps such accounts would be too vulgar. Or perhaps there are no accounts because there is normally little to detail; vocabularies of shared value and intellectual intimacy have the character of seeming inherited, and therefore, say, your adviser at one worthy institution passes you along through someone suitable to someplace equally worthy as if you were a legacy.

I believe some of the pressure for what has widely come to be termed "political correctness" can be explained as a displaced response to the persistence of old-boy networks. This response is the classic one of legalism to traditionalism, in Max Weber's familiar typology of authority. Traditional authority is, once again, characterized in terms of its confident, thorough prejudices; the old-boy network is taken to be rotten with them. Whether these have to do with age, gender, physical disability, or sexual orientation, they correspond point-by-point to the ideological uniformity now summarized by a legalistic agenda against all discrimination, which is taken to be repellent and socially retrograde. Prejudices belong to the days when the chairman was always a man and usually an autocrat, when academic stratification expressed a broader, fixed social hierarchy, and when, only 30 years ago, almost 9 out of 10 doctorates were awarded to men.

Or when religion represented still another basis for prejudice. I have an old Jewish friend who tells the story of when she and her husband were invited to the campus of a small Midwestern liberal arts college in order for him to be considered for the position of dean. Things went very well. They liked the atmosphere. They even liked the president. But on the last Sunday morning, while driving around town and observing all the locals spilling out of churches, the president's wife turned to my friend at one point and asked the fateful question: "And which church would you attend?" She paused. They needed this job. They were sure they already had it. Of course her husband did not get it after she told the president's wife that they would not, in fact, attend any church.

How could she be sure this proved to be the reason? Of course she could not be. In a similar sense, I suppose, any woman or any black cannot be sure even today that gender or race, respectively, provided the ultimate reason why an expected job offer was not forthcoming. To each hiring procedure its own vanishing point. The difference, however, is one of ideological climate, and it makes all the difference: because an older hiring process, on the model of the old boy network, functioned more informally, the exercise of prejudice was not subject to the checks and texts of official opprobrium. Professionals had no great need to distinguish themselves from bureaucrats and technocrats—a story Larson tells very well—and so could afford to be either ideologically complacent or naive. Now, whether your c.v. contains requisite professional service or one of your letters of recommendation is from an eminent scholar, each item appears to represent a far more objective measure of your prospects than whether you might be a lesbian or confined to a wheelchair.

But has offensive discrimination ceased to function? Ideological sophistication may simply indicate a sophistication about the very category of ideology—and not any one example of it, much less examples that are nothing more than old-time prejudices dressed-up and "empowered." One of the more uncomfortable moments of my professional life occurred some years ago while I sat watching a candidate for a departmental position smoke cigarette after cigarette during his interview. He gave a poor performance. Nobody had to mention his smoking. Yet I am not sure anybody would have mentioned his smoking if he had given a brilliant performance. They just would not have voted for him, either way.

And so it goes, I would argue. Today's hiring process merely allows the moment of prejudice to seem less decisive and to become diffused amid legalistic criteria. One result is that an individual applicant who is unsuccessful gets no knowledge at all about what the reasons were, and knows that she won't. I know a woman whose convention interview concluded with the interviewer stating quite fervently, "I hope it's you." How could she not be fairly certain it would indeed be—or at least that she would be invited to campus? She wasn't. Months passed before the letter came informing her that the position had been "terminated" because there were too many unfinished searches for administrators. There was also something about "reexamining institutional priorities." So what could she conclude about why she was not hired? That there had been "proceedings" that were already active at the time of her interview that excluded her, and any relation she could have either to the position or the department was already beside the point? But what sort of knowledge is this? How does it enable one to improve one's chances in the future? In such circumstances, it seems to me, it is almost more consoling to feel that the unexceptionable bureaucratic operations were actually a mask for blunter and more personal prejudice of some sort.

In fact this woman chanced to know some gossip to the effect that the most influential man in the above department wanted a senior appointment for his old professor, and just threw up his hands at any sort of position when the old professor decided to stay where he was. I think she came to prefer this explanation to any other. Whether or not it happened to be true in this particular case, I believe it stands for any number of others, each of which bears traces of some sort of indeterminate, subterranean "network," but all of which must proceed to the verdict according to impeccable professional standards and proper affirmative action guidelines. What gets taken for granted, however, is that because everything gets written up or spelled out, the process of getting hired is far more fair, responsible, and progressive than it was in the past. It's not. It's just more complicated, more problematized, and more mystified.

Can there be anyone active in higher education during the past 20 years who has not seen a routine hiring scenario play itself out, faultlessly from any legalistic standpoint, which in fact was devised purely for show? Prejudice on the part of key people, or the presence of a local favorite—it hardly matters why. What does is that the very factors consigned to the bad old days instead appear to flourish the more deeply because all are agreed that they have been stamped out. Why *do* people get hired today? If things are so much improved, everybody ought to know, which means having that knowledge count in specific instances. Instead, I am not sure anybody knows very much about general instances—which usually means it is a time for handbooks, so that something can be summoned into existence, disseminated, and propounded. "The best preparation for professorhood," states Wilbur, "is rapid intellectual growth and productive scholarship" (76). But we knew this already. We have always known it. What we do not know is *still* why scholarship so often matters so little, or not at all.

It would be very tempting to argue that things have gotten worse, not better. In order to tease out such a contention, let me compare the exercise of the same prejudice, this time against homosexuality, from two separate academic moments. The first has to do with a story of a former colleague, the product of another generation, about how he lost a chance at his best job prospect once his Ph.D. was completed. He had asked his dissertation director to write him a letter of recommendation. The director did. In order to cinch the case as much as he could, the director mentioned that my colleague's mother lived near the institution in question, so her son would be especially pleased to be there, since he was very close to his mother. The director, in addition, knew the chairman personally. My colleague was sure he would get his offer. He didn't. Only much later, through a series of events far too complex to detail, did he learn why: the chair, on the basis of the director's aside about his mother, had concluded that my colleague was homosexual.

We may laugh. If we are not emancipated from such absurd fears today, at least we have procedures in place that require that we be more circumspect, open, and just. Yet consider the recent account of Ed Cohen, who went "on the market" in 1986. His hopes, he writes, were high: awards, a few publications, the full support of an elite institution. There was only one problem: he was gay and his dissertation title suggested it. Of course Cohen cannot be sure this explains why he received not a single interview that year; his "deficiencies" ranged from the fact that his publications were not yet in print to the fact that he refused to waive his right to see his recommendations. All he can conclude, nonetheless, is that dropping "homo" from his dissertation title and not using the word "gay" made all the difference from one year to the next. In 1987 he got eleven MLA interviews and two job offers. "I decided that what I needed to do was to represent my work in a way that was respectful of the project I had undertaken and yet accessible to people who might not necessarily be sympathetic to the undertaking" (168). So ought we to regard Cohen's strategy as one fully authorized by the conditions of getting hired, or as one subversive of those same conditions?

At least, we could conclude, Cohen was considerably more knowing about the moment of his own hiring; my old colleague, alas, was victimized by his. Perhaps. He never told this story as a victim, though. He delighted in it each time. I think it spoke to him of the exquisite comedy of academic life, whether its sheltered ignorances or its formal entanglements. Interestingly, Cohen, in contrast, does tell his story as a victim. About "the experience of my own self-silencing—especially on a subject that it had taken me years to learn to speak and write about publicly," he declares it to be "acutely painful" (168). To sharpen the contrast, we might say that to Cohen his experience is a tragedy, because it speaks to him of essentially nothing except how hollow the conditions are; there seems to be little pleasure even in manipulating them to one's own advantage. So can we conclude: the emptier the process, the more formal it is? Of course it could be conceded that Cohen represents a special case. However, if the process of getting hired at present cannot deal satisfactorily with special cases, one could well ask exactly how it can be put forward as some sort of advancement, especially when the special case is an example of the "identity politics" that the rules were expected to arbitrate?

We believe that each of us, in our heart of hearts, is a special case. We present ourselves as best we can on paper. We hope that we will be even more triumphant, if we get the chance, in the flesh. Yet time after time what the contemporary process of hiring seems to produce are candidates who, if unsuccessful, emerge with the feeling of having been merely a structural feature of proceedings that did not so much exclude them as ignore them. For such people, even Cohen's despair might seem like a kind of blessing. Let me relate the story of another woman, for whom a position seemed more assured than anybody I have ever known. Many of the reasons why had to do with her best friend, the previous occupant of the position, who set it up for her. By the time she went the on-campus visit seemed just a formality. It wasn't. She didn't get the job. What had she done?

Since she had gone through all the motions cleanly enough, she could only guess. Had she offended one member of the department by a jaunty remark about one of her former professors, possibly an object of veneration to her colleague-to-be? Had she scandalized the men by the incipient "feminism" of her presentation (she had been warned), especially by being flippant over a translation of the word "castration?" Could one of the senior men have somehow associated her with bad luck because, after she met him, he discovered that he had lost his textbook? Or was it simply that she felt such an immediate, visceral dislike of the chairman, and (she was certain) he to her, although, like good academics both, not an antipathetic word was exchanged? It would have made more sense if she had eaten a hamburger during the interview and learned afterwards that the department was all vegetarian.

She will never know. It is, in a sense, the job of the hiring procedures under which she was considered is to prevent her from knowing, as well as to protect the department from whatever she might find out. A more acute question is: Should she know? To consider what departments term "recruitment" from the candidate's point of view, as I have been doing, prompts one to ask what could be the cost to the profession when so many who apply to enter it are not so much rejected as cast aside? Being rejected at least has the virtue of preserving a personal relation, however unfortunate or inevitable, to authority. Being ignored rebukes the very idea of such a relation. This might seem like, well, an academic distinction; if one cannot get a job because one is Jewish or gay, then one is rejected because, in another sense, everything else about oneself is being ignored. Nevertheless, for people such as the woman above, the distinction is crucial, because at stake is the possibility of finding the hiring process to have some meaning beyond its legalistic character. I have suggested, indeed, that the current emphasis on political correctness participates in the hiring process once the process is understood as an attempt, from the bottom up, to will meaning into the proceedings.

This attempt proceeds in two ways. First, by insisting that the verdict preserve the character of a *relation*, and then, second, by keeping open the notion that any one verdict has in fact come about because a relation has been abused. The trouble with this is not that willing it so is at best only some compensation for the terminal consequences of an exquisitely formalized system. The trouble is that a more "personalized" logic really proceeds on the basis of the very traditional model of authority that the legalistic one aims to replace; in fact the traditional one remains in place, now, paradoxically, in order to redress the injustices of the new legalistic one. Political correctness is actually at cross-purposes with itself, and hence its imperatives cannot be neatly, coherently explained either as agreeing with a liberal social agenda or conservatively reacting against one. Arguably, those under the sway of the academic hiring process have no coherent politics in response. They just do not have any power, and so they insist that they have been personally, irrationally alienated from the profession itself at the very point of entry. Meanwhile, elites respond, from the top down, by trying to refine the very criteria which have been responsible for the abuse.

So now the most readily available handbooks urge candidates for the job interview, under "Do's," to "shake hands firmly and stand until offered a chair" or, under "Don't's," not to "hang around after the interview." Meanwhile hundreds of candidates get regretful letters each year about how worthy they are—although not quite adequately so considering the hundreds of other candidates. I have a friend who told me that her year's rejections were much more bearable because one place wrote her a lovely letter. She showed me the sentence that moved her most: "The profession needs many, many more persons of your skills, dedication, and love for our discipline." What to say? That it is a formula nonetheless? I didn't. What should a candidate think after reading several of these letters? That they are all designed to conceal how total is the evacuation of any personal connection? Or should these candidates wonder instead if they sat down too soon at the interview? Or if they should have shown up at all? The cost to the profession is a widespread cynicism about the hiring process, which by now, I believe, is essential to the continuation of the process.

The clearest examples of this cynicism are textual ones, despite the fact that the verdict—that is, its justification, not its announcement—is not required by the proceedings to be epitomized in textual form. The statement that so-and-so university is "an Affirmative Action/Equal Opportunity employer" (sometimes followed by some statement to the effect that minorities are urged to apply) is in fact a code, and a bad one, because there is no way to accurately decipher it as meaning necessarily that a position is for minorities only. Letters of recommendation are possibly even more deceitful, with even less reason. A pseudoanonymous piece on a real affirmative action search in *Lingua franca* records the following result of the interview round at the national convention: "Virtually everybody was worse in person than on paper, which was inevitable, given the implausibility of their letters of recommendation: every applicant was the 'best in years.' (This was true, in one professor's letter, for each of three candidates he was recommending.)" (Kindrow 23).

Let me not linger over the curious intricacies of either of these two texts alone. One could assess them by saying that it is one thing to claim such textual practices continue because no better ones have been found. It is quite another to maintain that the practices continue because nobody much cares about them anymore, except as phases through which the verdict has to proceed. Because, furthermore, no definitive text is necessary for the verdict—at the end, administrations may inform departments that positions have been disallowed and departments are free to inform candidates or not that searches have been aborted—everybody can feel that the real action is going on off the page anyway.

Is it? What is going on? Let me now consider getting hired aside from the traditional and legalistic framework I have been discussing. The first thing to say is possibly the only thing: there may be no adequate way to describe "the real action" when it finally issues in the form of a verdict. Burke, describing the various facets of the visit to campus and noting the importance of "collegiality," then makes a somewhat surprising point: "Yet the basis of choice—the clincher that gets the job—was rarely described in personal terms by the chairpersons interviewed" (64). Instead it seems the terms were pretty much what obtained before the visit, from quality of research to "style," although of course such things as poise or warmth were also mentioned as factors, and there is never any substitute for "personal dynamism." If chairs are reluctant to mention "personal terms," it may not be because they are more comfortable with standardized, objective criteria but because "the clincher" is, at root, most often the result of factors that no one fully comprehends. The clincher may even be the result of factors no one cares to comprehend, for it has been the burden of all which preceded it to make the clincher appear inevitable and logical.

"At the gates of the professional world," writes Larson, "the professional minorities who control a field do not receive an undifferentiated mass of entrants, but a super-filtered, super-classified, specialized, and hierarchicized cohort" (204). Precisely. So once a gate swings open it makes no sense to think that a newly authorized professional strides through for reasons that were accidentally formed, deeply biased, and fundamentally undifferentiated. Hence it may be that the entire hiring process as it exists in academic life today constitutes a massive effort not so much to produce "the clincher" but to *create* it, as if, somehow, a group of human beings can consistently evaluate other human beings on an individual basis which is perfectly reasonable and just. No wonder, we might say, that those who are evaluated are just as consistently incredulous.

I believe that at the center of the hiring process, especially when it is legally mandated to have no center, is mystery. "The clincher" is a profoundly mysterious thing. There are those who are in touch with the mystery, and those who are not. Those who are can at present purchase their intimacy with an affective vocabulary of victimization, while those who are not preserve their distance with a bureaucratized vocabulary of ideological rectitude. At bottom what separates these two groups is not a vision of a profession, but of human relations. You do not necessarily have to be on one side of the hiring line or the other. Let me illustrate with another example from my own experience. One of the loveliest moments I ever witnessed during an interview occurred some years ago while my department was undergoing its annual search for someone to fill a position in linguistics. Everybody knew it was only for show. We continued to wait for the local favorite to get a Ph.D. This particular year yielded one of the most impressive candidates I had ever seen. Even on paper it was obvious she had to be invited to campus.

On the search committee that year our most vexatious member, smitten at the time by composition theory, made a point of asking every candidate about one particular theorist. None so far had heard of him; she was content. When she asked the fateful question to an unusually poised and articulate linguist, however, the woman just turned to her, smiled, and replied: "No, I haven't heard of him. Could you tell me something about him?" The member was so startled she forgot one of the main things he was known for; a colleague had to intercede in order to finish what she had fumbled.

The superb reply was wasted, of course. Participate in a hiring process even for a year and you are likely to see—or imagine—enough waste to last a career, especially when what goes under the name of "scholarship" has gotten sorted out among the candidates and you are down to human cases. The faction for the local favorite held firm that year and the department rolled the search over for another. I never had a chance to vote for the above woman. What I realized, perhaps because I knew the verdict was foreclosed, is that I would have voted for her solely on the basis of her reply. Of course I thought it epitomized everything about her, on paper as well as in person. I could have made a perfectly reasonable case had I been called on to do so. Yet what seems to me especially compelling is that I did not care. Her reply clinched things for me because it simply transcended the pointless occasion. Moreover, the contrast was just too garish between the shabby departmental stage and the radiant human actor. I wanted—what? Justice? Revenge? I couldn't say. I still can't. Perhaps I wanted an entirely different hiring process. Or maybe I was suddenly shocked at how cynical I had become about it, and then longed to vote as if the position were a lost belief still not too late to affirm.

Writing about it now, I make the power of my feelings less mysterious. Feelings are misleading, after all. So are words about them. This is why hiring has procedures and these procedures have guidelines. But this is also why procedures and guidelines are continually in danger of being overcome with stray thoughts, irrelevant considerations, symbolic possibilities, and deep-seated fears. Because of tenure, academics—uniquely among other professionals—have to make decisions about new people who could be colleagues for the rest of the lifetimes of all concerned. At stake is not merely evaluating the relative merit of submitted examples of scholarship. (It needs to be emphasized that this sort of thing only goes on at elite institutions, which is to say that it does not go on at most colleges and universities in the country.) It is not even weighing years of experience. (Just about the only category left no one is going to take immediate exception to.) What is at stake, each time, is deciding how old you want someone to be whom you hire, or how aggressive you want someone to be whom you interview.

I know people who only seem to care if a person will "fit in," which essentially means a ready smile at the departmental coffeepot rather than a quick excursion into the theoretical frontiers of the discipline. And, come to that, shouldn't people care about smooth passages across their daily surfaces? How can they be prevented from caring, or from getting the ceremonies of the coffeepot mixed up with the imperatives of multicultural pluralism? In a sense, if a candidate is black or female, the waywardness or indeterminacy of a negative judgment a group of people can make is too easily explicable as a prejudicial one; surely this is one reason why it continues to be insisted on—the sheer mystery of getting hired is as unendurable from the standpoint of someone who receives the verdict as from someone who delivers it.

Or someone in the position of feeling responsible for the whole system. Wayne Booth begins *The Vocation of a Teacher* by telling a familiar horror story: a former Ph.D. student reports that in her only interview at the national convention (one response to 29 letters of inquiry sent), the six people there had not read her dossier, repeatedly misunderstood one of the main points she emphasized about her dissertation, and got both her name and marital designation wrong. Booth is outraged. Now, some years later, he imagines a protest letter to the main offender, with the following postscript: "Your victim recovered; she now teaches and publishes—brilliantly, as you could have predicted if you had taken the trouble to see her" (4). Is it conceivable, nevertheless, that his student did not get her ideas out fast enough, or lacked the poise to deal adroitly with stupid objections? Is it appropriate, too, that Booth tells a story that has a happy ending? The waste of the hiring process is not really waste if it can be recuperated as success. Its injustice is not mysterious if it is always the result of rudeness and routinization. Getting hired in horror stories just is not mysterious—by which I mean, in part, that losing a job does not always make sense, and probably should not be continually recreated as if it ought to make sense, even if now there is every ideological reason or every professional good that it do so.

Let me give another kind of story. Alexander Theroux has a little essay in which he maintains, to his own venerable credit, that "trying to survive by means of one's pen is a noble but precarious alternative" to teaching. So what to do? "Many an autumn I've found myself standing cap in hand in some English department or other where various poke-nosed officials and subheads—often without my experience, sometimes without my degrees, almost always without my competence—gathered together, peevishly took my measurements, and generally regarding me as an outlaw or a mongrel or both, grudgingly threw a course my way" (36). Reading Theroux, one thinks that getting hired is so little written about because, like writing a dissertation, it is something to *get over with*. Theroux, however, defiantly remote from the tenure track, can excoriate academics with rare gusto. Therefore, we wonder, since he still needs a job, how does he get one? I would like to suggest one reason: academics like him. It makes some sense: Who else could appreciate the gusto? He comes across, on the page anyway, as just the sort of fire-in-his-eyes being, the creative writer, who makes everybody glow.

Why does anybody get hired? What is the clincher? It may be unrecoverable in most cases today. Legal narratives do not deliver the clincher; they just set up a storyline. The clincher is probably a fiction anytime, and better ones from which legality falls away like an encumbrance are always available. There is a hiring story of unusual resonance and beauty contained in Bernard Malamud's *A New Life* (1961). The first thing to say, however, is that there hardly seems any hiring process to be described; the hero, S. Levin, merely recalls at one point that he is relieved that a new colleague, the director of composition, apparently does not know he, Levin, applied to over 50 other places, included the more prestigious rival of the one that accepted him. (The novel takes place in the mid-fifties—when Reid, it will be recalled, got his dissertation and when O'Toole got his ascension. These three examples illustrate, I think, the difficulty of historicizing the hiring process. "We've been hearing from people from every state in the Union," muses the director. "For next year I already have a pile of applications half a foot high" (12). He could be speaking in 1997. The difference is that it is clear to him this pile constitutes recognition, not work—and certainly not work for a committee.) Perhaps we would have thought no more about why Levin was chosen, had he not asked another colleague, because he suddenly fears he accepted a cheaper salary than anybody else would have ($3,000). At least at this point the question comes to exert a shaping force in the novel.

Much later, when the director has learned that Levin is refusing to support his candidacy for chairman, he exclaims, "Sometimes I curse the day I brought you here" (284). He refuses to answer Levin about why. Not until very late in the novel does Levin learn that in fact he was chosen because the director's wife, with whom he is having an affair, was engaged by his picture, which he chanced to include with his application. He knows he did not have to. "It was an old picture. I wanted them to know what I looked like." "You looked as though you needed a friend," says the woman. "Was that the reason?" "I needed one," replies his lover, "Your picture reminded me of a Jewish boy I knew in college who was very kind to me during a trying time in my life" (331).

From among a number of ways to interpret this story, I would like to emphasize two: first, getting hired as a manifestation of human presence, and, second, getting hired as an amorous relation. Perhaps the second is more scandalous, but the first is bad enough. One thinks no further than how haunting the absence of a real human being is in letters of recommendation, or how grimly ironic actual presence may be (as in the affirmative action search above) in terms of these texts. It seems by the mid-fifties that the inclusion of pictures with one's application was already somewhat unusual; certainly in our own deprejudiced and undiscriminated day a real photograph could only be quite literally seen as providing far too provocative grounds for all sorts of retrograde judgments. Levin's lover-to-be makes one. Of course his attractiveness to her has, in one sense, absolutely nothing to do with his performance as a potential member of an English department teaching composition. In another sense, however, and a richer one that the novel explores, the qualities of sympathy, concern, and vulnerability that Pauline intuits are precisely those that Levin subsequently demonstrates effectively even in his professional capacity. There is a very real sense in which he was right for the job.

I take it that Malamud's text constitutes a rebuke to any process of getting hired, insofar as it is predicated on voiding all but the most abstract, impersonal registers of human presence. The more one restores this presence, the more unreasonable, subjective, and irrational one's response is likely to be—which is only an argument against such responsiveness if one has a conception of human relations in which much of what is human simply is not to be trusted. One thing is trust itself. What is the basis for it? Does Pauline, looking at Levin's picture, trust her response? What should she have other than a vision of remembered love or a conviction of human need in order to trust? Of course no hiring procedure can satisfactorily answer these questions. My argument has been that the one currently in place conducts itself as if the questions did not exist. In fact actual human beings are moved by answers to them anyway, because some sort of trust must be summoned, and will be, whether or not a few live candidates will eventually fly in. And my argument has been that they appear too late, just as often to unsettle as to clinch the proceedings from which they have emerged.

They do not offer themselves to be loved. Nevertheless, Malamud's narrative is one of love—the love that, so to speak, is embedded in the "calling" of a profession, or of the profession as a calling. No matter that love cannot express itself as such in this context and can only justify itself in another context. Levin presents himself as someone in need of love; the narrative provides someone to love him just as it provides him with a job. This is of course not exactly the same state of affairs expressed by any candidate in search of a college teaching position. But it is close enough. Many things about getting hired are clarified by its correspondence to an amorous relation. There are, for example, many of the feelings unsuccessful candidates are left with once the fateful letter comes, thanking them for their interest, mentioning the multitude of other candidates, and wishing them luck in the future: one feels envy at those chosen instead, bitterness over one's own unworthiness, baffled desire, lost innocence, blunt rejection. The illicit convertability of hiring into loving, and back again, also explains why an objectified hiring process has to exist, with so many measures taken to ensure against some "personal" connection, much less against some sexual advantage being gained by any party in the affair. Yet it remains an affair with more than one connotation, and so many amorous overtones abide (from how either party "woos" the other to how certain sorts of contracts are modeled on prenuptial agreements) that it would be tedious to list them. "Nobody wants me!" I heard a desperate friend with a dissertation nearly "in hand" cry awhile ago. She is a woman. In the erotics of hiring, is the candidate always in the feminized position? Of the two above whose prospects first seemed so good, it was as if the first was stood up (he had promised to call) and the second was abandoned at the altar (it was all a mistake).

I want to insist on getting hired as an amorous proceeding (Kafka's characterization about the verdict is so acute because it could just as easily apply to falling in love) because for some decades now a teaching job in American higher education has meant a job in the same place for the duration of one's career. It has become quite common to read about how some fields such as health science or business are already experiencing a lack of qualified faculty and how as many as two-thirds of the present faculty in all fields will be retiring. How much mobility have these people had? Apart from the upper echelons, very little, I believe, in the past 20 years. Reid or O'Toole each appear to have assumed far more, and got it. My impression is that they were from the last generation to enjoy substantial job mobility in their discipline.

Impressions count for much in this area: the lament that "I can't get out" is seldom based on statistics, and easily becomes a self-confirming one. Of course this applies to tenured professors only, not those who have had, by default, careers trying to get tenure or those who have never been able to get on the right track. The hiring procedures perfected during the last two decades were not designed for those with security and seniority; recruitment procedures are designed to converge on those seeking their first job. Yet there have been consequences for tenured people, and the most crucial one can be put in the following way: they have had professional marriages from which there was, effectively, no chance for divorce. Can it be any coincidence, therefore, that the specific amorous correspondence that has shaped the hiring process during recent decades has been the one of a fateful, dutiful, and perhaps even loveless marriage?

Susan Sontag has an essay on Camus that she begins in the following way: "Great writers are either husbands or lovers. Some writers supply the solid virtues of a husband: reliability, intelligibility, generosity, decency. There are other writers in whom one prizes the gifts of a lover, gifts of temperament rather than of moral goodness. Notoriously, women tolerate qualities in a lover—moodiness, selfishness, unreliability, brutality—that they would never countenance in a husband, in return for excitement, an infusion of intense feeling" (52). In precisely the same way, candidates for a job are either husbands or lovers. What has happened in recent decades is that a hiring process has evolved in order to solicit husbands. Of course it has not happened in any deliberate way and it has happened for a wide variety of reasons—lately, because of downsizing, for example, or earlier, as a response to the threatening presence of women. Furthermore, it has not developed because of any systematic discrimination against lovers. As Sontag concludes, "It's a great pity when one is forced to choose between them"; even academics can be presumed to be not entirely without regret in this area. Nonetheless, in both love and recruitment one is forced to choose. Husbands have been consistently chosen for college teaching because the people doing the choosing have been getting older and more conservative; there has simply been no reason to risk the secure pleasures of the civil coffeepot for the unknown ones of flashy candidates who probably will not stay or witty ones who somehow look as if they might not want to volunteer to head the curriculum committee. "He won't stay," I heard from more than one member about a particular candidate during my department's recent search. Translation: he will be unfaithful. Getting hired in the academic world during recent decades has been for life.

That is to say, nobody even gets fired anymore. What is the relation between getting hired and getting fired? What is the relation, that is, when, as an associate professor in another department remarked to me awhile ago, once you have tenure you couldn't even get fired if, while you were having sex with a dog outside the president's office, she came out and tripped over you? Few things other than the rarity of a tenured firing (or even a nontenured one) demonstrate how permanent the fact of a job in the academic world has come to seem—and therefore, to invoke Weber again, how bereft of charisma the sources of authority that legitimize the claim to a position.

Lately, we might say, things have changed somewhat. To continue with an amorous model: lovers have been insisting that they be regarded as husbands, while husbands have taken to lamenting that there are suddenly not enough lovers—or too many. But getting hired remains a pretty resigned business because the peculiar kind of marriage it has represented has not been infused by fresh energies, much less eroticized ones. The point of getting hired continues to be to pledge young Ph.D.s (who have themselves been getting steadily older) to the stable, permanent virtues of the tenure track. It is as if the point of falling in love were to get married. Teaching off the tenure track has, therefore, not been quite *respectable*—like being a single person looking for sex in a room full of married couples who do not smoke, drink, or disparage each other's children.

To put it another way, teaching off the tenure track has not been to have a career. What has it meant to have a career during recent decades? In a sense, nothing more than to get tenure. Fixed, not to say fixated, at the moment of entry, it is as if the very imagination of the profession has gotten very intricate about what it means to be hired in proportion to how it has gotten very slack about what it means to have a career. A career is not of course convertible into the conditions of its beginning. It is not even convertible into tenure. What has occurred instead is that these conditions have effectively converted the whole notion of a career into themselves. The project of what to do after tenure can be left to take care of itself once the imperative of what to do before tenure is substituted for it. Perhaps with so many competing for so few jobs this substitution was inescapable; no career, after all, without tenure first, and so the most attractive feature of a college teaching position more urgently becomes the occupational stability it promises. What this has meant in practice, however, is a transformation of an older conception of the academic profession as a "calling."

The idea of a "calling" is, I think, a charismatic one. Its very force is enshrined in academic lore by the professor whose way with learning is so vivid, or challenging, or maddening, that the student—and eventual professor-to-be—is enchanted. "Calling" has religious roots, as recalled memorably at one point in Lionel Trilling's story, "Of That Time, Of That Place," when the tortured student, Tertan, says the following in a letter to the Dean about his Professor Howe: "To him more than another I give my gratitude . . . a noble man, but merely dedicated, not consecrated" (100). To be called into a profession is not to be reduced to a mere *motive*. Perhaps Wilbur, in his handbook entry, marks the venerable conception when he forebears treating the question of why anyone would want to enter college teaching in the first place.

His own treatment, however, cannot avoid evoking a quite different, far more disabused, realistic, and instrumental conception. In the same way, I would argue, any hiring process re-creates in its own image those whom it would solicit. In Larson's remarks on a profession as representing a "calling," she stresses that, no matter how the calling comes to constitute "an essential dimension of the self," it remains for her an ideologically constructed notion. Therefore, the more instrumental its choice becomes, or the more material, the less peer esteem matters, and the more the idea of calling is eroded (227). I take it as obvious now that in the professional narrative of college teaching any conception of it as a calling is so submerged and domesticated as to be effaced. I read somewhere that intelligence agencies the world over measure a potential agent's vulnerability according to an American acronym known as MICE, for money, ideology, compromise, and ego. Departments in American institutions of higher education are not yet so ruthless. But I think it is widely understood that, for hiring purposes, noble ideals are beside the point, unless the occasion requires some judgment about how well a candidate can manipulate a rhetorical vocabulary.

Indeed, the discursive idiom these days in higher education appears to be to emphasize what one's job has in common with those in other professions, or even those that are not professions at all. At a concluding moment in *Work Time*, for example, Evan Watkins invokes the experience of an old junior-high friend, a baker, and his previous pages are filled with comparisons of English departments to advertising agencies or of *Hamlet* to a Wheaties commercial. Contra Larson, it is as if to Watkins what matters most in his profession is what it has in common with the larger labor market. At one point, he states, "English is not a workplace in the same way as a GM plant, but it governs the designation of work just as surely" (12). This sort of hedging occurs repeatedly. It seems to me to disclose that college teachers are no longer certain about what professional story to tell themselves. A stronger claim would be, since a career is not just the story we tell ourselves but the story we are told, that the old narratives have been exhausted. That one emphasizing the Calling may be especially embarrassing. Watkins would find it appallingly naive, even if he appears to have no better, or even any at all, with which to replace it.

This is why hiring is so important. Through it we are initiated not only into the "ideological solidarity" of a profession, but into the profession as the basis for a life plan. But the legalism that authorizes hiring today proposes no plan at all. Its concern is merely that minority or disadvantaged groups get the opportunity to have a career in the first place. Fair enough. Yet I have been maintaining that, no matter how laudable the goal, the process is vitiated by unacknowledged tensions and misplaced consequences. Not only have prejudices not been eliminated. They have not even been understood. It is perhaps debatable who understands them less—those who support the ideological rectitude of the legalistic agenda, or those who oppose it as mystified. No one understands them at all who will not acknowledge that this agenda has become so oppressive it threatens to transform the whole notion of a career in college teaching, which need not be as circumspect, placid, or even free from prejudice as the present profile suggests.

The traditional model of authority, when it was unchallenged, may not have countenanced wayward, eccentric, or deviant energies any better. All that may be claimed for it is that it was more intimate with some more charismatic license—the very license that today's legalistic model has to efface in order to enjoy any authority at all. There are of course many reasons for getting hired. Some of them may actually be more aberrant than the rules stipulate. A Theroux, after all, does get his bone, and there may be more Reids managing to thread their own ways than anybody imagines. Furthermore, there may still be just as many reasons for not getting hired, and some of these may be much better than the rules indicate. None of this will console my friends above, who would probably want to reply that they themselves are better than the rules. The trouble is, in any case, nobody's telling. Confidentiality reigns. Getting hired is not entering into a dialogue with anybody about it, but instead listening to what you need to know.

I have claimed that ultimately there may be very little to know that will prove decisive. Another way to put this would be to state that, at the end, getting hired is always very difficult to separate from getting chosen. You get chosen because you are exceptional. How do you know? On what basis? You only really know when you are chosen—and then, if you are adequate to the moment, you receive the knowledge as something to celebrate, as a confirmation of yourself. The moment is therefore nothing if not a fictional one, and I want to resort to a last fiction in order to illustrate it.

There is a lovely passage early in E. L. Doctorow's *Billy Bathgate* after Billy, juggling, has been rewarded a 10-dollar bill along with the judgment that he is "a capable boy" by Dutch Schultz. Dutch and entourage proceed to leave. Billy is suddenly surrounded by a gang of jealous boys, but he slips away and delivers the following exultation:

> Oh you miserable fucking louts, that I ever needed to attach my orphan self to your wretched company . . . you dumb-bells, that you could aspire to a genius life of crime, with your dead witless eyes, your slack chins, and the simian slouch of your spines—fuck you forever, I consign you to tenement rooms and bawling infants, and sluggish wives and a slow death of incredible subjugation, I condemn you to petty crimes and mean rewards and vistas of cell block to the end of your days. (41)

Is it conceivable that a professor of English—Ed Cohen, say—could direct such words to the hundreds above whom he is about ascend now that he rather than they has been hired? Probably not. It is hard to feel exceptional against a background of hundreds; the point about getting hired today is that you are simply not entitled to feel that you have been, in a profound sense, chosen. But among many other reasons Billy's exultation would not be appropriate, let me conclude with one more: Billy himself would most likely have long ago been excluded from consideration. Or rather he would have excluded himself. His notion of a career is that it sponsors a "genius" life. But this represents, in turn, another profession entirely. For the profession as it actually determines itself at the point of entry, the life to which Billy condemns his fellows, is precisely the same slow life with which everyone is presented.

Works Cited

Booth, Wayne. *The Vocation of a Teacher: Rhetorical Occasions, 1967–1988.* Chicago: U of Chicago P, 1988.

Burke, Dolores. *A New Academic Marketplace.* New York: Greenwood, 1988.

Cohen, Ed. "Are We (Not) What We Are Becoming? 'Gay Identity,' 'Gay Studies,' and the Disciplining of Knowledge." *Engendering Men.* Ed. Joseph Boone and Michael Cadden. New York: Routledge, 1990. 161–75.

Doctorow, E. L.. *Billy Bathgate.* New York: Harper & Row, 1989.

Hanna, S. S. *The Gypsy Scholar.* Ames: Iowa State UP, 1987.

Kindrow, G. "The Candidate." *Lingua franca* 1.4 (1991): 21–25.

Larson, Magali Sarfatti. *The Rise of Professionalism: A Sociological Analysis*. Berkeley: U of California P, 1977.

Malamud, Bernard. *A New Life*. New York: Dell, 1963.

O'Toole, Simon. *Confessions of an American Scholar*. Minneapolis: U of Minnesota P, 1970.

Reid, B. L. *First Acts*. Athens: U of Georgia P, 1987.

Sontag, Susan. *Against Interpretation*. New York: Dell, 1967.

Theroux, Alexander. "The Detours of Art." *The Review of Contemporary Fiction*. 11.1 (1991): 36–40.

Trilling, Lionel. *Of This Time, Of That Place and Other Stories*. New York: Harcourt Brace Jovanovich, 1979.

Watkins, Evan. *Work Time: English Departments and the Circulation of Cultural Value*. Stanford: Stanford UP, 1989.

Wilbur, Henry. "On Getting a Job." *The Academic's Handbook*. Ed. A. Leigh Deneef, Craufurd Goodwin, and Ellen Stern McCrate. Durham: Duke UP, 1988.

Chapter Thirteen

The Educational Politics of Human Resources: Humanities Teachers as Resource Managers

Evan Watkins

Although identified in many different ways, intellectuals in humanities departments in the university have not typically been seen as economic agents. Christopher Newfield reminds us of the importance of university structure in establishing a rather different role: "Dominick LaCapra once remarked that the research university is structured like a nuclear family: the scientists are the dads, and they go out and make the money, and the humanists are the moms, and they stay home and take care of the kids" (341). Men are not usually socialized to take care of the kids, and the men who set the agendas and terms of value for the humanities during the first half of the century not only borrowed liberally from a scientific vocabulary to describe their work, but also inscribed the morality of arduous effort and the masculine heroism of discovery onto the tasks. Registering the exact measure of ambiguous force to a verse fragment or the precise field of reference for a historical document was above all *difficult*; not just anyone could do it. Payday, however, was a reminder that no matter how rigorous, the economic value of their efforts was not commensurate with the value of their colleagues' work in the sciences and in the professional schools.

As Bruce Robbins has argued in *Secular Vocations*, one compensation for this economic marginalization in the university was the equation of "genuinely" critical positions with independence from the marketplace. Humanities intellectuals could never expect the financial support extended to colleagues, but conversely their scholarly work could claim to represent the best interests of a general public, uncontaminated by allegiances to financial interests. "Professional" position as academics then appeared ambivalent at best, registered in the many versions of fall narratives into professionalism that Robbins analyzes. Professionalism is suspect not only because professionals are assumed to represent only their own narrow areas of specialized expertise rather than the public interest, but also because the work objectives of professionals are to some necessary extent market driven. Particularly in English, "service" and "service courses" thus became dirty words, a reminder of the marketplace side of professionalism to be displaced whenever possible onto composition specialists, graduate students, and junior faculty. English became a "high volume" field, but most of the volume of student circulation through the discipline was handled by these lower-level workers.

The now familiar model of economic change from high volume, mass produced, standardized goods to high value, flexibly specialized goods and services immediately responsive to shifts in specifically targeted markets cannot be applied directly to the organization of work in English departments. Nevertheless, there are enough similarities between the model and the assumptions that inform directions of recent educational reform proposals to suggest a range of serious issues. These proposals imply that the educational "value" of departments like English will no longer lie in high volume, in terms of sheer numbers of faculty, courses taught, and student credit hours produced. Rather, it will appear in terms of a wide array of relatively specialized services to very different audiences, and the potential effects of such a shift are considerable. Financial and institutional support may well begin to be directed not at English, to be allocated within the department as the department sees fit, but at specific programs within English dependent on perceived demands for services. In such circumstances, programs will be tied first of all to their immediate sources of support. It is already evident that the familiar hierarchy consigning an indiscriminate collection of service courses and instructors to the bottom of the discipline is changing in any number of ways as new forms of those services are often in demand. Composition and composition theory, for example, stand out as the one relatively bright spot in an otherwise deeply depressed market for English Ph.D.s.

Suspending for the moment judgments of whether such changes represent a good or bad thing, it is necessary to remember that "culture" and "cultural discourses" have a specific contemporary status that extends well beyond the academic disciplines. In the midst of recent and variously theorized economic changes, corporations discovered culture. Or perhaps more exactly, corporate managers realized that what had seemed a "natural" organizational structure determined by the economic exigencies of market presence, production capacity and aggregate demand was in fact a complex construction, dependent on a delicately balanced form of "corporate culture." The discovery of culture in this sense was neither a function of the growing importance of marketing relative to production, nor an awareness of the market potential for new cultural goods of all kinds, but the enforced recognition that the very structure of corporate organization involved a constitutively specific cultural field of practices.

One of the effects of this realization has been that corporate human resources analysts have broadened the scope of their field, from the interpersonal dynamics of management skills to a larger process of education that engages political issues of "multiculturalism" and "diversity" every bit as intensely as those of us in the university. "If we ignore the statistics about workforce composition and education," management consultants John Fernandez and Jacqueline Dubois argue, "we will have a severe shortage of qualified workers and a country that continues to have large pockets of extremely disadvantaged people of color" (208). They stress that while educating "qualified workers" and eliminating the "disadvantages" faced by those "large pockets" of people of color may seem radical political goals, they are by no means incompatible with corporate objectives: "We must emphasize that companies that are willing to accommodate diversity will reap rewards in traditional dollars-and-cents terms as they listen to their most valuable resource: people" (206). Fernandez and Dubois see no necessary contradiction between a politics of "empowerment" for a large, diverse, multicultural population on the one hand, and corporations who expect to "reap rewards in traditional dollars-and-cents terms" on the other. In recent books like Fernandez's *Managing a Diverse Work Force*, Ann Morrison's *The New Leaders*, Sondra Thiederman's *Profiting in America's Multicultural Marketplace*, and R. Roosevelt Thomas, Jr.'s, *Beyond Race and Gender*, human resources management is understood as realizing empowerment in the marketplace terms of work and its organization no less than in the market of cultural products. Human resources intellectuals thus stand in a very different relation to the market than the humanities intellectuals in the university who are the subject of Robbins's argument.

In whatever terms they might disagree over specifics, consultants like Fernandez and others are unanimous in their recognition that effective human resources management involves more than internal corporate organization and policy. It requires changes in the orientation of *public* policy generally, and it must begin not in the corporate workplace but far earlier, in the classrooms of an educational system. It is a mistake, in any case, to think a "humanities education"—however defined—as something confined to an academic setting. Business writer Richard Crawford points out that "IBM can correctly boast that it runs the largest educational system in the country" (29), and much of that education has to do with the "traditional" subjects of the humanities: literacy skills, methodologies of critical thinking and problem solving, historical awareness, how to read cultural representations, the power of narrative construction, the dynamics of interpersonal relationships—the list of similarities is a long one. In short, corporations have "discovered" culture.

It does not seem to me a great leap of logic to assume that the emphasis on knowledge growth and knowledge workers that shapes corporate direction will also affect public policy with regard to educational institutions. To the extent that human resources management is itself a set of educational practices, I think it altogether likely that programs for educational reform will reposition those of us who teach in the humanities as an extension and corroboration of the intellectual work practices of human resources management. On the one hand, this means that like human resources professionals, humanities intellectuals would acquire a new status as economic agents. Rather than simply "taking care of the kids," humanities instruction becomes a valuable contribution to an economic productivity that depends on human resources, and "the kids" appear as a pool of well-trained and flexibly skilled adults. On the other hand, however, the attention to culture in the humanities would itself take on new meanings as an economic activity. In the new terms of corporate organization, cultural practices after all are everywhere linked to the realization of corporate goals.

I realize of course that some such vision of humanities instruction as a kind of subcontracted junior-level corporate human resources management would seem to justify the punch line of every co-optation narrative about the academic "success" of recent radical programs in the humanities. In any case my interest here is not to theorize how, antennae to the wind, we might learn to "survive" what will result from the complex of corporate and public policy changes. In focusing attention on the figure of the intellectual as corporate human resources analyst in this essay, I have two immediate aims in mind.

The pressures on the university from new adaptations of a conservative "social issues" agenda are considerable and scary, and in claims like those advanced by William Bennett or Roger Kimball, for example, that agenda often finds expression in some version or another within humanities departments. Business-oriented proposals for educational reform, however, are not necessarily congruent with new conservative social issues politics, and such proposals are much less likely in any case to have faculty representatives. Hence, unlike new conservative social issues, the effects of such directions cannot be anticipated or challenged in familiar ways, particularly when they arrive in the form of valuing diversity and multiculturalism rather than as an insistence on "crude" marketplace indices or as a nostalgia for the wonders of Western Civilization. And it is hard to do something about what you do not understand.

Second, human resources management cannot simply be dismissed out of hand as the most recent version of capitalism with a human face. Programs such as those advocated by Fernandez and other human resources experts offer a great many people a promise of opportunities for multiple forms of very different and better kinds of work than they are doing at the moment, and include a number of ideas for changing public policy, educational institutions, and marketplace forces toward the end of making those opportunities available for more people. The issue is not really a matter of whether such a promise is "genuine" or just another mask for economic business as usual. Posed in these terms, the "correct" answer is already presupposed, and critique is left in the familiar and frustratingly ineffective role of keeping a distanced watch on these guys as proof that at least we have not been fooled. If, however, educational reform directions position humanities intellectuals as low-level academic versions of human resources managers then it might well be the case that possibilities for effective oppositional practices appear in new ways that include economic practices. Being positioned as an economic agent is not necessarily a bad thing, nor is it deterministic to recognize that economics, too, must change dramatically in order for political change to become a reality.

❦ ❦ ❦

A now familiar corporate vocabulary ("flexible specialization," "flattened management hierarchy," and so on) projects often very different narratives and changes, but there is at least a certain agreement that the "new economy" will require new workplace skills and foreground new workers. The expanded role of human resources management owes a great deal to the corporate recognition of the importance of a "culture" that will encourage development of a different kind of worker. In a book significantly titled *Post-Industrial Lives*—rather than, say, "postindustrial economics" or "postindustrial society"—business sociologists Jerald Hage and Charles Powers suggest a way of understanding recent economic developments that focuses attention on these new workers.

"Long-term change," they argue, "can be viewed as a composite of two contending forces that shape the way in which knowledge is embedded in activity. For want of better terms, we call these forces the processes of (a) rationalization and (b) complexification. Both processes influence the way social life is constructed. And a shift in the relative importance of these forces recently occurred" (43). Rationalization, as Weber described it, dominated the development of industrial society; complexification has emerged as the dominant force in postindustrial society. As in other accounts of economic change, Hage and Powers assume the development of new technologies is crucial: "What is important to recognize in order to understand this process [of industrial deskilling] is that it was predicated on embedding increasing levels of knowledge in machines precisely so that workers could function effectively without much knowledge or experience" (44). In contrast, the recent "impact of complexification on occupational roles is the exact opposite of that of rationalization, for machines don't always simplify or replace roles. Their introduction can also be associated with the creation of new occupational specialties and the addition of new activities to existing roles" (50).

Machines were introduced on the assembly line to replace hand labor. More often than not in small, specialized operations they appear instead as instruments that enlarge the field of available data, project a number of alternative possibilities, and require considerable, "creative" problem-solving ability on the part of their users. Rather than machine operatives assigned to repetitive task performance, employees then become skilled knowledge workers who expect and demand control over the determination of what counts as a "task" in the first place. Knowledge workers in this sense must be highly educated, and they must assume that their education will be a continuing process as situations change and still newer technologies become available. As educated workers, they will likely be educated consumers as well, which can lead among other things to dissatisfaction with mass produced, standardized goods of all kinds, and thus to an increasing demand for the sort of specialized goods and services they themselves oversee at work. In such an account, new technologies are not assumed as the "cause" of a change from mass production to specialized production, any more than they cause higher levels of education. Their function in Hage and Powers's argument is rather more like an available code that translates back and forth among different variables of change.

On the one hand, then, the concept of complexification yields a positive narrative of economic and cultural change across the development of new technologies. On the other hand, however, Hage and Powers's refocusing of sociological attention toward this positive dynamics of knowledge growth and away from the unequal distribution of wealth and power that preoccupied earlier sociologists (such as Weber) makes the persistence of social inequalities seem virtually incomprehensible, as they are forced to admit:

> The mechanisms of exploitation, which have produced a great underclass and denied large segments of society a realistic opportunity to develop to their human capital potential have simultaneously denied society the contributions these people are capable of making. A society that easily discards millions of people is unlikely to succeed in PI [postindustrial] competition. That path is so obviously dysfunctional that ignoring the problems of the underclass seems incomprehensible. (209)

The route by which Hage and Powers arrive at that conclusion is similar to the arguments of human resources management consultants like Fernandez, who likewise express astonishment at the "dysfunctional" myth that would justify the "discarding" of millions. What seems the inherent cost of the controlling profit dynamic of the corporation from a perspective like Weber's is merely a surviving relic of past beliefs and assumptions whose "dysfunctional" effects will soon become apparent even to the most obdurate corporate representatives for Hage and Powers and for Fernandez.

Thus while perhaps not strictly technological determinists, Hage and Powers—and a great many other theorists of a postindustrial society—nevertheless tend to locate "solutions" to the "problem" of persistent inequalities within a recognizable tradition of technocratic thinking. As William Leiss puts it:

> The concepts of 'information revolution,' 'information economy,' and 'information society' constitute an important new stage in the tradition of technocratic thinking in modern society. In large part their importance lies precisely in how perfectly they represent this tradition. They enable us to see clearly what role public policy is thought to have in the interaction between technology and society: namely, to 'soften up' public opinion so that a compliant response to a new technology may be delivered. (283–84)

Theorists of a knowledge-driven information society would thus function, in a familiar phrase from Gramsci, as "experts in legitimation" for shaping a politics of consent. Whatever "solutions" they might offer are a matter of better adaptation to an inexorable "logic" of events, shaped ultimately by changes in technologies.

Yet Leiss does not stress nearly enough how recent theorizing represents "an important new stage in the tradition of technocratic thinking." In that tradition, public policy remains reactive. Given the assumed inevitability of technological change, the most significant policy question is expressed in terms of how best to "adjust" to it. In this "important new stage," public policy also has an important role in creating conditions that make technological innovation possible. That is, public policy assumes a directive rather than a reactive role. Thus information and postindustrial society theorizing itself functions as propaganda that helps create conditions that assign high priorities to and rewards for innovative technological developments. Public policy in this sense is where such theorizing intersects with the work of management consultants like Fernandez, who stress the human resources necessary to implement these developments, and sociologists like Hage and Powers, who describe the shifting role requirements of knowledge growth and complexification. At the intersection of these currents of thought, the aim of public policy is the *creation* of new human resources rather than, as Leiss speculates, the reactive management of an "underclass."

In Hage and Powers's view, the new directive role of public policy implies that the dynamic of change no longer preserves the equilibrium of "top" and "bottom." For the task of creating new human resources must occur across the entire spectrum of the social formation, regardless of what might currently exist as "top" or "bottom." Similarly, "managing diversity," as consultants like Fernandez and Thomas understand it, is not a matter of "assimilating" traditionally excluded groups into an existing corporate culture. It is about changing corporate culture to maximize human resources. The pedagogical function of a directive public policy thus must be directed first at now "dysfunctional" attitudes found in reactionary corporate management.

What this "new stage" preserves from the tradition of technocratic thinking Leiss identifies is a certain perception of inevitability, of inexorable "forces" at work, if now embodied in "knowledge growth" or simply "information" as well as in technology itself. While in the past agency had been understood as a question of individual choice, Hage and Powers argue "that this conceptualization is inappropriate for our times" (210). The individual can no longer appear the determinate node of agent choice: "We demonstrate that knowledge growth, and more specifically the ways in which new knowledge is implanted in minds, in machines, and in patterns of social organization, determines the structural need for the exercise of agency as a functional prerequisite to flexible adaptation in the face of uncertain and changing conditions" (211). The curiously passive voice construction—"the ways in which new knowledge is implanted"—squatting in the midst of this discussion of "agency" signals not only the persistence of a technocratic assumption of inevitability but also a change in the very notion of "change."

Daniel Bell responds with some considerable irritation to the endlessly repeated reminder that "change" has accelerated: "We have heard much of the acceleration of the pace of change. It is seductive but ultimately a meaningless idea other than as a metaphor. For one has to ask, 'Change of what?' and, 'How does one measure the pace?' There is no metric that applies in general, and the word change is ambiguous" (96). All that can be said with some certainty, he continues, "is that the scale of change has widened . . . the growth of an enterprise, for example, requires specialization and differentiation and very different kinds of control and management systems when the scales move from, say, $10 million to $100 million to $1 billion" (97). In other words, for Bell no independent measure exists by which relative rates of change might be assessed; the fundamental characteristic of change in the present is to absorb more and more surrounding territory that thereby becomes unavailable to function as a stable point of reference for rate. Counterpoised against Hage and Powers's discussion of agency, Bell's comments suggest that "inevitability" now has less to do with the linear progress and acceleration rates emphasized by technocratic thinking in the past and more to do with structural saturation. For "$10 million to $100 million to $1 billion" is not a measure of rate or even movement, but an index of completeness, of "spread" across a field. Bell's perception registers change by reference to an alteration of the whole.

It should not then be surprising that "agency" in Hage and Powers's discussion likewise appears as a matter of "scale" rather than as some autonomous, unilateral exercise of choice at a determinate, causal node. Agency is distributed across a process requiring "negotiation and co-determined agreement among people who must cooperate" (210). Much of the analysis in *Post-Industrial Lives* thus has to do with networks and their role structures, as the ensemble of occasions that links the inevitable scale enlargements across the social formation with cooperatively negotiated powers of agency at any given point anywhere in the social field: "We predict that the fluid network will be the defining form of social organization in the PI era" (204), a form that reconstructs "the society from the bottom up" (205).

This reversal of a more traditional vision of change moving from the top down in every sector (with public policy functioning to "soften up" the bottom to accept change) explains why it is that the persistence of massive social inequalities, together with "ignoring the problems of the underclass," should seem so "obviously dysfunctional" as to be "incomprehensible" (206). It flies in the face of the inevitability of scale saturation. A linear vision of rapidly accelerating change could easily accept the social disjunction that emerges between a few leaders and the great many left behind, even when it might portend a "society that easily discards millions of people." Change as scale enlargement, in contrast, assumes the inevitability of permeating the entire social formation, wherever it might begin.

Over the last two decades, however, the rhetoric of corporate restructuring invokes instead a vocabulary of "scaling down" rather than the steady spread of scale implied by Bell's comments. Downsizing, flattened management hierarchy, flexible specialization, precision concentration on critical points in the value-added stream, regionally autonomous operating units, implemented automation, and so on, are all expressive of *reductions* of scale. Relatively sanguine information society theorists like Benjamin Compaine dismiss the fears about job loss, the replacement of workers with machines, the "information gap" between rich and poor and between nations, and the disparities in the availability of new technologies that have resulted from these forms of restructuring, by appealing once again to inevitabilities of scale, in even broader terms: "As seen in the figures representing the constant dollar price of electricity, automobiles, telephone service and television sets, the combination of declining costs, thanks to improvements in technology, and a wealthier work force, has lessened the difference in life style between the poorer and richer in society. Today, with many manufacturing jobs being transferred to the developing industrial nations, there are signs that a similar process is taking place on a global scale" (189–90). That is, in Compaine's vision at least, what worries Hage and Powers as an "incomprehensible" persistence of inequalities only appears as a problem because the scale of their own analysis is simply not wide enough yet.

As Bell reminds us, however, changes in scale are rarely uniform across the social formation of any specific country, let alone globally. The long historical curve plotted by Compaine not only ignores "local" disruptions, but depends on a structural scheme possessed by the analyst that conveniently permits a synchronicity of "before" and "after" at any given moment in the process of change. Bell argues in contrast that public policy in the form of deliberate political decisions must intervene to compensate for uneven developments: "The problem for future information societies is to match the scales between political and economic institutions and activities" (97), in other words, between an information *society* and an information *economy*. Even if one took, for example, the statistics generated in Marc Porat's massive nine-volume study in 1977, *The Information Economy*, as a Q.E.D. for the existence of an economy driven primarily by "information work" in some form or another, Bell's point is that nothing would warrant assuming an egalitarian information society as an automatic corollary, as Compaine implies.

More radically, Herbert Schiller argues in *Who Knows: Information in the Age of the Fortune 500* that the more complete the scale of economic transformation toward an international, information-based capitalism, the more it becomes necessary to recognize that we live in a society of deliberately calculated *mis*information about social inequalities that have in fact been widened and intensified by the organization of an information economy. That is, in Schiller's argument not only is there a growing gap between information "haves" and "have-nots," but public policy has deliberately encouraged the dissemination of misinformation calculated to maintain the gap. Thus Bell's hope of "matching scales" would be merely a familiar utopian fantasy of liberal political "tinkering." It ignores both the investment of dominant interests in preserving inequalities and the power of controlling the availability of information on which to base the political decisions Bell would urge as necessary. For Schiller, the existence of a genuine information society—with equal access to, and possibilities of empowerment by, information skills and knowledges—would make the current form of an information economy with its controlling interests an impossibility.

Schiller's arguments have not gone unanswered, of course. In one of the more careful responses, Jorge Reina Schement points out that Schiller has rather too quickly assimilated the organization and control of informational activities to a uniform development of capitalism: "They [Schiller, Vincent Mosco and others] can explain the role played by capitalism in the formation of the pattern of informational activities, but they are unable to distinguish the relative influence of industrialization, apart from capitalism. By examining only the dynamics of capitalism, their critique remains incomplete" (37). As Schement goes on to argue, capitalism and industrialism cannot be understood as necessarily synonymous: "The United States was already a capitalist society before entrepreneurs began adapting the industrial system to the pursuit of profit" (41). Likewise, while an information economy may indeed be capitalistic, there is no reason to assume that "adapting" the control of information "to the pursuit of profit" will yield exactly the same results as industrial capitalism. Understanding social inequalities requires analysis of the specific conditions of an information economy rather than simply assigning inequalities to some uniform "dynamics of capitalism" as an underlying cause.

Schement's argument also suggests good reason to question Hage and Powers's perception of the survival from the past of "rationalized," routine work practices in an information economy. In an information economy even flexibly specialized manufacturing involves *local* sectors of "routine" work existing in isolation not only from other and "complex" work sectors, but more often than not—as subcontracted or leased—from the organization and location of any central corporate structure. In other words, such local forms of routine, rationalized work are not holdovers from a now vanishing form of production, as Hage and Powers imply, but indispensable to and produced by the current requirements of complex work and its ends. Even if capitalism remains in place, structural patterns of inequalities and forms of exploitation will then differ significantly.

To a great extent the "secular vocations" in the humanities that Robbins analyzes have projected a self-understanding of their work as occupying a kind of "negative" space, "outside" this entire complex of marketplace forces and economic exploitation. While perhaps now a familiar picture of intellectual work, it must be altered considerably in turning to consider the work, affiliations, and positions of consultants like Fernandez or business sociologists like Hage and Powers in current economic conditions.

Like earlier scientific management planners, human resources analysts understand their work as directly engaged on behalf of corporate objectives. "True, all groups will benefit," R. Roosevelt Thomas argues in *Beyond Race and Gender*, "whether they are different in terms of age, lifestyle, gender or race. But their benefit is not the driving motivation. Managing diversity presumes that the driving force is the manager's, and the company's, self-interest" (168). That "self-interest," Fernandez reminds us, is typically expressed as "rewards in traditional dollars-and-cents terms" (206). Given this admitted commitment to corporate profit objectives, Hage and Powers's assertion that they are theorizing change "from the bottom up"; Fernandez's concern for the necessity to educate everybody and for the elimination of the disadvantages faced by people of color; and Thomas's argument that managing diversity requires a radical change in "corporate culture" rather than attempts to assimilate "others" into an existing culture, are all likely to seem hollow claims indeed, nothing but a mask for economic business as usual.

Nevertheless, if in the past "traditional" corporate profit objectives did not seem to require much attention to "diversity," then something must have changed significantly to have occasioned the current ensemble of linkages. The answer supplied by management diversity theorizing lies in demographics. Dramatized in the Hudson Institute's 1987 Report, *Workforce 2000*, corporations will face a radical shortage in skilled labor and a labor force growth rate fueled overwhelmingly by white women and people of color in circumstances where "quality and innovation," as Hage and Powers argue, "are now more important in the marketplace than price" (35). Quality and innovation come from the availability of more and more highly skilled people educated to produce and take advantage of changing conditions rather than from an "efficiently" organized mass of relatively unskilled workers.

Likewise, in terms of marketing the success of flexibly specialized production depends on the identification of very specifically targeted consumer "needs." And what from the side of production looks like a shortage of skilled labor and an influx of white women and people of color into the workforce looks from the marketing side like a shortage of knowledge about how to target goods and services to this influx. With respect to both production and marketing, demographics is intended to supply the "reality check" of hard data that reveals how profit potential must be linked with an attention to diversity. At the same time, however, demographics also projects a powerful politics of selection that alters fundamentally the very conditions of "incorporation" as a public citizen of a democracy.

❦ ❦ ❦

The dream of a "universal" public education system involved a claim to create uniform, fair, public standards for the enormously complicated process of identifying appropriately qualified people for different occupational positions. Schools were the location where the interests of "private" enterprise intersected with the interests of the State as representative of the general public, with ideologies of merit—the best person for the requirements of any given position—providing a shared set of norms. The State's responsibility was to provide an educational system that could ensure equal access to and equal opportunity for training to everyone; private enterprise was assumed to be driven by its own interests to hire the best available people emerging from educational training programs; educators in the schools, meanwhile, were simultaneously in charge of training and positioned at the controls of finely tuned discriminations of respective "merit" among the student population whose work they monitored.

In practice of course the process always seemed flawed, the indices skewed, corrections and adjustments a continual necessity, "exceptions" more and more obvious. Further, as critics pointed out with increasing frequency determinations of merit were no more race- or gender- or class-blind than the actual selection decisions made at workplaces. In relation to occupational stratification, merit seemed little more than a complicated form of ideological legitimation. Even such ideological critiques of merit, however, tend to ignore how merit and selection implied fundamentally distinct grounds of decision making. For all that the results often looked similar in excluding specific population groups, merit directly addresses the identification of differences among people against the background of a public discourse that invoked ideally knowable, uniform standards. Thus it was possible that once shown to be discriminatory or exclusionary in practice, either actual decisions or the norms of public discourse could be modified.

In contrast, the process of workplace selection begins not with differences among individuals, but with the organization of work itself, with differences among tasks. At the upper levels of occupation—prestigious professions, corporate management, and so on—these two distinct fields of merit and workplace selection could appear to coalesce insofar as the "quality" of the person and the precise nature of the work "tasks" performed seemed mutually defining. But down the scale of occupational stratification, the disjunction becomes more visible not only in terms of the fit between personal qualities and task-determined responsibilities, but also with respect to the relative indices of differentiation to which individuals are subjected.

For instance, person X with a high school diploma and two years of community college working as a convenience store clerk is not only overeducated and underemployed, as the familiar refrain has it. From management perspective, person X is also "overmerited," having been the subject of far too many and "redundant" merit decisions than "necessary" to determine via workplace selection practices an "appropriate" worker. Thus educational theorists like Bowles and Gintis, for example, have argued that the real function of such "overmeriting" is instead psychological. It has little directly to do with selection, but rather with the necessity to convince large numbers of the population to accept the "fact" that they do not really have what it takes to occupy better paying and more prestigious positions. In a great many cases the persuasion may take some considerable time. Person X may be one of those for whom four years of high school humiliation was not enough; however "redundant" from the perspective of workplace requirements at a convenience store, the two extra years of community college may well have been psychologically necessary to complete the "education."

Such reasoning, however, underestimates the way in which ideologies of merit also contribute powerfully to a psychology of workplace *rights*. Two years of community college may finally have persuaded person X that he or she really is dumb, but there is nothing that automatically prevents the possibility that in specific circumstances person X would be convinced instead that he or she had immense untapped potential finally being realized. The authority invested in merit decisions to "cool off" student expectations can also yield a potentially "dangerous" psychology should the student come to feel "empowered" by such decisions. The disjunction between indices of merit and of workplace selection necessary for merit to function as ideological legitimation carries a potential for disruption, familiarly targeted by conservative social theorists as a general "breakdown of standards" in educational systems.

Unlike conservative social theorists, however, corporations who see themselves presently facing a shortage of highly skilled labor worry less about the breakdown of standards and its effects on large numbers of the school population than about the educational training required for skilled positions. Corporate management fears focus at the top of the job ladder where merit decisions and selection practices can seem to coalesce under the name of "human resources." Corporate human resources analysts thus occupy a stress point between what Robert Reich identifies as the *global* field of reference for the work of symbolic analysts employed by transnational corporations, and the educational and occupational expectations of a potential *domestic* workforce in the process of training.

For the former, global mobilities require continually learning new work skills and ways of adapting to unfamiliar conditions in both marketing and production. Human resources programs have an important role in this continual process of retraining, and the so-called environmental scans produced by resources management professionals contribute to the identification of global market potential as well as feasibility projections for relocating or opening new corporate units. But environmental scanning also functions to isolate demographic factors that might yield a locally available source of new workers. Thus the presence of a major research university, for example, whose programs are addressed to a large, multicultural population, offers an attractive incentive for opening a new regionally autonomous corporate unit that would have immediately available a source of qualified workers. Human resources professionals who help define for the corporation what counts as "qualifications" are then engaged simultaneously in defining educational goals for those in school at particular locations. Likewise, the assessments of the desirability or not of regional locations, produced by human resources analysis, affect people's conditions of choice of school in the first place.

Seen through the lens of merit, selection procedures had seemed a generalized process, ideally at least answerable to uniform, known, public standards, and enforceable by public policies such as affirmative action. In this new scenario, however, selection from an available pool of educated workers at any given location is dependent entirely on a corporate management "read" of immediate conditions, produced by the demographic technologies of environmental scanning and the like. Conceptions of merit do not disappear by any means, but the ground of merit decisions is dislocated from the realm of public discourse and reinscribed within the demographic studies of corporate human resources analysis. Demographics, that is, make possible a constructed identity of merit decisions and selection practices by "privatizing" merit. The expansion of private education is often viewed by conservative social theorists as a welcome alternative to the "radical" ideologies that have infiltrated public education systems. In the sense I have been describing, however, a corporate expansion has already taken place. For what is "private" about "private enterprise" in this vision is not really its economics, but its power to control the educational authority of merit decisions as grounded in the technologies of demographic studies.

Despite claims that demographics are intended to spur corporate commitments to genuine diversity in the workforce, Avery Gordon has explained how this ostensible "reality check" involves a rather remarkable sleight-of-hand: "For example, diversity management rarely attributes increased rates of white female labor force participation to the economic crisis of the mid-1970s, preferring the more idealistic explanation of heightened feminine consciousness" (16). In larger terms, diversity as a "new" reality made visible by demographics "allows the corporation to ignore the fact that it was instrumental in keeping American business more homogenous than American society" (16). Demographics can thus project diversity management as politically progressive only "because in effect it has no history, only progress and the future" (16). Whatever may have been the case in the past for whatever reason, demographics keeps the focus resolutely on meeting the challenges of the future, and identifies diversity management as the best tactical means of aligning progressive political reform with newly redesigned corporate business practices and inclusive forms of corporate culture.

Thus in R. Roosevelt Thomas's understanding managing diversity is a more effective form of "empowerment" for employees than public policy dictates such as affirmative action because it "doesn't seek to give relief to a system's negative consequences by adding supplementary efforts" (26). That is, Thomas's quarrel with affirmative action as public policy is neither with its politics nor with its "intrusion" of politics into economics, but with its effectiveness. Managing diversity in contrast "is a holistic approach to creating a corporate environment that allows all kinds of people to reach their full potential in pursuit of corporate objectives" (167). It involves an internal process of cultural education that leads to the "natural creation of a diverse work force," and a "natural upward mobility for minorities and women" (28) within the corporation.

As Gordon points out, Thomas's work is explicitly couched in the cultural terms of corporate reorganization that seems oblivious to the social history of corporations in the United States. Nevertheless, arguably it is informed by a powerful historical vision. The "corporate environment" Thomas describes offers a way of rethinking a great many fundamental premises of liberal democracy as now recentered around the *corporate* citizen rather than the citizen of the State. That is, managing diversity as a cultural education is also a political education in citizenship, and ultimately corporate selection practices thereby identify the process of incorporation into a body politic. Managing diversity must then also function within the privatized selection process for a corporate workforce.

While the political role of human resources analysts may be imagined as oppositionally committed to new, more publicly open and more democratic forms, their function as economic agents is already circumscribed by the politics of this division between public and private. Thus the "problem" is not that human resources analysts are also economic agents and hence inevitably "compromise" their politics or allow their work to be "co-opted." It is that the privatization of selection within internal corporate control also demarcates which zones of political power are available to which economic agents. Privatization in this sense makes the process of "incorporation" into a workforce synonymous with political "incorporation" as citizens. Managing diversity is finally about the political management of citizenship.

One visible effect produced by this double field of reference of incorporation is the special role "profession" begins to occupy in the mutation of a so-called middle class and its social expectations. A profession appears as less a carefully controlled avenue of upward mobility and social prestige than as a way to use economic practices as an avenue of political incorporation. "Profession," that is, identifies a pathway of incorporation by which agents engaged in market organized economic practices can also attempt to secure at least some visible authority within the organization of corporate capital politics. Professional services are sold; they are market-appropriate resources. But to the extent that professional services are also imagined as having general, public value, professional agents can have a claim to political authority in the "public" world.

As I argued in *Throwaways*, the growth and diversity of services is a distinctive feature of recent economic trends. Services of all kinds, however, are increasingly sold within the terms of a complex symbolic system designating service workers themselves as professional providers. To take one example, business cards were once limited to relatively traditional and prestigious fields such as law but are now a feature of virtually any service transaction from periodontal specialists to fitting room technicians at major department stores, mechanics at K-Mart, and housecleaning personnel. A quick glance at any *Yellow Pages* will reveal not only dozens of usages of "professional" on every page, but also a remarkable proliferation of accreditation guarantees that attest to a professional level of service. This symbolic system may seem at best just a marketing ploy and at worst merely a source of humor, as in the nominal transformation of garbage collectors into sanitation engineers. Yet even in what may appear bizarre circumstances, the signs designating the professional also continue to focus a claim to general, public value for the service sold. That is, the privatization of corporate selection processes simultaneously permits this refocusing of *public* as a mediating term by which profession can link economic value to political incorporation and worth. One result is that what "the public" seems to value most are not necessarily the services supplied by the profession and the opportunity to purchase those services, but rather an opportunity to become oneself a professional in the field and thereby secure a form of political incorporation. "Public" thus mutates into multiple, strategic forms of political practice.

As part of a public education curriculum, literary study was often imagined as something of great potential value to every citizen. Even though the majority would never become professional literary scholars, that education had value to the citizens of a democratic political state. However, R. P. Blackmur was once led to comment that such education "is producing a larger and larger class of intellectually trained men and women the world over who cannot make a living in terms of their training and who cannot, because of their training, make a living otherwise with any satisfaction" (8). In current circumstances, in contrast, students who get enough of a literary education construct a sense of its value linked to the possibilities of becoming a professional literary teacher and scholar. As this happens, the gap Blackmur notes is dramatically foreshortened. "Intellectual training" and "making a living" begin to seem an indissoluble complex, as "training" now includes an education in the multiple practices of what you do day-to-day, "making a living" as a professional literary scholar and teacher. Thus the "job" that may or may not appear just beyond the horizon of the "training" period no longer looks like the beginning of "making a living," but rather the *political* guarantee of social position and authority to extend the complex of intellectual and economic practices at another level.

Although still generally regarded as an alien force in the profession of literary scholarship, economics appears at precisely this point of identification between intellectual training and making a living. The diminished job market for English Ph.Ds, we tell ourselves over and over, means that it is "unethical" to continue to support high-volume graduate programs, educating people who will never be able to find jobs in the field. It is the economic "realities" of the market that put a cap on how many literary scholars we can "turn out." So we have to pay considerably more attention to standards, make our selection processes tighter, accept the necessity to put more energy into general undergraduate rather than specialized graduate training—and be sure to tell those undergraduates most "successfully" trained that they had better not even think of grad school in English. All of which makes for an interesting notion of "ethical," and one that folds us neatly into the human resources project of carefully managing diversity.

Markets, however, define economic practices, not the other way around. Markets are complex ensembles of social relations in which the resources produced at specific points in the formation can be designated as exchangeable within conditions thereby identified as economic. Thus "economic realities" do not intrude from the outside to set a limit on how many Ph.Ds we should "ethically" produce; economic practices are part of the training from the beginning. Limits are a matter of the politics of markets. Possible ways to create, multiply, and extend avenues of political incorporation against the consolidation and privatization of selection practices depend on changing the politics of markets, not on the freedom of a position "outside" marketplace forces.

If such possibility implies very different practices and programs than those offered by Fernandez, Thomas and other human resources analysts in their attempts to coordinate "people issues" and "business issues," there remains nevertheless an indispensable lesson from their work. Like it or not, anyone positioned as an economic agent will represent the interests of a great many people. It is silly to overestimate the potential authority of such a position in the humanities, relative even to the work of corporate consultants like Fernandez, let alone those who shape the larger parameters of public policy. But it is a mistake to imagine that it is possible to avoid "speaking for" anyone else, somehow edenically free from the contaminations of representation in its various forms. In addition to issues of whether academic study might actually "co-opt" or "appropriate" or "colonize" other cultures and cultural traditions by representing them, there is also an economics of multiculturalism that positions our work.

There is little reason to seek a return to the ideologies of merit that informed the history of a public educational system in the United States. For any number of people the dream of "universal" public education was never quite an idyll. Rather than aligning them with traditionally prestigious professional fields such as law or medicine, understanding literary and cultural studies as a profession inserted within the multiple, diverse market fields of professional service providers functions like Gramsci's redefinition of the "intellectual," enlarging both positional reference and representational affiliations. Which is not quite the same as training more

English majors, but has everything to do with the specific linkages of economic professionalization and political incorporation. For the idea of the "The Market" has become more than an economic fiction. It is a politics of colonizing control and "management," against which the proliferation of self-designated professions and the mazy intricacies of the "informal sector" from which they emerge function as a reminder that actual markets are always collision zones of political struggle.

The existence of multiple, differently organized markets thus renews the urgency of that familiar question within socialist traditions: Whose market, for whom? Likewise, the politics of a university position in the humanities raises at every level of everyday practice issues of economic direction. No one can hope to plot in advance how to forestall the ways in which corporate privatization of selection also redefines the social configurations of a public world. Nor is it possible to escape the often contradictory imperatives that come with a professional, academic position. But the encounters with multiple publics in such positions nevertheless encourages new forms of tactical maneuver where what we learn as educators is not only a matter of cultural resistance. Equally important, as professions multiply before our eyes, we learn how to leverage economic practices into a weapon in the struggles for political change. We learn possibilities for making use of an economic agency.

Works Cited

Bell, Daniel. "Communication Technology: For Better or for Worse?" Salvaggio 92–101.

Blackmur, R. P. "Toward a Modus Vivendi." *The Lion and the Honeycomb: Essays in Solicitude and Critique*. New York: Harcourt, Brace, 1955. 3–31.

Compaine, Benjamin. "Information Gaps: Myth or Reality?" *Issues in New Information Technology*. Ed. Benjamin Compaine. Norwood: Ablex, 1988.

Crawford, Richard. *In the Era of Human Capital: The Emergence of Talent, Intelligence, and Knowledge as the Worldwide Economic Force and What It Means to Managers and Investors*. New York: HarperCollins, 1991.

Fernandez, John P. *Managing a Diverse Work Force: Regaining the Competitive Edge*. Lexington, MA: Heath, 1991.

———, and Jacqueline Dubois. "Managing a Diverse Workforce in the 1990s."

Human Resource Forecasting and Strategy Development: Guidelines for Analyzing and Fulfilling Organizational Needs. Ed. Manuel London, Emily Bassman, and John Fernandez. New York: Quorum, 1990. 202–10.

Gordon, Avery. "The Work of Corporate Culture: Diversity Management." *Social Text* 44 (1995): 3–30.

Hage, Jerald, and Charles Powers. *Post-Industrial Lives: Roles and Relationships in the Twenty-First Century*. Newbury Park: Sage, 1992.

Leiss, William. "The Myth of the Information Society." *Cultural Politics in Contemporary America*. Ed. Ian Angus and Sut Jhally. New York: Routledge, 1989. 282–98.

Morrison, Ann M. *The New Leaders: Guidelines on Leadership Diversity in America*. San Fransisco: Jossey-Bass, 1992.

Newfield, Christopher. "What Was Political Correctness? Race, the Right, and Managerial Democracy in the Humanities." *Critical Inquiry* 19 (1993): 308–36.

Porat, Marc. *The Information Economy*. 9 vols. Special Publication 77–12. Washington, DC: Office of Telecommunications, 1977.

Reich, Robert. *The Work of Nations: Preparing Ourselves for Twenty-First Century Capitalism*. New York: Knopf, 1991.

Robbins, Bruce. *Secular Vocations: Intellectuals: Professionalism, Culture*. New York: Verso, 1993.

Salvaggio, Jerry, ed. *The Information Society: Economic, Social and Structural Issues*. Hillsdale: Erlbaum, 1989.

Schement, Jorge Reina. "The Origins of the Information Society in The United States: Competing Visions." Salvaggio 34–51.

Schiller, Herbert. *Who Knows: Information in the Age of the Fortune 500*. Norwood: Ablex, 1981.

Thiederman, Sondra. *Profiting in America's Multicultural Marketplace*. New York: Macmillan, 1991.

Thomas, R. Roosevelt. *Beyond Race and Gender: Unleashing the Power of Your Total Workforce*. New York: AMACOM, 1991.

Watkins, Evan. *Throwaways: Work Culture and Consumer Education*. Stanford: Stanford UP, 1993.

Workforce 2000: Work and Workers for the 21st Century. William B. Johnston, project director. Indianapolis: Hudson Institute, 1987.

Contributors

Crystal Bartolovich teaches at Syracuse University. She has published widely on cultural studies and early modern British culture, and her book, *Boundary Disputes: Primitive Accumulation and the Origin of (Un)common Culture*, is forthcoming.

Michael Bérubé recently moved to Penn State University to take the Paterno Family Chair, though responsibilities do not include coaching football. His most recent books are *Life as We Know It: A Father, a Family, and an Exceptional Child* (1998) and *The Employment of English: Theory, Jobs, and the Future of Literary Studies* (1998).

Terry Caesar currently teaches at Mukogawa Women's University in Japan. He has published three books on academic life, *Conspiring with Forms* (1992), *Writing in Disguise* (1998), and, also from SUNY, *Traveling through the Boondocks* (2000), as well as books on travel writing.

Lennard J. Davis is currently head of the English department at the University of Illinois-Chicago. Following several books on the novel, his most recent books include *Enforcing Normalcy: Disability, Deafness and the Body* (1995) and *My Sense of Silence: Memoirs of a Childhood with Deafness* (2000), as well as the edited anthology *The Disability Studies Reader* (1997).

Grant Farred teaches at Duke University. He is editor of *Rethinking C. L. R. James* (1996) and author of *Midfielder's Moment: Coloured Literature and Culture in Contemporary South Africa* (1999) and *What's My Name? Organic and Vernacular Intellectuals* (forthcoming).

Vincent B. Leitch holds the Sutton Chair in English at the University of Oklahoma. He is the general editor of the new *Norton Anthology of Theory and Criticism* (2001) and author of several books, including the standard *American Literary Criticism from the 1930s to the 1980s* (1988).

Devoney Looser currently teaches English and Women's Studies at Louisiana State University. She is the author of *British Women Writers and the Writing of History, 1670–1820* (2000) and the editor of *Jane Austen and Discourses of Feminism* (1995) and *Generations: Academic Feminists in Dialogue* (coedited with E. Ann Kaplan; 1997).

Louise Mowder did her doctoral work in English at Rutgers University, and was a president of the MLA's Graduate Student Caucus.

David R. Shumway teaches at Carnegie Mellon University. He is the author of *Michel Foucault* (1989) and *Creating American Civilization: A Genealogy of American Literature as an Academic Discipline* (1994), and coeditor, with Craig Dionne, of *Disciplining English*, also from SUNY (2001).

James J. Sosnoski teaches at the University of Illinois-Chicago. His most recent books are *Token Professionals and Master Critics: A Critique of Orthodoxy in Literary Studies* (SUNY, 1994) and *Modern Skeletons in Postmodern Closets: A Cultural Studies Alternative* (SUNY, 1997).

Paul Tremblath teaches at Colorado State University. His work has appeared in *Postmodern Culture*, *Philosophy and Literature*, *the minnesota review*, and other journals, and he is completing a book on what "aesthetics" can mean after poststructuralisms and cultural materialisms.

Evan Watkins teaches at Penn State University. He is the author of four books, including *Work Time: English Departments and the Circulation of Cultural Value* (1989), *Throwaways: Cultural Work and Consumer Education* (1993), and *Everyday Exchanges: Marketwork and Capitalist Common Sense* (1998).

Jeffrey J. Williams teaches at the University of Missouri-Columbia. He is the author of *Theory and the Novel: Narrative Reflexivity in the British Tradition* (1998) and a co-editor of *The Norton Anthology of Theory and Criticism*. Since 1992 he has edited *the minnesota review*.

Index

Arnold, Matthew, 81–82

Balsamo, Anne, 117
Baumgarten, Alexander, 50, 55n.7
Baym, Nina, 62, 65
Bell, Daniel, 271–73
Benjamin, Walter, 50, 55n.7, 124, 140
Bennett, Tony, 111
Bérubé, Michael, 111
Beverley, John, 144–45n.21
Bhabha, Homi, 89, 116–17
Birmingham Centre for Contemporary Cultural Studies, 78
Bloom, Allan, 118
Bloom, Harold, 95–97, 108
Booth, Wayne, 254
Bourdieu, Pierre, 13–14n.1, 154, 212–14, 221n.12
Bové, Paul A., 29, 45
Bowen, William, and Neil Rudenstine, 230–33
Bromwich, David, 97–100
Brooks, Cleanth, 30–34
Brooks, Peter, 37–38
Burke, Kenneth, 4–7
Butler, Tudith, 191–93

Campbell, Colin, 181
Carby, Hazel, 88
Childers, Mary, 69
Chomsky, Noam, 218–19
Clark, Bruce, 166
Clarke, John, and Janet Newman, 141–42n.5
Cohen, Ed, 248
Compaine, Benjamin, 274–75
Craigie, Jonathan, 97–100
Cultural Studies (Grossberg et al.), 49, 102–03, 109n.1, 136–37

Davion, Victoria, 68
Deleuze, Gilles, 44, 49–51, 54–55n.6, 55n.8, 68
de Lauretis, Teresa, 67
de Man, Paul, 184–85
Denning, Michael, 87, 89–90
Derrida, Jacques, 27, 44, 50, 53n.1, 56n.10, 181, 191
Dewey, John, 47
Doctorow, E. L., 261–62
Dollimore, Jonathan, and Alan Sinfield, 46

Ehrenreich, Barbara, 213–14

Farid, Elashmawi, and Philip R. Harris, 132–33
Fernandez, John, and Jacqueline Dubois, 267–69
Fish, Stanley, 186, 191–92, 193–95, 222n.19
Fisher, Philip, 126–27
Foucault, Michel, 9, 45–53, 53n.1, 54n.5, 55n.7, 120, 139, 190
Frye, Northrop, 95–96

Gallop, Jane, 61, 66, 186
Gates, Henry Louis, Jr., 184
Graff, Gerald, 6, 9, 137, 157
Gramsci, Antonio, 45
Greenblatt, Stephen J., 29, 35–36; and Giles Gunn (*Redrawing the Boundaries*), 114–40
Gross, Bertram, 144n.20
Group for Early Modern Cultural Studies (GEMCS), 162–67, 170–71n.10–11
Guillory, John, 8

Habermas, Jurgen, 48
Hage, Jerald, and Charles Powers, 270–76
Hall, Stuart, 84, 119, 137, 141n.1

Haraway, Donna, 62, 69
Harris, David, 86–87
Harris, Philip R., and Robert T. Morgan, 131–32
Hartman, Geoffrey, 181
Henry, William, III, 96
Hirsch, Marianne, 63; and Evelyn Fox Keller, 63, 66
hooks, bell, 69
Hyman, Stanley Edgar, 32

James, C. L. R., 86, 123–24
Jameson, Fredric, 26, 111–12, 122, 198n.16
Johnson, Richard, 128

Keller, Evelyn Fox, and Helene Moglen, 66
Kittredge, George Lyman, 173–74, 188–89
Klein, Renate, 64
Kolodny, Annette, 62, 65
Kramarae, Cheris, and Dale Spender, 65

Lacan, Jacques, 26–27
Laclau, Ernesto, and Chantal Mouffe, 47, 53–54n.2
Landry, Donna, 62, 67, 68
Leavis, F. R., 81–82
Leavis, Q. D., 82
Leiss, William, 271–73
Leitch, Vincent, 39–40n.1
Lentricchia, Frank, 44, 48, 184
Levine, George, 99–100, 109n.2
Lukács, Georg, 159–60, 161
Lyotard, Jean François, 48

Makaryk, Irena, 39–40n.1, 40n.3
Malamud, Bernard, 255–57
Marcus, Leah, 138–39
Marxist Literary Group (MLG), 171n.16
Miller, J. Hillis, 181
Miller, James, 49
Miller, Nancy K., 63–64
Modern Language Association (MLA), 101, 161; convention, 7, 155–56, 184, 187
Montrose, Louis, 122–23

New Criticism, 30–34, 44, 80, 92–93, 107
New Historicism, 29–30, 35–37, 46, 48, 122–23
Nietzsche, Friedrich, 43

Ohmann, Richard, 9, 14n.2, 184, 190n.2
O'Toole, Simon, 243–44

Paglia, Camille, 68, 70n.4, 198n.5
Perloff, Majorie, 145n.22
Phelan, James, 206–19
professionalism, 204–19, 266, 282–84
Propp, Vladimir, 26, 37–38
PMLA, 102, 194

Rajchman, John., 49
Ransom, John Crowe, 40n.2
Reich, Robert, 279–80
Reid, B. L., 242–44
Robbins, Bruce, 217–18, 265–66; and Gerald Graff, 134
Roiphe, Katie, 68, 70n.4
Rorty, Richard, 47–48, 53–54n.2

Sahlins, Peter, 119
Said, Edward, 45–46, 197–98n.4, 215–17, 222n.18
Schement, Jorge Reina, 276
Schiller, Herbert, 275–76
Sedgwick, Eve Kosofsky, 192–93
Sherman, Stuart, 173–74
Solomon, Robert and Jon, 106
Sontag, Susan, 258
Sosnoski, James, 198n.9
Spenser, Edmund, 132
Spivak, Gayatri Chakravorty, 112, 120, 186
star system, academic, 157, 163, 173–97; cinematic, 175–80
Stimpson, Catherine, 127

Tansey, Mark, 184–85, 198n.7
Theroux, Alexander, 254–55
Thomas, R. Roosevelt Jr., 277, 281
Tichi, Cecilia, 142–43n.8
Tompkins, Jane, 193
Trilling, Lionel, 180, 259–60

Watkins, Evan, 141n.4, 260
Webster, Grant, 32–33
West, Cornel, 47, 53–54n.2, 197–98n.4
Wilbur, Henry, 241–42
Williams, Raymond, 82–84, 87, 125–26, 138